P9-DGU-884

INSTALL ELECTRICAL BREAKERS FOR ENTIRE SHOP WITHIN EASY REACH, CIRCUIT-RATED FOR SUFFICIENT AMPERAGE
STOCK FIRST AID KIT WITH MATERIALS TO TREAT CUTS, GASHES, SPLINTERS, FOREIGN OBJECTS AND CHEMICALS IN EYES, AND BURNS
HAVE TELEPHONE IN SHOP TO CALL FOR HELP
INSTALL FIRE EXTINGUISHER RATED FOR A-, B-, AND C-CLASS FIRES
WEAR EYE PROTECTION AT ALL TIMES
LOCK CABINETS AND POWER TOOLS TO PROTECT CHILDREN AND INEXPERIENCED VISITORS
USE DUST COLLECTOR TO KEEP SHOP DUST AT A MINIMUM
WEAR SHIRT SLEEVES ABOVE ELBOWS
WEAR CLOSE-FITTING CLOTHES
WEAR LONG PANTS
REMOVE WATCHES, RINGS, OR JEWELRY
KEEP TABLE AND FENCE SURFACES WAXED AND RUST-FREE
WEAR THICK-SOLED SHOES, PREFERABLY WITH STEEL TOES
3"
8½"
1½"
13½"
LAMP-ON FINGERBOARD
1½"
3"
6"
2"
5"
1½"
14½"
AND-HELD FINGERBOARD
PROTECTION
WEAR FULL FACE SHIELD DURING LATHE TURNING, ROUTING, AND OTHER OPERATIONS THAT MAY THROW CHIPS
WEAR DUST MASK DURING SANDING AND SAWING
WEAR VAPOR MASK DURING FINISHING
WEAR SAFETY GLASSES OR GOGGLES AT ALL TIMES
WEAR RUBBER GLOVES FOR HANDLING DANGEROUS CHEMICALS
WEAR EAR PROTECTORS DURING ROUTING, PLANING, AND LONG, CONTINUOUS POWER TOOL OPERATION

THE WORKSHOP COMPANION®

MAKING TABLES AND CHAIRS

TECHNIQUES FOR BETTER WOODWORKING

by Nick Engler

Rodale Press
Emmaus, Pennsylvania

Printed in the United States of America on acid-free ∞, recycled ♻ paper

If you have any questions or comments concerning this book, please write:
Rodale Press
Book Readers' Service
33 East Minor Street
Emmaus, PA 18098

About the Author: Nick Engler is an experienced woodworker, writer, teacher, and inventor. He worked as a luthier for many years, making traditional American musical instruments before he founded *Hands On!* magazine. He has taught at the University of Cincinnati and gives woodworking seminars around the country. He contributes to woodworking magazines and designs tools for America's Best Tool Company. This is his fortieth book.

Series Editor: Kevin Ireland
Editors: Bob Moran
Roger Yepsen
Copy Editor: Barbara Webb
Graphic Designer: Linda Watts
Illustrator: Mary Jane Favorite
Master Craftsman: Jim McCann
Photographer: Karen Callahan
Cover Photographer: Mitch Mandel
Proofreader: Hue Park
Indexer: Beverly Bremer
Interior and endpaper illustrations by Mary Jane Favorite
Produced by Bookworks, Inc., West Milton, Ohio

Library of Congress Cataloging-in-Publication Data

Engler, Nick.
Making tables and chairs/by Nick Engler
p. cm. — (The workshop companion)
Includes index.
ISBN 0–87596–655–1 hardcover
1. Furniture making. 2. Tables. 3. Chairs. I. Title.
II. Series: Engler, Nick. Workshop companion.
TT197.5.T3E538 1994
684.1'3—dc20 94–34413
CIP

2 4 6 8 10 9 7 5 3 1 hardcover

The author and editors who compiled this book have tried to make all the contents as accurate and as correct as possible. Plans, illustrations, photographs, and text have all been carefully checked and cross-checked. However, due to the variability of local conditions, construction materials, personal skill, and so on, neither the author nor Rodale Press assumes any responsibility for any injuries suffered, or for damages or other losses incurred that result from the material presented herein. All instructions and plans should be carefully studied and clearly understood before beginning construction.

Special Thanks to:

Bergman Upholstery
Englewood, Ohio

Larry Callahan
West Milton, Ohio

Bob Menker
West Milton, Ohio

Israel Sack, Inc.
New York, New York

The Workshops of David T. Smith
Morrow, Ohio

Tom Stender
Boston, New York

Wertz Hardware
West Milton, Ohio

Willow Tree Inn
Tipp City, Ohio

Contents

Techniques

PROJECTS

Techniques

1

Designing Tables and Chairs

Although tables and chairs seem commonplace to us nowadays, they were once symbols of power and wealth. The first settlers to come to this continent had only rudimentary furniture. Tables were makeshift affairs — a wide plank thrown across sawbucks. When seated at the *board* (as these knockdown tables were called), most people sat on simple plank benches. If there was a chair available, it was reserved for an important person — the *chairman* of the board.

As the woodworking trades in America developed, tables became more sophisticated, and chairs more commonplace. We also developed a vast array of styles and types. Today, there are tables of every conceivable size and shape, from tiny plant stands to huge dining tables. The variety of chairs is equally amazing, from outdoor Adirondack chairs to plush, upholstered rockers and recliners. Additionally, there is a wide choice of methods of construction and materials from which to build. Your first task in building a table or a chair is to sort through these possibilities, defining the type, the style, and the dimensions of your project.

Types and Styles

For a woodworker, the most useful way to categorize tables and chairs is by their *purpose* and *method of construction* — how the pieces are used and how they are assembled. The purpose of a table or chair determines the overall dimensions and configuration of the piece; its construction determines the size and shape of the parts.

HOW TABLES AND CHAIRS ARE USED

Given the almost endless variety of tables and chairs, they seem difficult to classify, whether by purpose or any other criteria. But when you look them over carefully with a woodworker's eye, you'll discover there are only a few basic types. Tables, for instance, can be organized into just four broad categories (SEE FIGURE 1-1):

- *Dining tables* are used primarily for eating meals. The tops can be almost any shape or size, but on the average they are big enough to accommodate four to eight people.
- *Worktables,* such as workbenches and serving tables, are designed to be used standing up. They tend to be taller and narrower than dining tables, making it easier to stand and work at them and to reach across the entire width. They often have drawers or cupboards beneath the tops to store tools and utensils.

1-1 There are four common categories of tables. ***Dining tables*** (1) are designed primarily for eating. They are meant to be used sitting down, and they usually accommodate four to eight people. ***Worktables*** (2), such as this workbench, are meant to be used standing up. ***Specialty tables*** (3) are designed for a single purpose. This writing table, for example, was built for paperwork. ***Occasional tables*** (4) are small, portable tables with a variety of purposes — side tables, coffee tables, displays, and stands.

■ *Specialty tables* are engineered for a specific purpose. A writing table, for example, is a comfortable size and height for writing or typing. A card table is designed for playing games; a drafting table is made for artwork.

■ *Occasional tables* include any small, portable table that can be used for a variety of purposes. This category includes side tables, coffee tables, candlestands, and similar pieces.

There are also four categories of chairs when organized according to purpose (SEE FIGURE 1-2):

■ *Dining and desk chairs,* also called standard chairs, are designed to be used with tables and desks. They sometimes have armrests. Those without arms are often referred to as *side chairs.*

■ *Easy chairs* are made for relaxing. Although they are generally upholstered, they don't have to be — you can build a comfortable chair without padding. Easy chairs are more roomy than other chairs, and the angle between the back and the seat is increased slightly to make them more comfortable.

■ *Rockers* are also made for relaxation, but their uniqueness and their popularity earn them a category all their own. They are an American invention — they first appeared in the Colonies in the eighteenth century.

■ *Specialty chairs,* like specialty tables, are designed for a specific purpose or action. A swivel chair, for example, allows you to work at several stations at once. A drafting chair perches you above the artwork, helping you to focus on the entire picture.

1-2 Chairs can also be grouped into four broad categories. Standard or ***dining and desk chairs*** (1) are designed for sitting at a table or desk. Dining chairs are often part of a matching set that accompanies a table. ***Easy chairs*** (2) are built for relaxation and are used for resting, reflection, reading, conversation, and similar activities. They tend to be larger and more comfortable than standard chairs. ***Rockers*** (3) are also made for relaxation, but they are carefully balanced on curved runners to rock back and forth.

Specialty chairs, like specialty tables, are designed for a specific purpose. The ***library chair*** (4), for example, converts to a stepladder. The small ***pouting chair*** (5) is also intended as a step stool.

METHODS OF CONSTRUCTION

Classifying tables and chairs by their construction methods reveals that there are just a few simple ways to build them. Consider what it takes to create a table — each table has only two major components, the *top* and the *supports,* and each component can be assembled in several ways. There are three types of tabletops (SEE FIGURE 1-3):

■ A *slab top* is made from a single wide plank, several planks glued up to make a single board, or sheet material such as plywood.

■ A *folding top* consists of one or more *leaves* hinged to a slab. With the leaves folded, the table can be stored in a smaller space than a slab-top table of the same size.

■ An *extension top* may have detached or sliding leaves. If it has detached leaves, the top is divided into two halves, which pull apart so you can insert the leaves between them. Sliding leaves pull out from under the top.

1-3 Most small and medium-size tables have simple ***slab*** tops (1) — a single board, a sheet of plywood, or several boards glued edge to edge to make a wide plank. Larger tables often have ***folding*** tops (2) or ***extension*** tops (3) with leaves. When it's not necessary to use all the available table space, these leaves fold down or slide away or can be removed to conserve space.

There are also three types of table supports (SEE FIGURE 1-4):

■ The most common type is *leg-and-apron* supports. Four legs are joined to four aprons and hold up the top.

■ *Trestles* support a tabletop like a plank laid across sawhorses. Often, the trestles are joined by one or more *rails*.

■ A *pedestal* consists of a single column or *post* with three or more *feet*. The tabletop is attached to the upper end of the post.

Like tables, chairs have two component assemblies — the *seat* and the supporting *frame*. There are two possible ways to make a seat (SEE FIGURE 1-5):

■ A *slab* seat is solid wood. The top surface is often shaped or scooped to fit the posterior comfortably.

■ A *frame* seat is made up of four *rails* joined at the ends. Usually, a pliable material such as cloth tape or leather is stretched over the frame to fill the space between the rails. In some chairs, a separate seat (usually an upholstered board) rests on top of the rails.

A chair frame is almost always assembled with mortise-and-tenon joints. However, there are two ways to make the frame members (SEE FIGURE 1-6):

■ A chair constructed in the ***joiner's tradition*** has members with a rectangular cross section and is assembled with square mortises and tenons.

■ One built in the ***turner's tradition*** has cylindrical frame members with a round cross section and is built with round mortises and tenons.

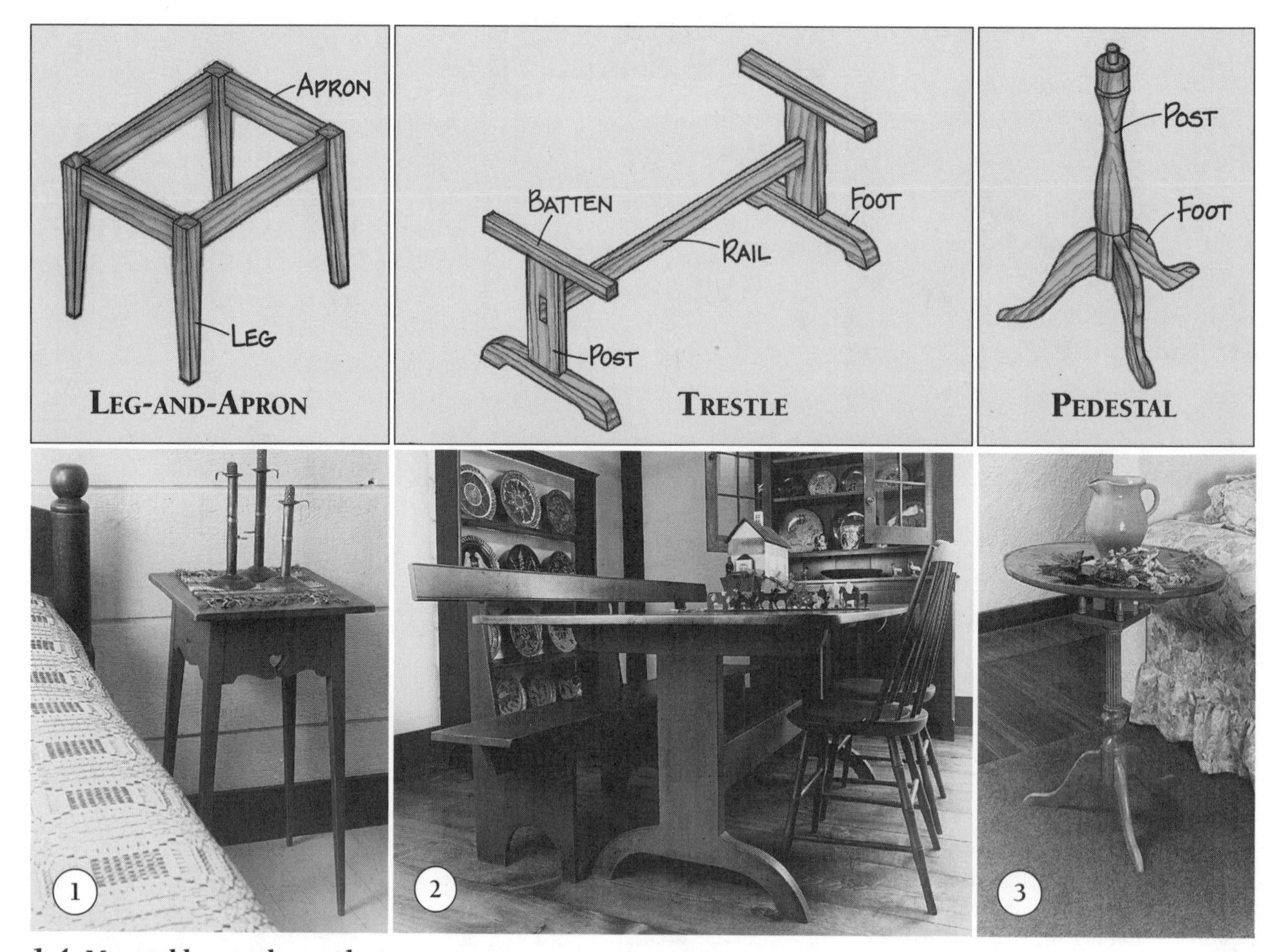

1-4 Most tables perch on a *leg-and-apron* assembly (1) — four legs joined by aprons. However, you can also use ***trestles*** (2) or a ***pedestal*** (3) to support a tabletop.

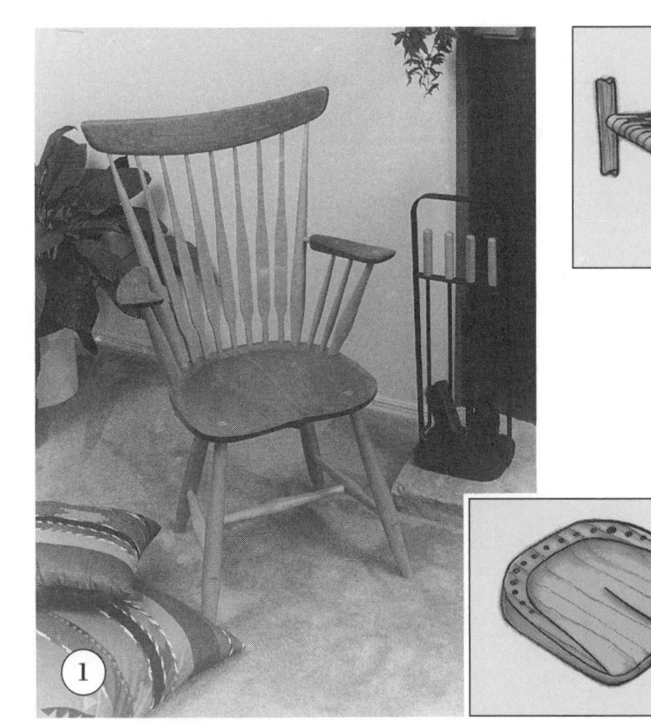

1-5 This Windsor chair has a *slab* seat (1) — a solid block of wood. When the wood is shaped or scooped to fit your backside, as

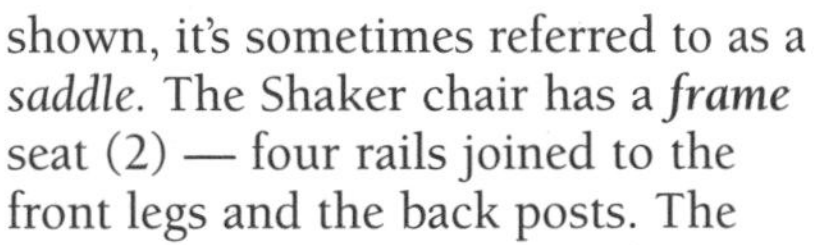

shown, it's sometimes referred to as a *saddle.* The Shaker chair has a *frame* seat (2) — four rails joined to the front legs and the back posts. The space between the rails has been filled with woven cloth tape.

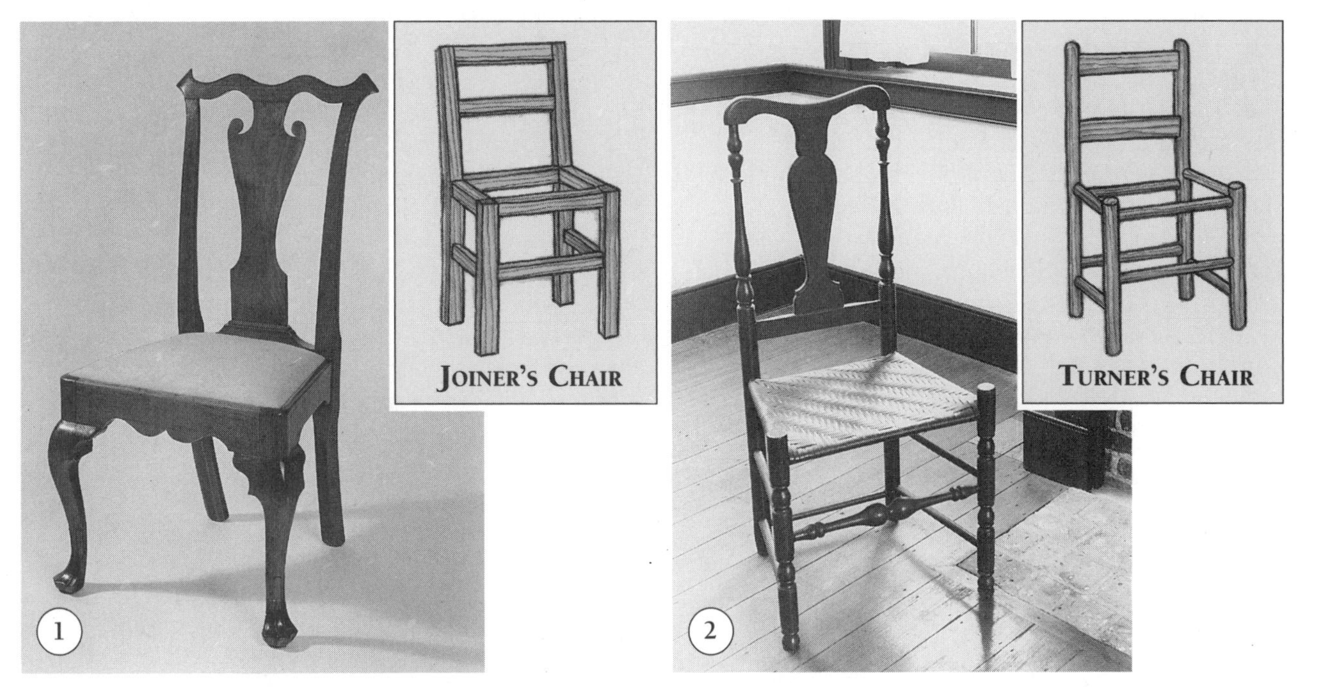

1-6 Shown are two Queen Anne– style chairs. The upholstered chair is made in the ***joiner's tradition*** (1) — the parts of the supporting frame are rectangular and are joined with square mortises and tenons. The side chair is built in the ***turner's tradition*** (2). With the exception of the back rails and splat, all the parts are turned on a lathe and joined with round mortises and tenons. *Upholstered chair photo courtesy of Israel Sack, Inc.*

STYLE

Table and chair designs become more complicated when you consider style. Over the centuries, dozens of furniture styles have evolved, each with endless variations. These styles range from simple and unadorned to highly ornamental. Nineteenth-century Shaker tables and chairs, for example, were almost devoid of decoration. The style was purely functional, as is the Contemporary style in the twentieth century. On the other hand, eighteenth-century Chippendale tables and chairs sported cabriole legs, ball-and-claw feet, and other ornamental woodworking, as did the Victorian Revival styles of the nineteenth century. And there are many, many styles that fall somewhere in between these extremes. (For a broad overview, refer to "American Table and Chair Styles" beginning on this page.)

If you have not decided on the style of your project, or wish to refine its design, it helps to look through collections of furniture photographs. One of the most comprehensive is *American Furniture,* by John S. Bowman (Exeter Books, 1985), a survey of styles from the earliest Colonial times to the present day. Here are several additional references:

- *Furniture Treasury,* by Wallace Nutting (Macmillan, 1928)
- *Three Centuries of American Furniture,* by Oscar P. Fitzgerald (Gramercy Publishing Company, 1982)
- *The Heritage of Upper Canadian Furniture,* by Howard Pain (Key Porter Books, Ltd., 1984)
- *American Country Furniture,* by Nick Engler and Mary Jane Favorite (Rodale Press, 1990)
- *The Knopf Collectors Guides: Furniture, Volumes 1 and 2,* by William C. Ketchum, Jr. (Alfred A. Knopf, 1982)

There are also several magazines that you may want to look through:

- *Antiques,* Old Mill Road, P. O. Box 1975, Marion, OH 43085
- *Antiques and The Arts Weekly,* The Bee Publishing Company, 5 Church Hill Road, Newtown, CT 06470
- *The Antique Review,* P. O. Box 538, Worthington, OH 43085

Remember that style, although important, has little to do with the purpose of a table or chair. Furthermore, it may not affect construction at all. A functional Contemporary chair is used for sitting, as is a highly decorated Chippendale chair. And although they look to be two completely different projects, their basic structure and overall dimensions are much the same.

AMERICAN TABLE AND CHAIR STYLES

There are four major furniture *traditions* in America — design aesthetics that have developed and blossomed over hundreds of years. Each tradition has produced one or more styles of tables and chairs.

- *Southwest Tradition, 1521 to present* — The first American furniture was crafted by Indians thousands of years ago. The Southwest Indians, in particular, had a rich woodworking heritage. They made *tollicpalis* (chairs) and several types of low tables. When the Spanish conquered the area in 1521, immigrant *ensembladores* (joiners) taught native American woodworkers to make furniture in the conquistadors' style. The Spanish designs were a unique blend of European and African art forms. (The African Moors who ruled Spain during medieval times left their mark on Spanish art and architecture.) The aesthetics of three continents — Europe, Africa, and North America — blended to create the Southwest style. This was overshadowed by the Eastern tradition in the late nineteenth and early twentieth centuries, and then revived.
- *Southern Tradition, 1718 to 1803* — When the French founded New Orleans in 1718, immigrant woodworkers began making furniture in French styles. These were copied throughout much of the South during the eighteenth century, then blended into the Eastern tradition when the French sold Louisiana to the United States.
- *Eastern Tradition, 1607 to present* — The Eastern design tradition has been far and away the most influential and prolific furniture aesthetic in America. It began with the arrival of the first European settlers in Virginia and Massachusetts. At first, while they were concerned more with survival than design, they produced only *primitive* pieces. By 1640, however, they were producing massive, blocky *Jacobean* tables and chairs, copied from English designs. Later, they reproduced *William and Mary, Queen Anne,* and *Chippendale* designs as these developed in England.

After the American Revolution, there was a backlash against all things English, and American furniture designers looked to France for inspiration. France had revived the design principles of classical Greek and Roman architecture, and the American *Federal* and *Empire* styles of the late eighteenth and early nineteenth centuries were copied from the "neoclassical" aesthetics of the French.

The Victorian era brought the extremely decorative *Gothic, Rococo,* and *Renaissance Revival* styles. America was also fascinated with the gadgetry of the Industrial Revolution, including *patent* furniture — mechanical tables and chairs that folded, swiveled, or converted from one form to another. As more and more furniture was produced in factories, styles developed that lent themselves to machine production. One of the most popular was *Victorian Oak,* or simply *Oak* furniture. Toward the end of the nineteenth century, there was a reaction against excessive ornament and mass production. Charles *Eastlake* and his followers created *Art Furniture* as a simpler, tasteful alternative to the ornate Victorian Revival styles. Woodworkers who built *Arts and Crafts* or *Mission* tables and chairs revived old medieval forms and advocated a return to individual craftsmanship.

By the first quarter of the twentieth century, the reaction against factory-made furniture had dissipated, but the swing away from ornament continued. It culminated in the aesthetic of functionalism — "form follows function" — and the ultra-functional *International* style. However, not all designs were completely devoid of decoration. *Art Deco* tables and chairs used exotic veneers and materials for embellishment. *Modern* or *American Moderne* furniture combined elements of both International and Art Deco styles.

After World War II, the International style spawned lighter, more versatile, and more economical furniture forms that came to be called the *Contemporary* style. However, since the 1970s, some designers have rebelled against the lack of ornament. They have combined older neoclassical elements with newer forms to create an innovative *Post-Modern* style. Additionally, many individual craftsmen are exploring new designs, techniques, and materials in a riot of personal creativity collectively called the *Handicraft Revival* movement.

■ *Folk Tradition, 1700 to present* — There are also several important American furniture styles that did not follow prevailing trends. For religious, cultural, or sometimes just plain practical reasons, craftsmen developed their own aesthetics and stuck to them. *Windsor* chairs, for example, are based on traditional English country forms that first appeared in the sixteenth century. *Pennsylvania German* furniture followed peasant traditions imported from Germany and Switzerland. *Shaker* tables and chairs evolved from a religious belief in the sanctity of utility and handwork.

In addition to the four different traditions in American furniture design, there is also a distinction between ***classic*** (1) and ***country*** (2) furniture. Classic furniture was built by cabinetmakers (usually residing in large cities) for trendy upper-class customers. The design of these pieces was on the cutting edge of American decorative arts. Country furniture was built for the common folk. Often the builders were just as skilled as classic craftsmen, but their clientele didn't have the wherewithal to pay for high style. So their pieces were practical, inexpensive, simplified versions of the current upper-class styles. *Classic furniture photo courtesy of Israel Sack, Inc.*

(continued) ▷

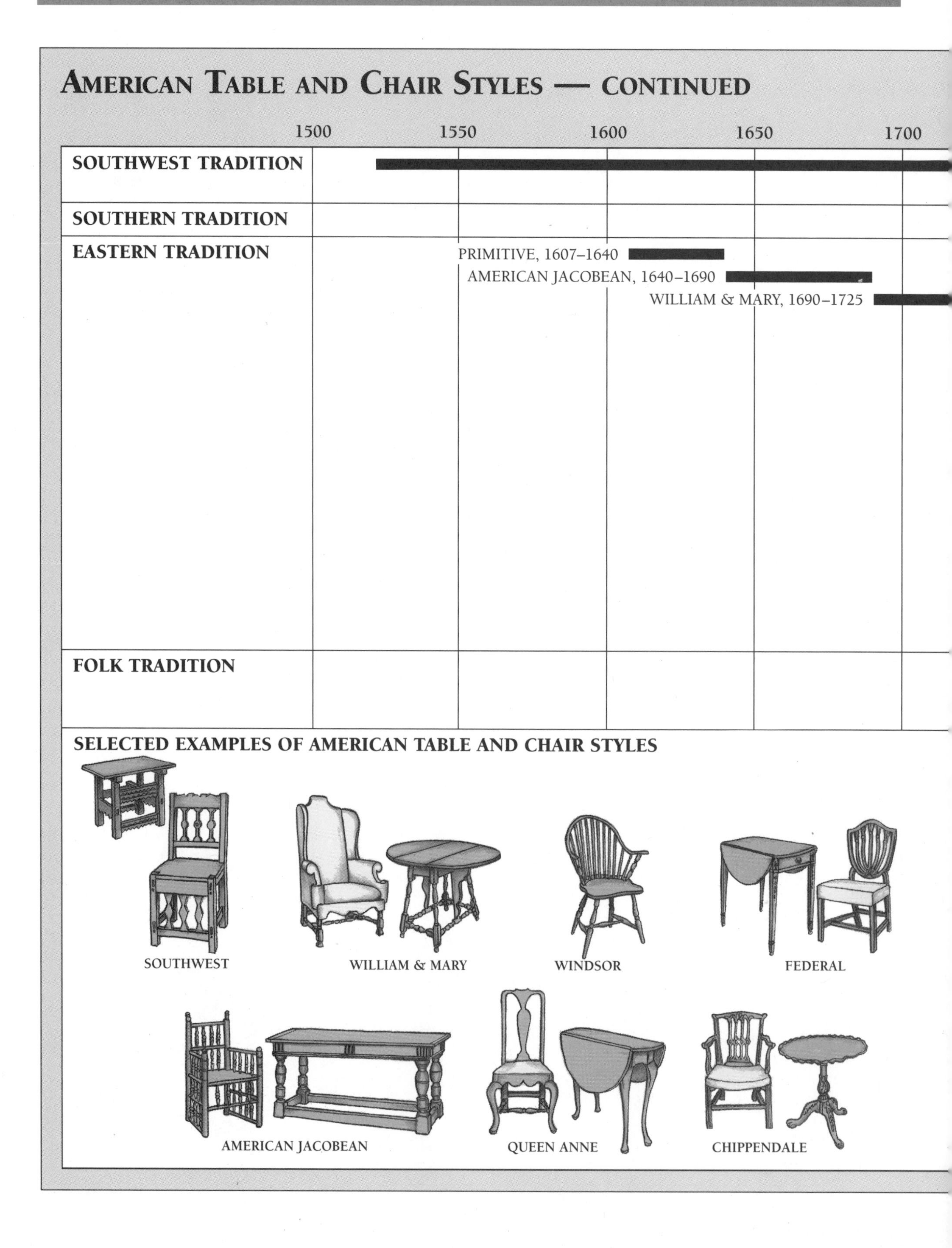
AMERICAN TABLE AND CHAIR STYLES — CONTINUED
1500
1550
1600
1650
1700
SOUTHWEST TRADITION
SOUTHERN TRADITION
EASTERN TRADITION
PRIMITIVE, 1607–1640
AMERICAN JACOBEAN, 1640–1690
WILLIAM & MARY, 1690–1725
FOLK TRADITION
SELECTED EXAMPLES OF AMERICAN TABLE AND CHAIR STYLES
SOUTHWEST
WILLIAM & MARY
WINDSOR
FEDERAL
AMERICAN JACOBEAN
QUEEN ANNE
CHIPPENDALE

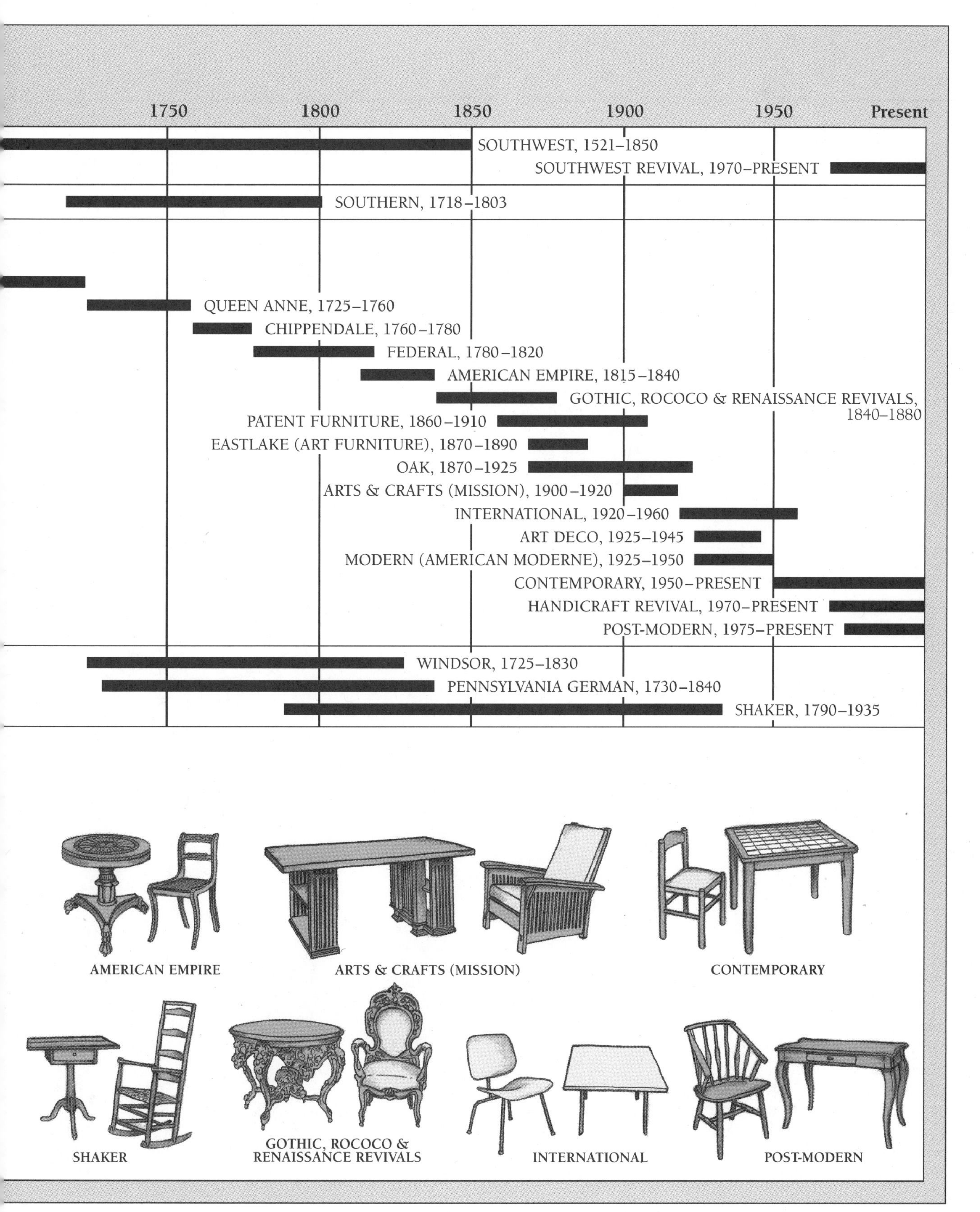
1750
1800
1850
1900
1950
Present
SOUTHWEST, 1521–1850
SOUTHWEST REVIVAL, 1970–PRESENT
SOUTHERN, 1718–1803
QUEEN ANNE, 1725–1760
CHIPPENDALE, 1760–1780
FEDERAL, 1780–1820
AMERICAN EMPIRE, 1815–1840
GOTHIC, ROCOCO & RENAISSANCE REVIVALS, 1840–1880
PATENT FURNITURE, 1860–1910
EASTLAKE (ART FURNITURE), 1870–1890
OAK, 1870–1925
ARTS & CRAFTS (MISSION), 1900–1920
INTERNATIONAL, 1920–1960
ART DECO, 1925–1945
MODERN (AMERICAN MODERNE), 1925–1950
CONTEMPORARY, 1950–PRESENT
HANDICRAFT REVIVAL, 1970–PRESENT
POST-MODERN, 1975–PRESENT
WINDSOR, 1725–1830
PENNSYLVANIA GERMAN, 1730–1840
SHAKER, 1790–1935
AMERICAN EMPIRE
ARTS & CRAFTS (MISSION)
CONTEMPORARY
SHAKER
GOTHIC, ROCOCO & RENAISSANCE REVIVALS
INTERNATIONAL
POST-MODERN

Sizing Tables and Chairs

Once you have decided what type of table or chair to make, you must figure its size and configuration. In short, you must make the piece *functional* and *comfortable.*

TABLE DIMENSIONS

When sizing a table, consider the height and size of the tabletop, the placement of the legs, and the width of the aprons. The tabletop must rest at a comfortable height for whatever purpose you want the table to serve, and there must be adequate space for that activity. If you sit at the table, the legs and aprons should not interfere with the seating.

DINING TABLES

■ *Height.* The tops of dining tables should be between 27 and 30 inches high, depending on the height of the chair seats. The higher the table, the more formal it feels. Lower tables tend to be more comfortable.

■ *Space.* Allow 23 to 26 inches of elbow room and 12 to 15 inches of space in front of each person seated at the table. People will be close enough to feel intimate, but not so close that they will be cramped. (See Figure 1-7.)

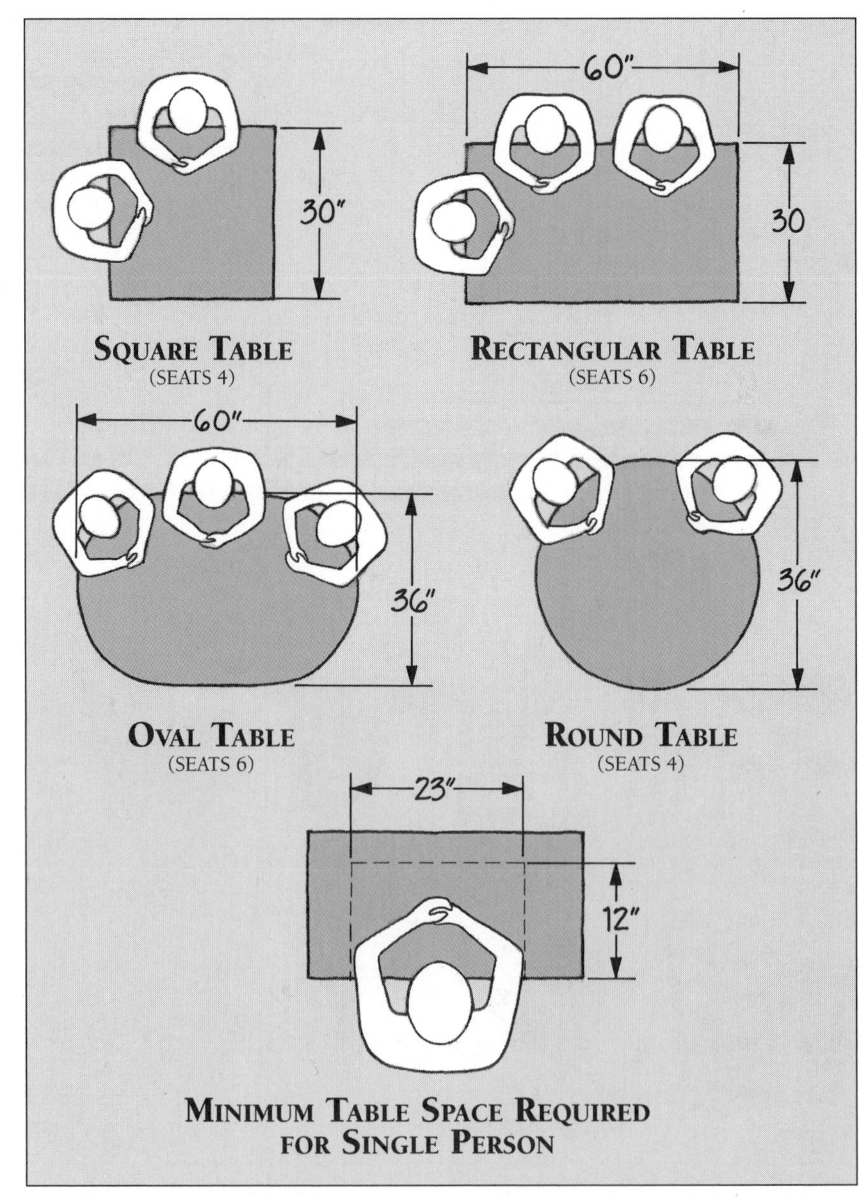

1-7 As a rule of thumb when designing a dining table, you should allow a space at least 23 inches wide and 12 inches deep for each person. However, this isn't an absolute. These dimensions change depending on the shape of the tabletop and how the people are arranged around it. For planning purposes, it's often wise to draw a scaled top view of the table, arranging silhouettes of people around it, as shown.

■ *Legs and aprons*. Place the table legs where folks won't bump into them. There should be 18 to 24 inches of toe room under the table for each dining position. The bottom edges of the aprons should be no closer than 24 inches to the floor to provide adequate knee clearance. (SEE FIGURE 1-8.)

WORKTABLES

■ *Height*. A worktable may be anywhere from 30 to 40 inches high, but most are between 34 and 36 inches. The optimum height depends on the work that is to be done and the tools used. It also depends on the height of the person who does the work. If you build a worktable that will be used by one person predominantly, you may want to size it according to his or her height. Refer to "Adjusting for Height" on page 17.

■ *Space*. The tops can be any size, but most are between 15 and 30 inches deep, and 30 to 72 inches long. There must be adequate space to hold the tools and the work, and you should be able to reach across the tabletop easily.

■ *Legs and aprons*. Since you usually stand at a worktable, knee clearance is not a consideration. Toe room is greatly reduced — allow the tabletop to overhang the aprons 2 to 4 inches to accommodate your toes. Design the legs and aprons to provide maximum support and stability.

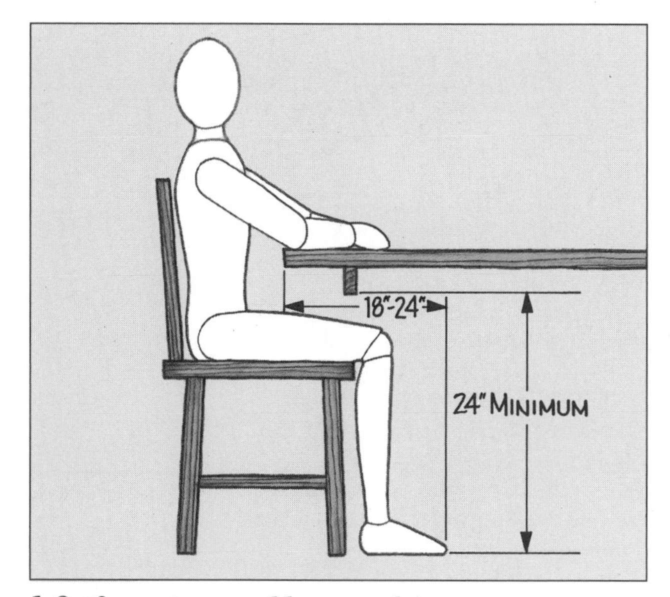

1-8 **If you sit at a table, not only** must there be enough room on top of it, there should also be adequate room underneath it. Leave at least 18 inches horizontally for toe room and no less than 24 inches vertically for your knees and thighs.

STANDARD TABLE DIMENSIONS

The dimensions shown for the following tables are averages. They are intended as guidelines, not absolutes. Use them as a jumping-off point in designing your own tables.

DINING TABLES

	NUMBER OF SEATS	HEIGHT	LENGTH	DEPTH OR WIDTH
Square	2	27″–30″	24″–26″	24″–26″
	4	27″–30″	30″–32″	30″–32″
	8	27″–30″	48″–50″	48″–50″
Rectangular	2	27″–30″	24″–26″	30″–32″
	6	27″–30″	30″–36″	66″–72″
	8	27″–30″	36″–42″	86″–96″
Round	2	27″–30″		24″–26″ dia.
	3	27″–30″		30″–32″ dia.
	4	27″–30″		36″–39″ dia.
	5	27″–30″		42″–45″ dia.
	6	27″–30″		48″–52″ dia.
	7	27″–30″		54″–58″ dia.
	8	27″–30″		62″–66″ dia.
Oval	4	27″–30″	42″–48″	28″–32″
	6	27″–30″	60″–66″	32″–36″
	8	27″–30″	72″–78″	48″–52″

WORKTABLES

USE	HEIGHT	LENGTH	DEPTH
Food prep	34″–36″	30″–72″	23″–24″
Serving	36″–42″	42″–60″	15″–18″
Workbench	30″–40″	30″–72″	24″–30″

OCCASIONAL TABLES

USE	HEIGHT	LENGTH	DEPTH
Coffee table	15″–18″	30″–60″	22″–30″
End table	18″–24″	18″–24″	18″–24″
Hall table	34″–36″	36″–72″	16″–20″
Nightstand	24″–30″	18″–20″	18″–20″
Side table	18″–24″	24″–28″	18″–20″
Candlestand	24″–32″	15″–24″	15″–24″

SPECIALTY TABLES

USE	HEIGHT	LENGTH	DEPTH
Child's table	20″–22″	26″–30″	18″–22″
Computer table	25″–28″	36″–60″	22″–30″
Drafting table	32″–44″	31″–72″	23″–44″
Dressing table	29″–30″	40″–48″	18″–22″
Game table	29″–30″	30″–32″	30″–32″
Typing table	25″–28″	36″–42″	16″–24″
Writing table	28″–30″	36″–42″	20″–24″

OCCASIONAL TABLES

The dimensions of occasional tables depend on their use, as shown in "Standard Table Dimensions" on page 13. They are usually small enough to be moved easily. And since you don't sit at these tables, the location of the legs and the size of the aprons don't affect their function.

SPECIALTY TABLES

Again, the dimensions of these tables depend on their use. Refer to "Standard Table Dimensions" on page 13 for the average sizes of several common specialty tables. Remember that because you must sit at these tables, the placement of the legs and the size of the aprons are important. Allow enough room for toes and knees, as shown in *Figure 1-8.*

CHAIR DIMENSIONS

Chair sizes do not vary as widely as those for tables, because tables are built to accommodate activities, while chairs are made to accommodate people. People — at least, most adult people — are relatively close in size. There are several useful rules of thumb to help figure chair size, based on how the average person fits a chair *(see Figure 1-9):*

- The occupant's feet should rest flat on the floor when seated upright so there's no pressure on the legs behind the knee.
- The seat should either be level or slope *slightly* toward the back so the occupant does not slide forward. The more slanted the back, the more it becomes necessary to give the seat some slope.
- If you must sit for long periods in a chair, a flat seat is often better than a scooped seat; it allows you to shift positions. A framed seat, filled or covered with a material that has some give, is more comfortable than a hard slab seat. An upholstered seat — provided the upholstery is sufficiently thick — is usually the most comfortable choice.
- The chair back should curve to fit or have an opening for the lumbar region at the base of the spine. This also allows room for the buttocks.
- The chair back should be slanted backward so it supports the back without pressing into the shoulder blades. Chairs used for eating or work are slanted less than those used for relaxation.
- If the chair has arms, these should be positioned to support the occupant's arms without raising his or her shoulders. The chair's arms should be about 2 inches shorter than the depth of its seat.
- The chair mustn't be so low or tilt back so far that the occupant has trouble getting in and out of it.

Nonetheless, it's impossible to design one chair that will fit everyone for every occasion. To a large extent, the optimum size for a chair depends on what the occupant will be doing while seated there — working, eating, reading, relaxing, and so on. There is a subtle but important difference in the sizes and configurations of rockers, easy chairs, and dining and desk chairs.

DINING AND DESK CHAIRS

The average seat height of a standard chair is between 16 and 17 inches, but it can go as low as 14 inches or as high as 19. The seat is usually about 16 to 16½ inches deep and perfectly level. If the seat slopes, it's angled backward no more than 4 degrees off hori-

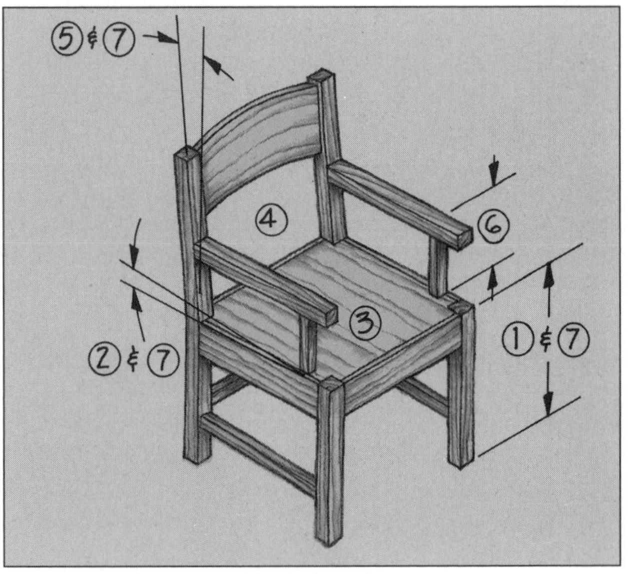

***1-9* When designing a chair, think** about how the human body fits it. Here are some suggestions: (1) Choose a height for the seat that allows the occupant to put both feet on the floor. (2) Make the seat level or sloped back slightly. (3) If you expect that the occupant will sit for a long time, cushion the seat. (4) Create an opening in the chair back where it meets the seat to make room for the buttocks. (5) Slant the chair back slightly so it does not press against the shoulder blades. (6) Position the chair arms so they support the occupant's arms without raising his or her shoulders. (7) Don't make the chair so low or tilt it back so far that the occupant has to work to get in and out of it.

zontal. (It should drop no more than 1 inch, front to back.) Most seats are about 18 inches wide at the front, tapering 2 to 3 inches toward the back. The seat may be about 2 inches wider if the chair has armrests, and these should be approximately 8 inches above the seat. The back is usually 30 to 36 inches high and slanted backward 5 to 15 degrees off vertical.

EASY CHAIRS

The dimensions of an easy chair are similar to those of a dining chair, but *slightly* larger. The seat is 1 to 2 inches wider and 2 to 4 inches deeper. The front edge of the seat may be slightly lower — about 15½ inches high — and sloped backward 10 to 15 degrees off horizontal. The angle of the back should increase with the slope of the seat, up to 30 degrees off vertical. This puts the occupant in a semireclining position, taking some weight off the spine.

ROCKERS

Since a rocker is also intended for relaxation, the seat is slightly broader, deeper, and lower than a standard chair — 19 to 22 inches wide, 16 to 18 inches deep, and 15½ to 16 inches high. The rockers should be about 30 inches long with a radius of 37 to 38 inches. The back is usually about 40 inches high and 105 degrees from the seat. The chair assembly should be joined to the rockers so the back rests about 25 degrees off vertical — about the same position as the back of an easy chair. *(SEE FIGURE 1-10.)*

"Standard Chair Dimensions" on page 16 shows the dimensions and configurations for these chairs.

FOR YOUR INFORMATION

A child's chair is built to the same proportions as a standard chair, but about two-thirds the size. The seat should be about 13 inches high, 14 inches wide, and 13 inches deep. The back is usually about 24 inches high.

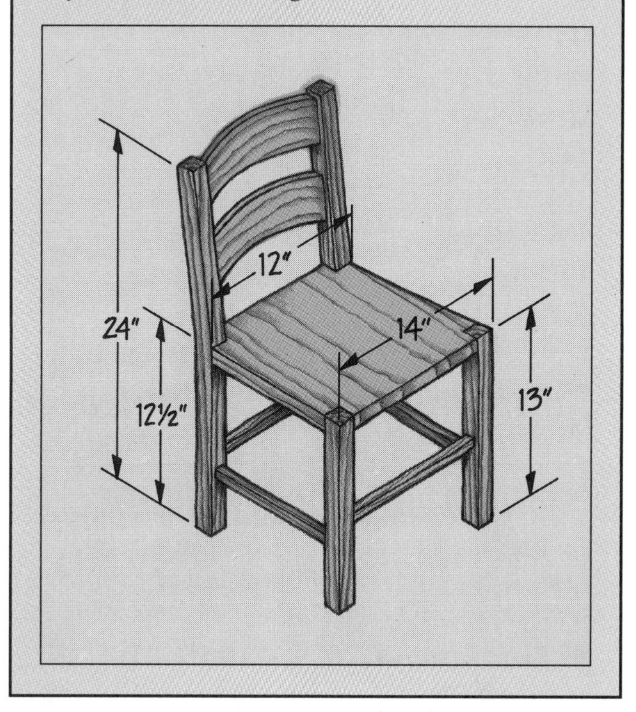

1-10 **When designing a rocker,** the *balance* is just as important as the dimensions. Not only must the chair fit the body comfortably, it must be balanced on its rockers to come to rest in a comfortable position. This Cape Cod rocker, for example, rests with the back and the seat tilted back slightly — the same position that you'd likely find most comfortable when seated in it. Balancing a rocker is a simple matter of positioning it properly on the rockers. If you're working out a new design, assemble the chair frame (and seat frame, if there is one) *without glue* and rest the assembly on the rockers. Move it forward and backward until you find the right balance point. If you move it all the way forward and it still won't balance properly, try shortening the back posts.

Try This Trick

To find the most comfortable configuration for a chair, make a mock-up from scraps of wood. Rest the seat on bricks or blocks of wood until you find a comfortable height and slope. Then add a back, leaning the boards against a wall.

Standard Chair Dimensions

Like the chart "Standard Table Dimensions" on page 13, the following numbers are intended as guidelines to help design a usable chair. Designing a truly *comfortable* chair will require some experimentation to find the best possible configuration.

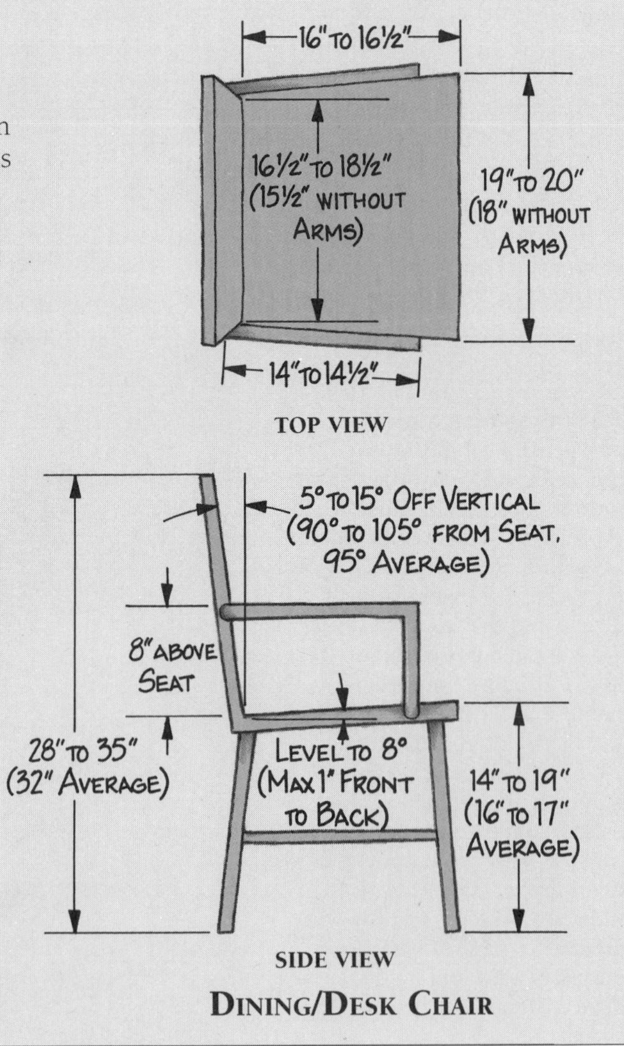

Dining/Desk Chair

ADJUSTING FOR HEIGHT

The optimum (most comfortable) height for a table or chair changes with the height of the person using it. If you are building one or the other for a specific person, you may want to adjust the height of the chair seat or the tabletop accordingly.

Height of Person	Height of Chair Seat	Height of Dining Table	Height of Typing Table	Height of Worktable
60″	13.8″	24.5″	21.5″	32.4″
61″	14.1″	25.1″	22.1″	33.0″
62″	14.5″	25.8″	22.8″	33.7″
63″	14.9″	26.4″	23.4″	34.3″
64″	15.2″	27.0″	24.0″	34.9″
65″	15.6″	27.6″	24.6″	35.6″
66″	15.9″	28.3″	25.3″	36.2″
67″	16.3″	28.9″	25.9″	36.9″
68″	16.8″	29.5″	26.5″	37.5″
69″	17.1″	30.1″	27.1″	38.2″
70″	17.5″	30.8″	27.8″	38.8″
71″	17.7″	31.4″	28.4″	39.5″
72″	18.1″	32.0″	29.0″	40.1″

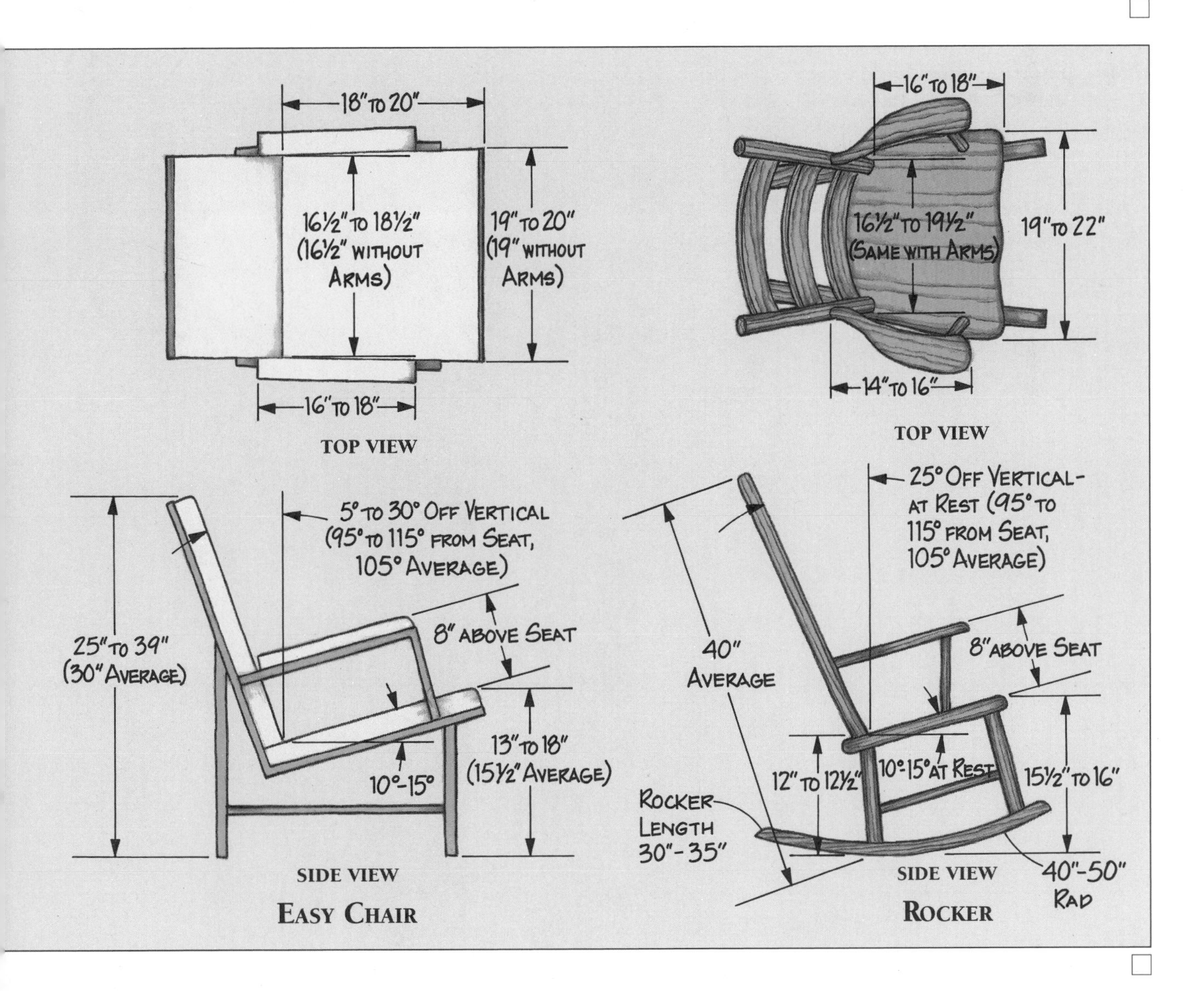

EASY CHAIR **ROCKER**

2

Leg-and-Apron Construction

Although there are several methods you can use to build the supporting framework for a table, most frameworks have leg-and-apron supports — four vertical legs joined to horizontal rails or aprons. Despite the simplicity of this construction, it's extremely versatile. You can use it to make tables of all sizes, shapes, types, and styles.

Furthermore, you have a choice of construction techniques. There are a variety of joints that can be used to assemble the legs and aprons, as well as different woodworking methods to make the legs and aprons.

Joining Legs and Aprons

The first step in making a leg-and-apron framework is to prepare the stock and join the legs and aprons. Cut these joints even before you shape the legs or cut the profiles of the aprons. It's much easier to cut the joints when the parts are rectangular, with flat sides and straight edges.

PREPARING THE LEGS AND APRONS

To cut accurate, tight-fitting joints, you must make sure that the legs and aprons are true and square. An uneven leg or a warped apron will make assembly difficult and may weaken the joints.

To prepare the legs and aprons, bring the stock into your shop and let it rest for several weeks until the moisture content of the wood reaches an equilibrium with the shop environment. When the wood has "shop-dried," cut the parts slightly longer, wider, and thicker than you need — this will release most of the internal tension within the wood. Joint two adjacent surfaces of the legs perfectly square to one another, then plane the remaining surfaces. When the leg stock is square, cut it to length. *(See Figures 2-1 and 2-2.)*

Treat the aprons in much the same manner. Joint two adjacent surfaces — a face and an edge — then plane the remaining face until the stock is the proper thickness. Rip the stock to width, truing the remaining edge, and cut the aprons to length. *(See Figure 2-3.)*

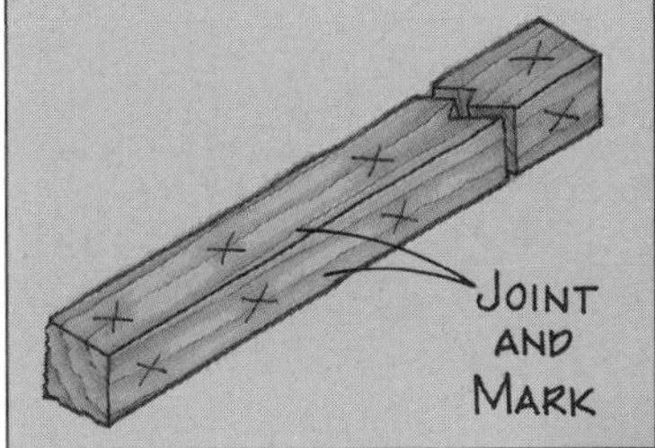

2-1 To true a leg, you must cut it perfectly straight and square. Begin by jointing two adjacent surfaces of the rough stock so they are straight, flat, and 90 degrees to one another. With a pencil, mark the surfaces you have just jointed.

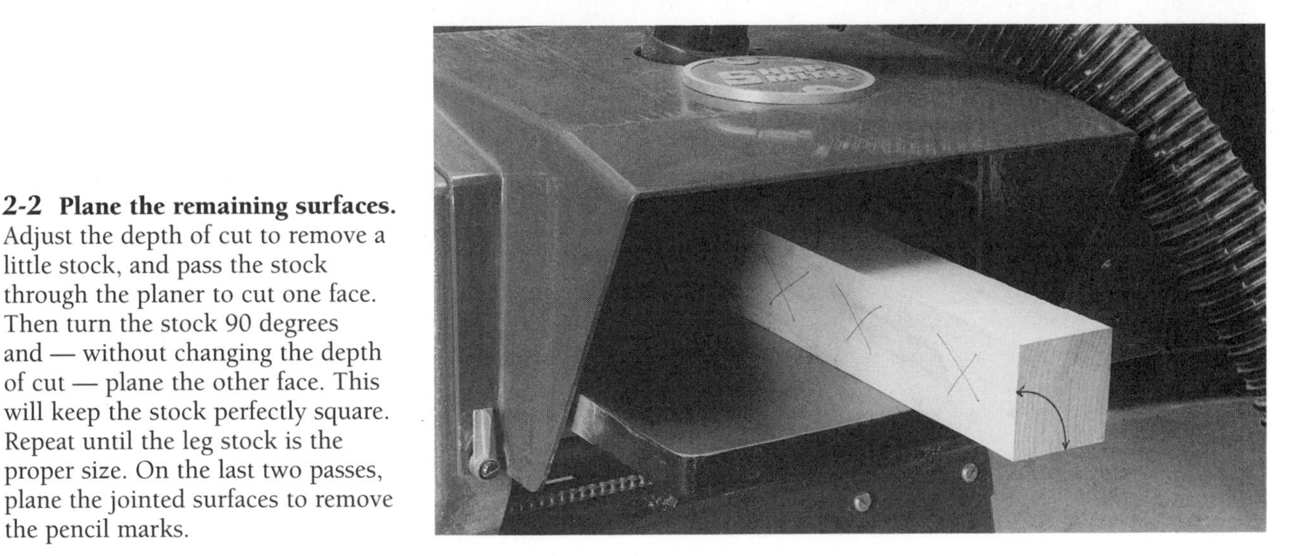

2-2 Plane the remaining surfaces. Adjust the depth of cut to remove a little stock, and pass the stock through the planer to cut one face. Then turn the stock 90 degrees and — without changing the depth of cut — plane the other face. This will keep the stock perfectly square. Repeat until the leg stock is the proper size. On the last two passes, plane the jointed surfaces to remove the pencil marks.

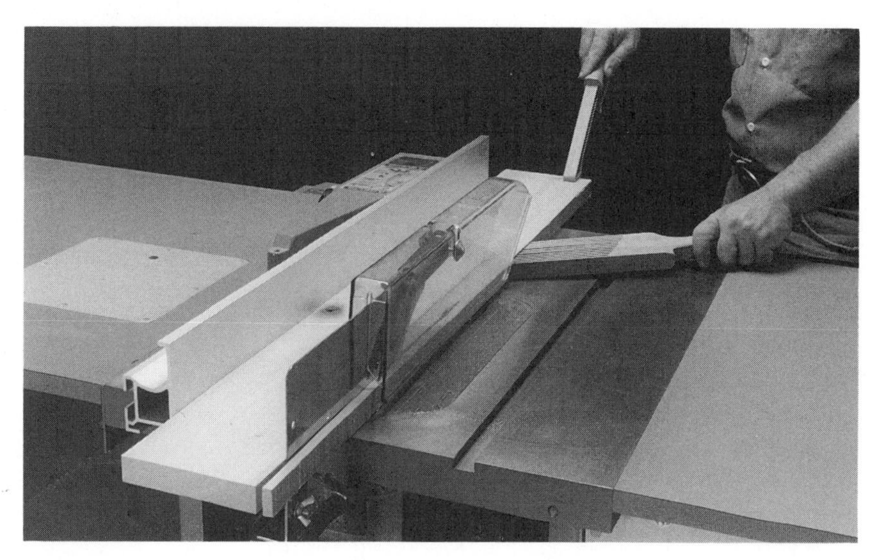

2-3 The process for truing aprons is similar to that for truing legs. Joint an adjacent face and edge; plane the remaining face to reduce the stock to the proper thickness; then rip it to width on a table saw, removing the remaining rough edge. Some woodworkers prefer to rip the stock 1/32 inch wider than needed, then remove the last 1/32 inch on a jointer. However, this extra step isn't always necessary, provided you use a sharp blade that leaves a reasonably smooth edge. Mark the ripped edge "up" so it will be hidden by the tabletop on the assembled table.

MAKING MORTISE-AND-TENON JOINTS

Traditionally, legs and aprons are joined with mortise-and-tenon joints. *(See Figures 2-4 and 2-5.)* The shoulders of the tenons keep the legs from racking, enabling the assembly to withstand the sideways pressure that occurs every time you lean on the table or scoot it across the floor.

Make the mortises in the legs first, then fit the apron tenons to them. Inspect the leg stock and choose the outside faces — the leg surfaces that you want to be seen. Measure and mark the mortises on the inside surfaces, then cut them with a mortiser, drill press, or table-mounted router. Cut the tenons with a router or a table saw, fitting them to the mortises. Try for a slip fit — the pieces should slide together easily with little slop. If they're too tight or too loose, you won't get a good glue joint.

There are also several variations on the mortise-and-tenon joints that you might use — dowel joints, loose tenons in matching mortises, and dovetail tenons in dovetail slots. *(See Figure 2-6.)*

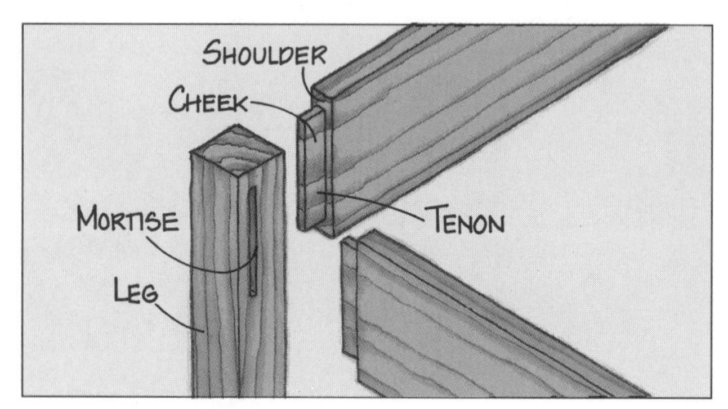

2-4 One of the best ways to join a leg to an apron is with a mortise-and-tenon joint. Make the mortise in the leg and the tenon in the apron. The tenon should have substantial shoulders — these prevent the leg from racking — but it must also be sufficiently thick to withstand daily use and abuse. Cut the tenon no thinner than 1/4 inch for small tables and 3/8 inch for medium-size and larger ones. You must also make the tenon long enough that the cheeks form a strong glue bond with the sides of the mortise. As a rule of thumb, make the tenon no shorter than 3/4 inch for small tables, 1 inch for medium-size tables, and 1 1/2 inches for large tables.

2-5 Because you want to make the tenons as long as possible, the mortises that fit them sometimes intersect inside the leg. When this happens, you must miter the ends of the tenons where they meet.

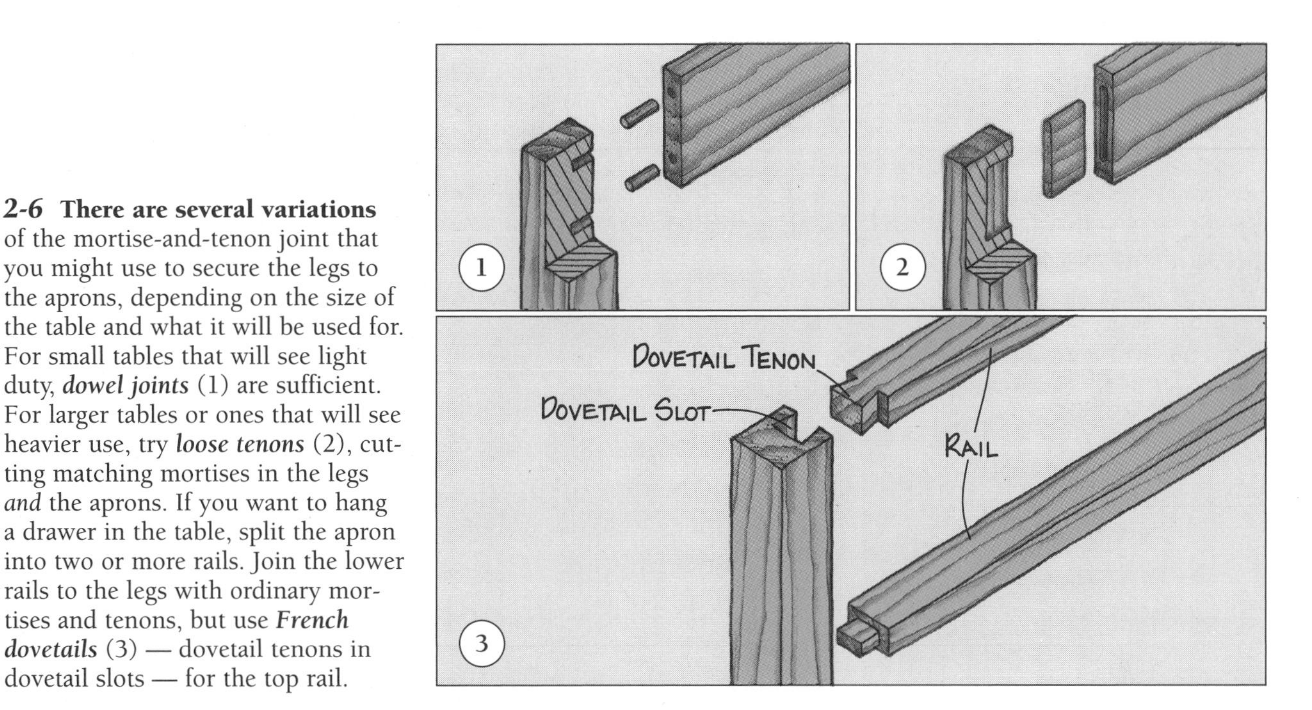

2-6 There are several variations of the mortise-and-tenon joint that you might use to secure the legs to the aprons, depending on the size of the table and what it will be used for. For small tables that will see light duty, ***dowel joints*** (1) are sufficient. For larger tables or ones that will see heavier use, try ***loose tenons*** (2), cutting matching mortises in the legs *and* the aprons. If you want to hang a drawer in the table, split the apron into two or more rails. Join the lower rails to the legs with ordinary mortises and tenons, but use ***French dovetails*** (3) — dovetail tenons in dovetail slots — for the top rail.

INSTALLING CORNER BRACES AND HANGER BOLTS

If you need a knockdown table, corner braces and hanger bolts are a popular alternative to mortises and tenons. *(SEE FIGURE 2-7.)* The aprons are joined by the corner braces, then the legs are bolted to the braces. This arrangement is surprisingly strong, even though it does not join the aprons and legs permanently. If you need to take the table apart to store it, you can remove the legs by simply loosening the nuts that hold them in place.

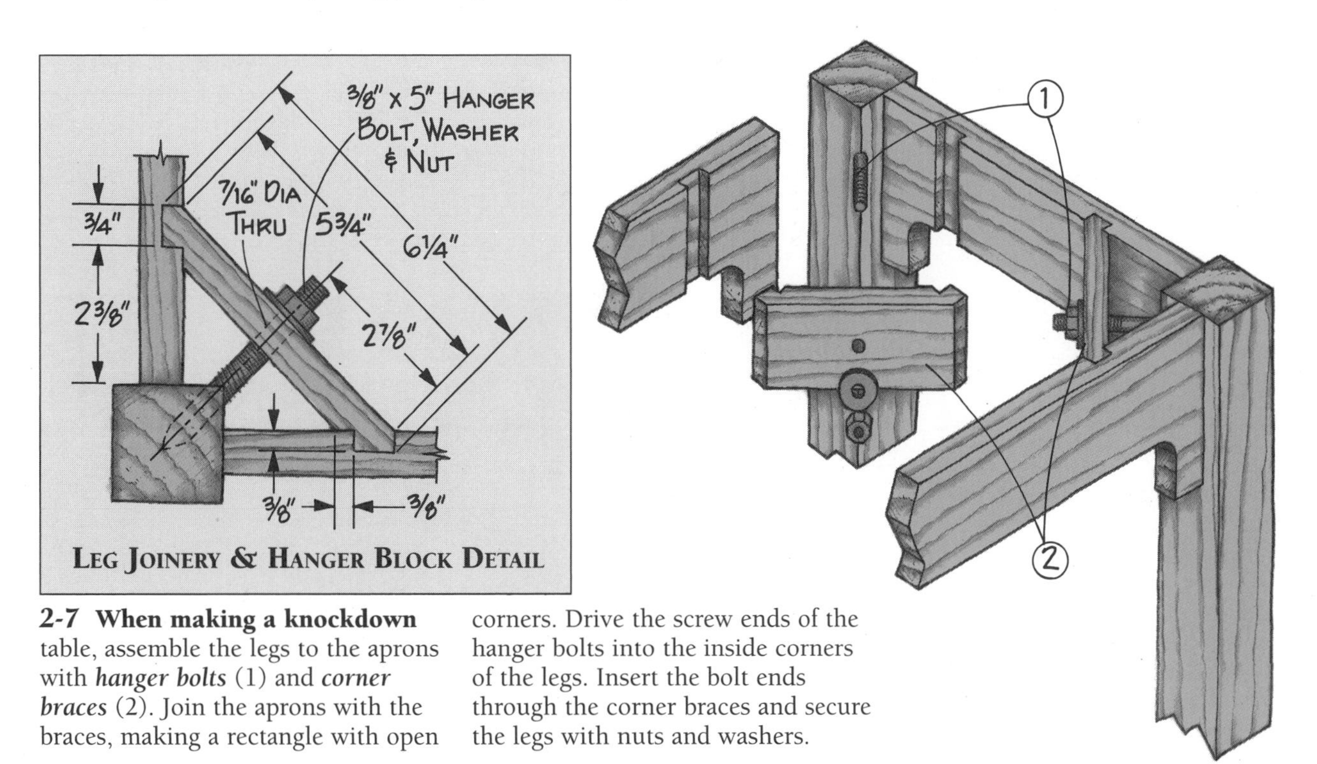

2-7 When making a knockdown table, assemble the legs to the aprons with ***hanger bolts*** (1) and ***corner braces*** (2). Join the aprons with the braces, making a rectangle with open corners. Drive the screw ends of the hanger bolts into the inside corners of the legs. Insert the bolt ends through the corner braces and secure the legs with nuts and washers.

You can purchase ready-made metal corner braces from most woodworking suppliers, or you can make your own. (SEE FIGURES 2-8 AND 2-9.) To install them, fasten the braces to the inside faces of the aprons. Commercial corner braces are secured with screws or they have tabs that fit in saw kerfs. The shop-made braces shown rest in dadoes.

Drive the screw ends of the hanger bolts into the *inside* corners of the legs. (SEE FIGURE 2-10.) Insert the bolt ends through the corner braces so the inside faces of the legs rest against the ends of the aprons. Secure the legs with nuts and washers. To remove the legs, loosen the nuts and pull the hanger bolts out of the corner braces.

FOR BEST RESULTS

Wait until *after* you've shaped the legs before installing the hanger bolts. Otherwise, the hardware may interfere with the shaping.

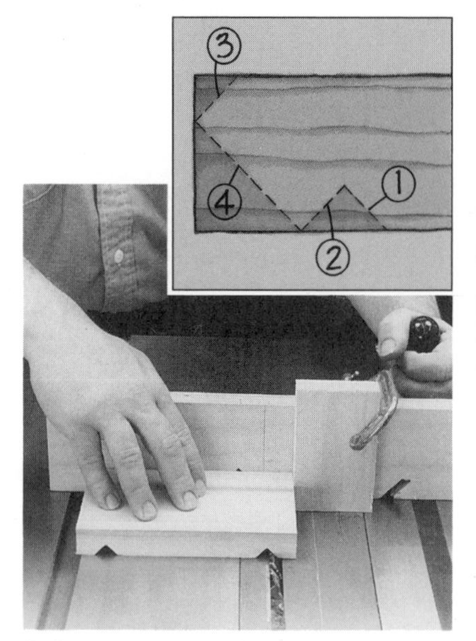

2-8 To create a corner brace, you must make four angled cuts in each end of the brace stock, cutting them in the order shown. Tilt the saw blade to 45 degrees, and make two passes to create a V-groove near each end. Use a miter gauge extension and a stop block to position the stock before making each cut.

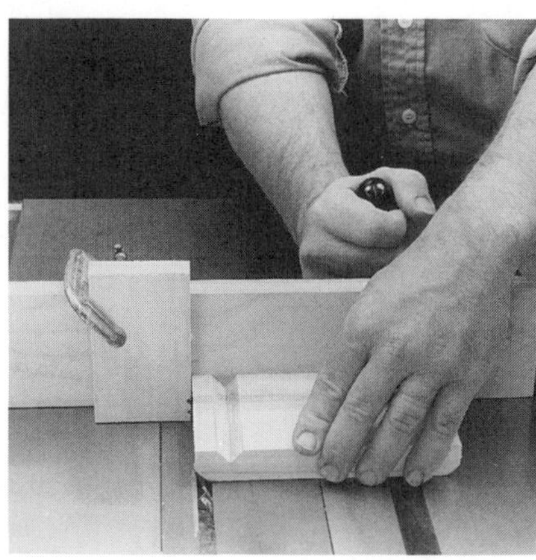

2-9 After cutting the V-grooves, make a narrow bevel in each end of the brace. The V-grooves should face up as you cut these bevels. Turn the block over so the grooves face down and cut wider bevels in the ends. When making the last cut, position the stop block very accurately so you don't shorten the brace as it's cut. To finish the brace, drill a hole the same size as the hanger bolt through the center of the face.

2-10 To install a hanger bolt, cradle the leg in a V-block while you drill a pilot hole in the inside corner. Thread two nuts onto the bolt end of the hanger bolt, jam them together by turning them in opposite directions, and use them to turn the bolt as you drive the screw end into the pilot hole.

Shaping Legs and Aprons

Once you've cut the joinery, you can shape the legs and aprons. There are several common treatments for table legs:

- *Taper* the legs, cutting them narrower at the bottom than at the top.
- *Turn* the legs on a lathe, reducing the bottom portions below the aprons to cylinders with coves, beads, and other shapes.
- Create S-shaped ***cabriole*** legs by making compound cuts on a band saw.
- Or, leave them ***square***. (You'll be in good company; Thomas Chippendale often left the legs of his tables square.)

TAPERING THE LEGS

To taper table legs, you must rip one or more surfaces at a gentle angle, slicing away slightly more stock near the bottoms of the legs than at the tops. *(See Figure 2-11.)* There are several tools you can use to do this, but one of the most accurate is a table saw.

To cut a taper on a table saw, you hold the board with its length at a slight angle to the blade as you rip it. The "Tapering Jig" on page 25 will prove to be a big help — it holds the leg at an angle as you push it past the blade.

2-11 All five legs on this bowfront hall table are tapered. The four corner legs have *single tapers* — two adjacent sides of each leg are tapered while the opposite sides are left straight. (In this project, the *inside* surfaces are tapered.) The middle leg has a single taper and a *double taper*; that is, it has three tapered sides. The right and left sides are double-tapered — both opposing sides are cut. The front and back sides are single-tapered — only the back is cut.

To set up for a taper cut, you must know the slope of the taper, and whether you will be cutting a *single taper* (on a single side or two adjacent sides) or a *double taper* (with tapers on opposing sides). The slope is determined by the *rise* and *run* of the taper. To find the rise, measure from the starting point of the taper to the end. To determine the run of a single taper, figure the amount by which the width of the board will be reduced. For a double taper, divide that amount by 2. *(See Figure 2-12.)*

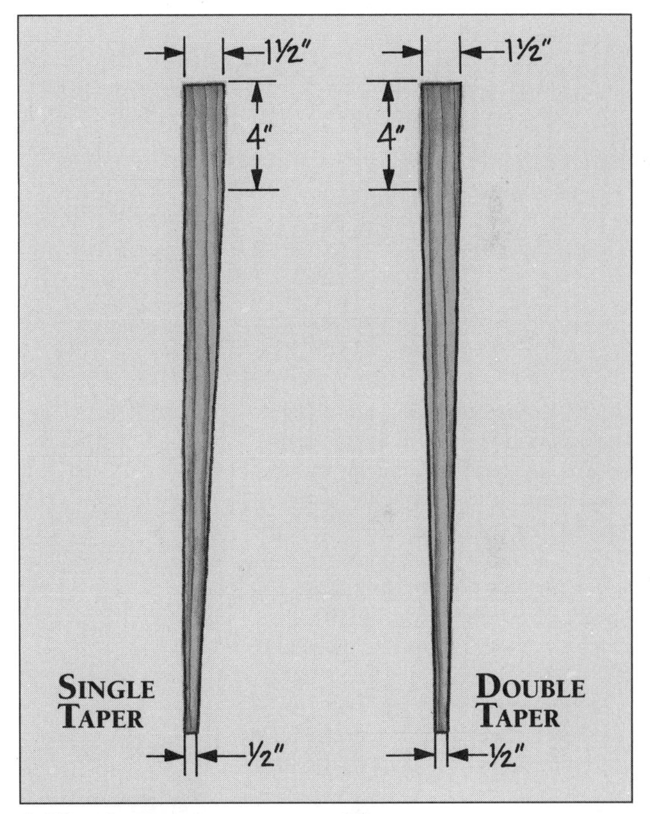

2-12 Shown are two tapered legs, each 24 inches long. The one on the left has a single taper; the one on the right, a double taper. The taper on both legs is the same length and narrows to the same width. The rise is equal — on both legs, the taper begins 4 inches from the top, making it 20 inches long. The run, however, is not equal. Although both legs are 1½ inches wide at the top and then narrow to ½ inch at the bottom, the single-taper run is 1 inch (1½ – ½ = 1), and the double taper run is ½ inch ([1½ – ½] ÷ 2 = ½).

Lay out the taper on a test piece the same size as the legs. Mount the test piece in the tapering jig with the layout lines up and place the jig on the table saw, against the fence. Adjust the tapering jig to cut the slope, and position the fence so the blade will begin cutting the leg the proper distance from the top end. *(See Figure 2-13.)* Cut the taper, using the fence to guide the jig. *(See Figure 2-14.)* When you're satisfied the setup is correct, cut the leg stock.

If you're cutting a double taper, you must make a wedge-shaped shim with the same rise and run as the taper. Make the first pass across the saw blade as if you were making a single taper. Then rotate the leg 180 degrees so the cut surface faces the jig. Insert the shim between the leg and the jig, and make the second pass. *(See Figure 2-15.)*

2-13 Before tapering good leg stock, cut a test piece to check the setup. Lay out the taper on the test piece and mount it in the "Tapering Jig" on the opposite page. Place the jig on the table saw against the rip fence. Adjust the tapering jig to cut the slope — the layout line that indicates the taper should be parallel to the fence. Position the fence so the inside edges of the saw teeth (those closest to the fence) brush the layout line that marks the start of the taper.

2-14 Turn on the saw and slowly push the tapering jig forward, feeding the stock into the blade. As you do, monitor the cut to make sure the blade is following the layout line. If it does, the setup is correct. If not, readjust the angle of the jig or reposition the rip fence. When you're satisfied with the setup, cut tapers in the legs.

2-15 To cut a double taper, make a wedge-shaped shim with the same rise and run as the taper. After setting up the jig and the rip fence, move the rip fence ⅛ inch toward the blade (to compensate for the saw kerf) and slice a wedge off the test piece. Remember to move the rip fence back into position! Make the first pass of the double taper as if you were cutting a single taper. Then rotate the leg 180 degrees so the cut surface faces the jig. Insert the wedge between the leg and the jig with the thick part of the wedge against the bottom end of the leg. This will hold the leg at the proper angle for the second pass.

Note: Depending on the slope of the taper, you may have to attach the shim to the leg with carpet tape to mount them both in the jig.

Tapering Jig

This tapering jig differs from others that you may have seen in two important respects. First of all, it grips the stock. The leg is pinched between the ledge and the sliding clamp. Serrated teeth, made from cut-off brads, dig into the top and bottom of the leg, securing it to the jig. You don't have to hold the stock in the jig with one hand as you work. And second, the jig is wide enough that you can push it past the saw blade without bringing your hands near the whirling teeth. Both of these features help you keep your fingers on your hands.

To make the jig, you must rout two slots in the holding arm — a long, straight, counterbored slot and a semicircular slot. Make the counterbored slot with a table-mounted router, using a fence to guide the stock. Rout the slot through the stock with a ⅜-inch straight bit. Then, without altering the position of the fence, change to a 1-inch straight bit and make the counterbore. To rout the semicircular slot, use a ⅜-inch straight bit and circle-cutting jig.

To create the "teeth" for the clamp and the ledge, drive *brass* tacks partway into the wood, then clip off the heads close to the surface with side cutters. Brass is much softer than steel or carbide, and it will not hurt the teeth of your blade should you accidently nick the tacks when cutting a taper.

1 Before mounting a leg in the tapering jig, lay out the taper on the wood surface that will face up as you cut. Rest the leg against the face of the holding arm and the bottom end against the ledge. Slide the clamp until it touches the top end. Using a mallet, *lightly* tap the clamp. This will set the teeth in the clamp and the ledge so they grip the leg. Tighten the wing nut that secures the clamp.

2 To set the angle of the tapering jig to cut the proper slope, rest it against the rip fence of your table saw. Pivot the holding arm right or left until the layout line that indicates the taper on the leg stock is parallel to the fence. Measure the distance between the fence and the layout line at several locations — the line is parallel when all measurements are equal. Tighten the wing nut that secures the holding arm.

(continued) ▷

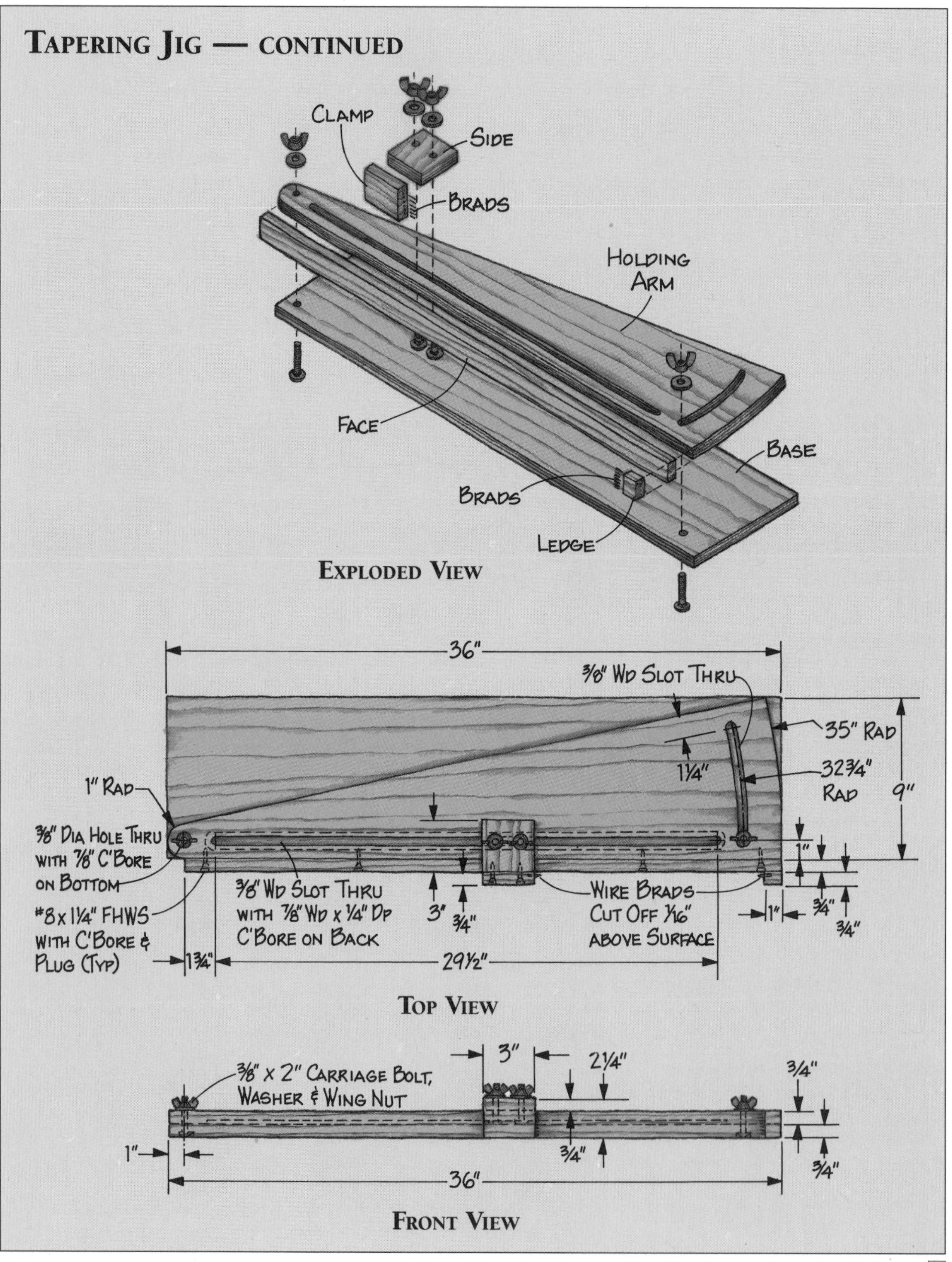

Tapering Jig — continued
Clamp
Side
Brads
Holding Arm
Face
Base
Brads
Ledge
Exploded View
36"
3/8" Wd Slot Thru
35" Rad
1 1/4"
32 3/4" Rad
9"
1" Rad
3/8" Dia Hole Thru with 7/8" C'Bore on Bottom
#8 x 1 1/4" FHWS with C'Bore & Plug (Typ)
3/8" Wd Slot Thru with 7/8" Wd x 1/4" Dp C'Bore on Back
3"
3/4"
Wire Brads Cut Off 1/16" above Surface
1"
1"
3/4"
3/4"
1 3/4"
29 1/2"
Top View
3"
2 1/4"
3/4"
3/8" x 2" Carriage Bolt, Washer & Wing Nut
1"
3/4"
3/4"
36"
Front View

TURNING LEGS

To turn table legs, you must mount them on a lathe, reduce the bottom portion of the legs to a cylinder, then cut beads, coves, and other shapes in the cylinder. These shapes combine to make a design, and this design is repeated on all four legs. *(SEE FIGURES 2-16 AND 2-17.)*

2-16 Turned table legs can be plain or fancy. The legs of the porringer serving table (left) are just gently tapered, while those on the book stand (right) sport beads, coves, flats, and tapers. Note that on both sets of legs only the *bottom* portion is turned. The top portion, where each leg joins the aprons, has been left square.

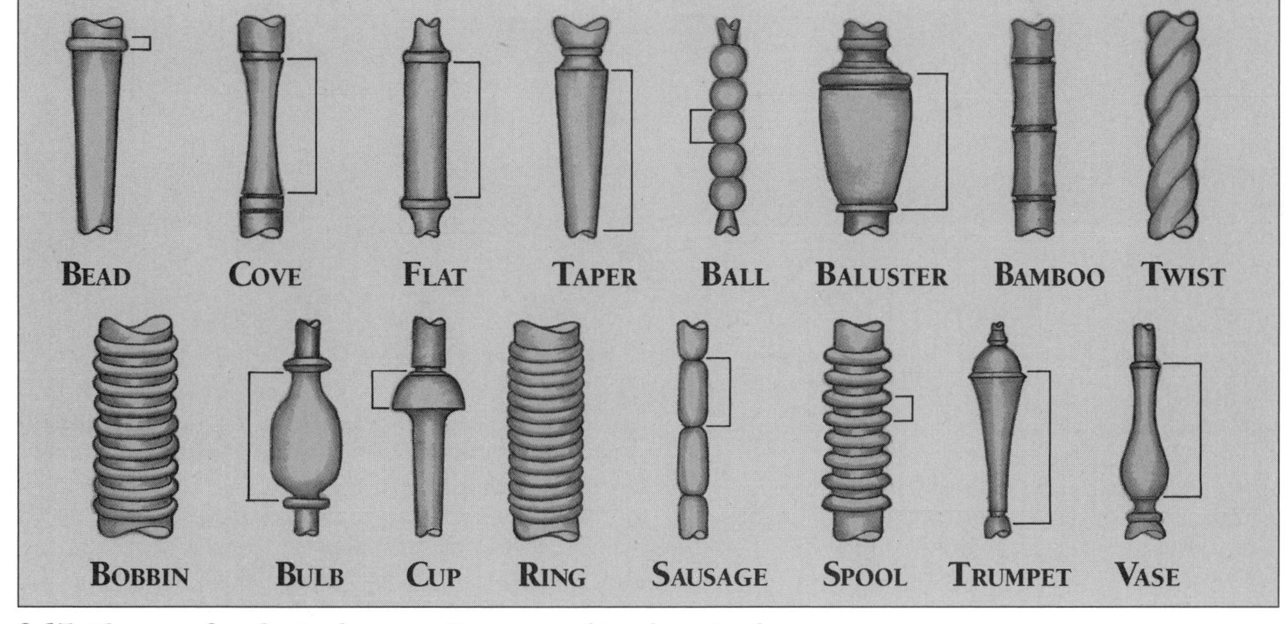

2-17 There are four basic shapes in spindle turning. A convex curve is called a *bead,* while a concave curve is a *cove.* You can also turn a *flat,* or simple cylinder, and a *taper,* or cone. You can combine these simple shapes to create more-complex designs. Shown here are several popular spindle patterns used in turning table legs.

The trick is to duplicate the same design on all four legs as closely as possible. You don't need a lathe duplicator to do this; the technique is very simple. Draw up a full-size pattern of the turned leg and measure the changing diameters all along the length of the turning. (*See Figure 2-18.*) Turn each leg to make a rough cylinder and mark the locations of the diameters on it. (*See Figure 2-19.*) Using a parting tool and calipers, turn the cylinder down to the appropriate diameter at each of the locations you have marked. (*See Figure 2-20.*)

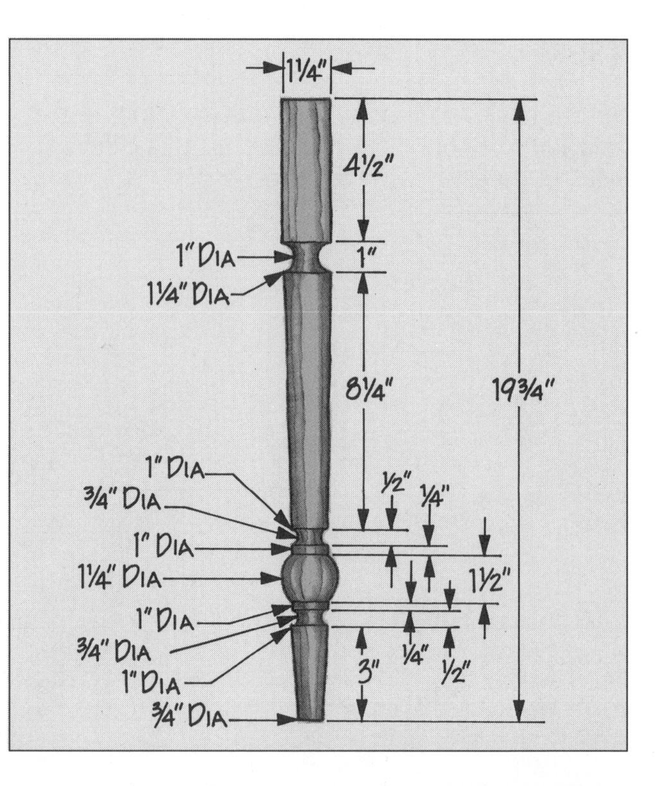

***2-18* The first step in turning a** set of table legs is to draw a full-size pattern. Carefully measure the *major* and *minor* diameters. The major diameters include the crests of beads, flats, and the widest portions of tapers. Minor diameters include the bottoms of coves and the narrowest portions of tapers. Also measure the locations of these diameters along the length of the leg.

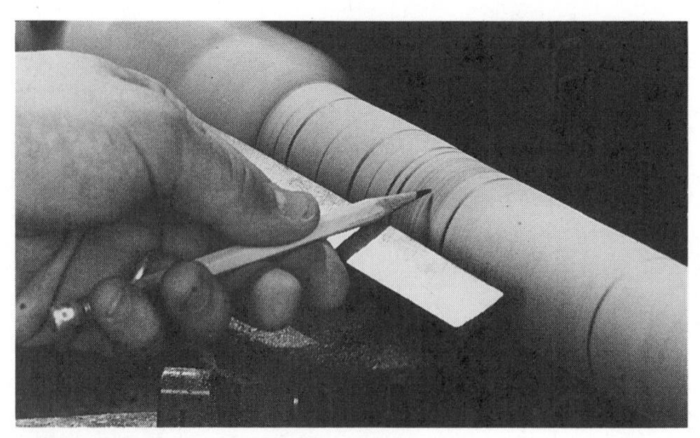

***2-19* Turn each leg to a rough** cylinder, slightly larger than the largest diameter in your pattern. With a pencil, mark the locations of the diameters along the length of the leg. Indicate the major diameters with marks that are thicker and darker than those that show the minor diameters, so you can easily tell the difference between the two. Many turners also shade the beads and coves, making the beads darker and the coves lighter. The flats and tapers are left unshaded. This takes a little time, but it eliminates confusion and the need for you to constantly check your pattern when turning a complex design.

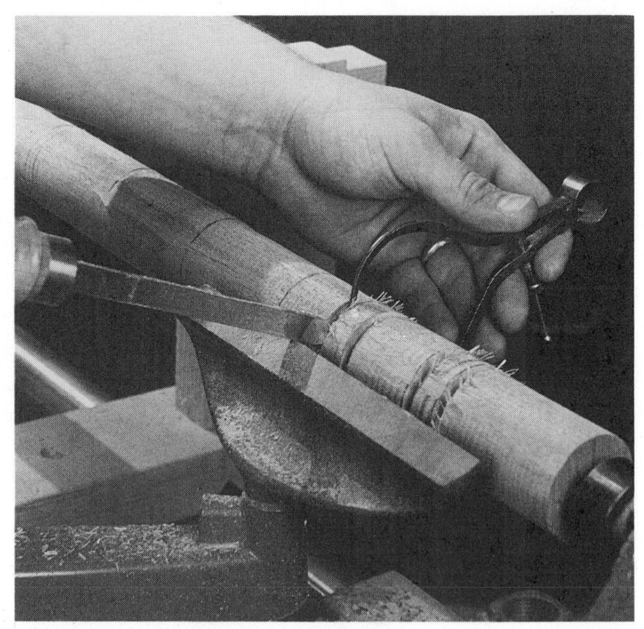

***2-20* At each mark, turn the leg** down to the appropriate diameter with a parting tool. Use calipers to gauge the diameter as you work. The parting tool will cut a narrow groove only a little wider than a saw kerf. Stop turning when you reach the desired diameters, then shade the narrow flat at the bottom of each groove with a pencil.

Then turn the beads, coves, flats, and tapers in your pattern, stopping at the diameters you have already turned. *(SEE FIGURE 2-21.)* As you work, compare the leg to the pattern from time to time. *(SEE FIGURE 2-22.)*

As long as you have correctly marked the location of the diameters and you don't turn down past them, the completed leg will look very much like the pattern. If you use this procedure for all four legs, they will look very much like each other. There will be some minor differences, of course, but the eye accepts small deviations in patterns without registering them. Few people, other than yourself and some fellow craftsmen, will ever notice.

TRY THIS TRICK

If there are many different diameters in your turning, make a set of *fixed calipers* — one for each diameter used — from scraps of plywood, as shown. This will save you the hassle of constantly readjusting your adjustable calipers.

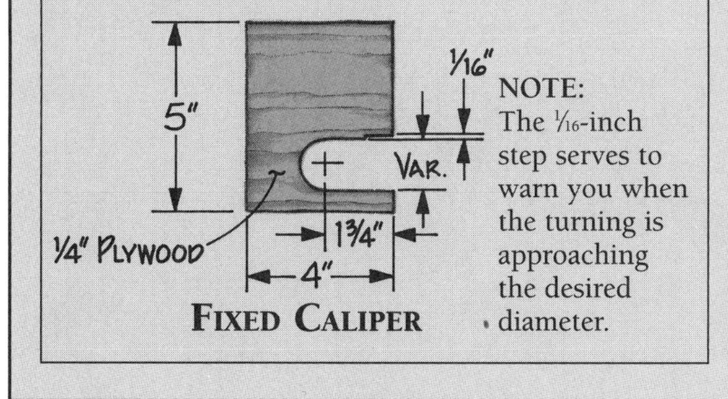

FIXED CALIPER

NOTE: The 1/16-inch step serves to warn you when the turning is approaching the desired diameter.

2-21 Turn the beads, coves, flats, and tapers in the design, using the appropriate turning tools for each shape. Cut each shape down to the pencil mark at the bottom of the groove left by the parting tool, but no farther. Stop cutting when the turning chisel begins to remove the mark.

2-22 As you work, compare the evolving leg to the full-size pattern. Then, after you've turned the first leg, use it as a comparison when turning the remaining legs. If you're careful when marking and turning the diameters, the legs will turn out remarkably similar to one another. There may be some minor differences, of course, but these won't be distracting.

MAKING CABRIOLE LEGS

Cabriole legs are often used on classic and traditional tables. These S-shaped legs come in many shapes and sizes, but all of them have several features in common — post, knee, ankle, and foot. Some cabriole legs also have "ears" or *transition blocks,* which make the curved legs seem to flow out of the aprons to which they're attached. *(SEE FIGURE 2-23.)*

These curved legs are usually cut on a band saw, using a technique called *compound cutting.* To make a cabriole leg without transition blocks, trace the pattern on the two adjacent inside surfaces of the leg stock. Cut the profile of one side on the band saw, saving the waste. Tape the waste back to the stock to make it square again, and cut the second side. When you remove the tape and the waste, you'll have a leg that curves through all three dimensions. *(SEE FIGURES 2-24 AND 2-25.)*

If the legs have transition blocks, the procedure is slightly more complex. You must glue the blocks to the leg stock, then trace the patterns on all the parts — legs *and* ears. When cutting, you must cut through both parts at times. *(SEE FIGURES 2-26 AND 2-27.)*

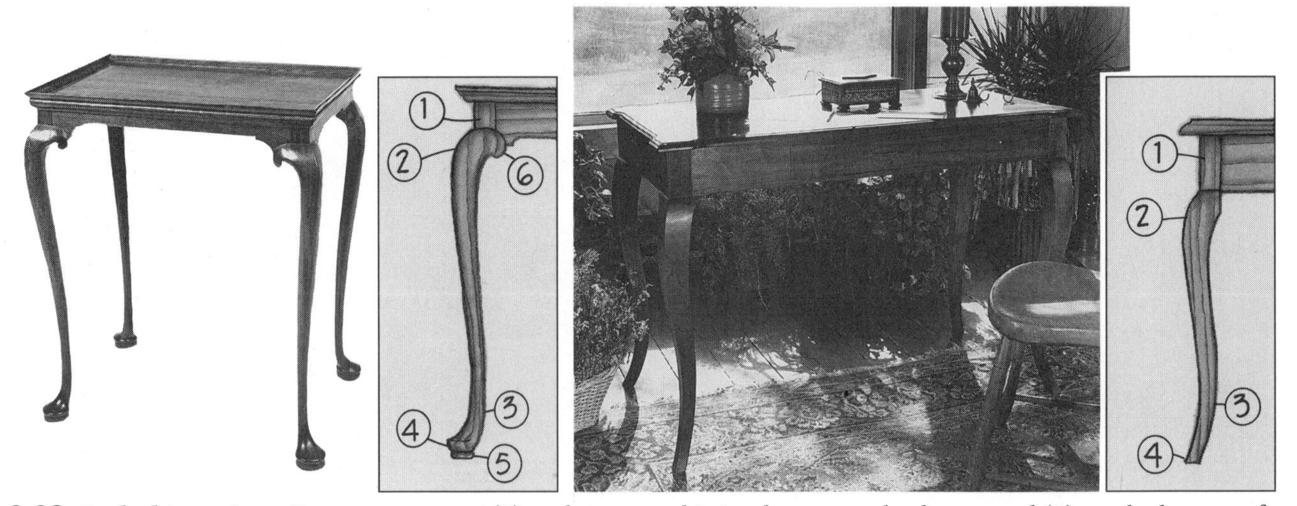

2-23 Both this antique Queen Anne table and this Post-Modern writing table have S-shaped cabriole legs. While cabriole legs come in many different sizes and designs, they all have a straight section or ***post*** (1) at the top — this is where the leg is joined to the aprons. The shaped portion begins at the ***knee*** (2), which curves out. The curve reverses at the ***ankle*** (3), then ends in a ***foot*** (4). Some cabriole legs may also have a ***pad*** (5) on the bottom of the foot. Others have decorative ***ears*** or ***transition blocks*** (6) on the sides, near the knees. *Queen Anne table photo courtesy of Israel Sack, Inc.*

2-24 To make a cabriole leg with-out transition blocks, first make a stiff leg pattern from posterboard or thin hardboard. Trace the pattern on the two adjacent inside surfaces of the leg stock. Flip the pattern over when marking the second side so each layout is a *mirror image* of the other. **Note:** Be careful that the parts of the layout — post, knee, ankle, and foot — line up with each other horizontally. The most critical part is the transition from the post to the knee. To make sure that it's aligned, mark a horizontal line on the pattern through this point. Measure the position of the post/knee transition on both surfaces of the leg, and using a square, mark horizontal lines on the stock. When positioning the pattern on the stock, align the horizontal lines.

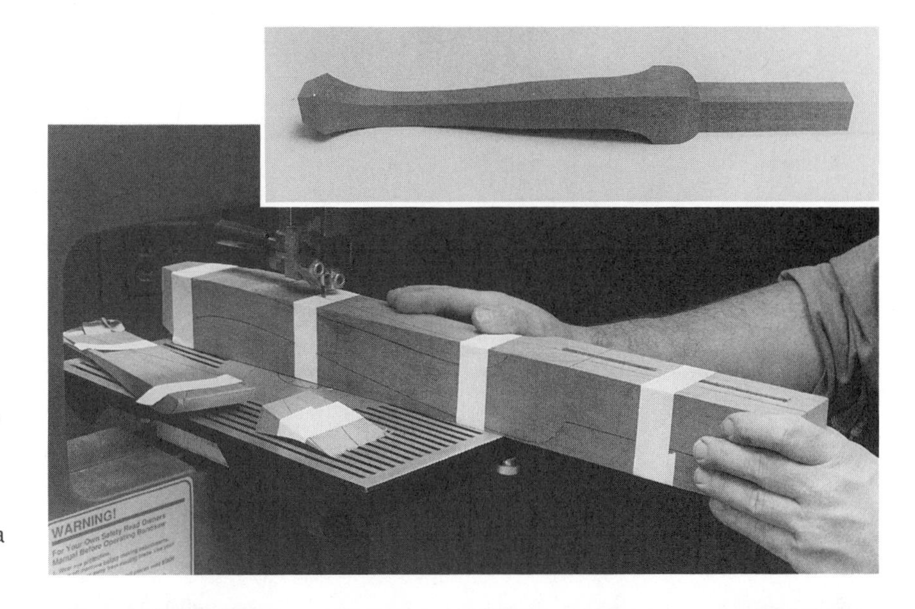

2-25 Cut the pattern on one surface of the leg, saving the waste. Tape the waste back to the stock — this makes the stock square again. Turn the stock 90 degrees and cut the second side. When you remove the tape and the waste, you'll have a cabriole leg.

2-26 To cut a cabriole leg with transition blocks, make *three* patterns — one for the leg, one for the knee, and one for the blocks. Glue the blocks to the leg stock, making sure that the grain directions match. Trace the patterns on the inside surfaces of the legs and the blocks. Once again, the patterns should be mirror images of each other. Note that each transition block must be marked on two sides, just like the leg stock. One side shows the shape of the ear; the other, the shape of the knee.

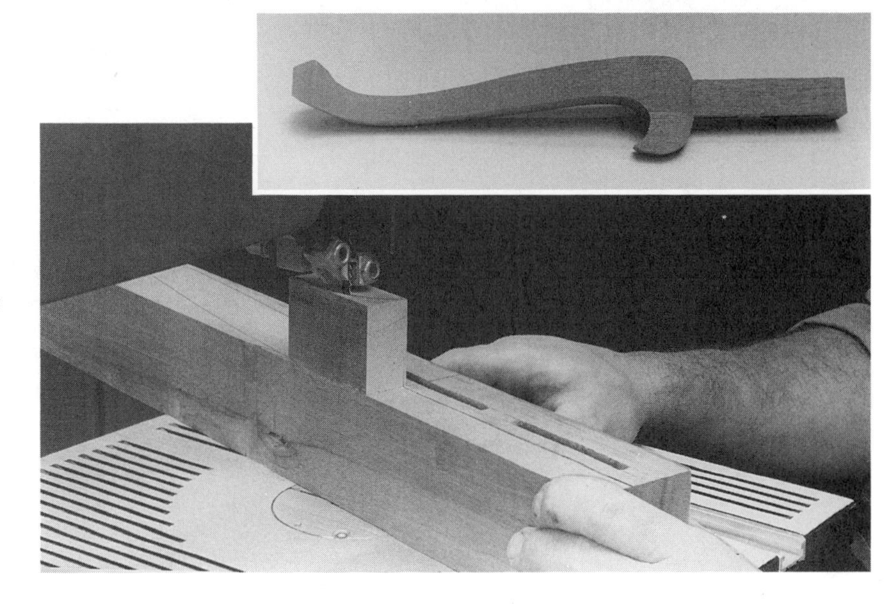

2-27 As you make the compound cuts, you must keep the upper blade guide the proper distance from the leg stock. This means that you must occasionally turn off the band saw, wait for the blade to coast to a stop, adjust the blade guide, and restart the saw. The blade guide must be raised to cut through both the ear and the leg, and lowered when cutting just the leg.

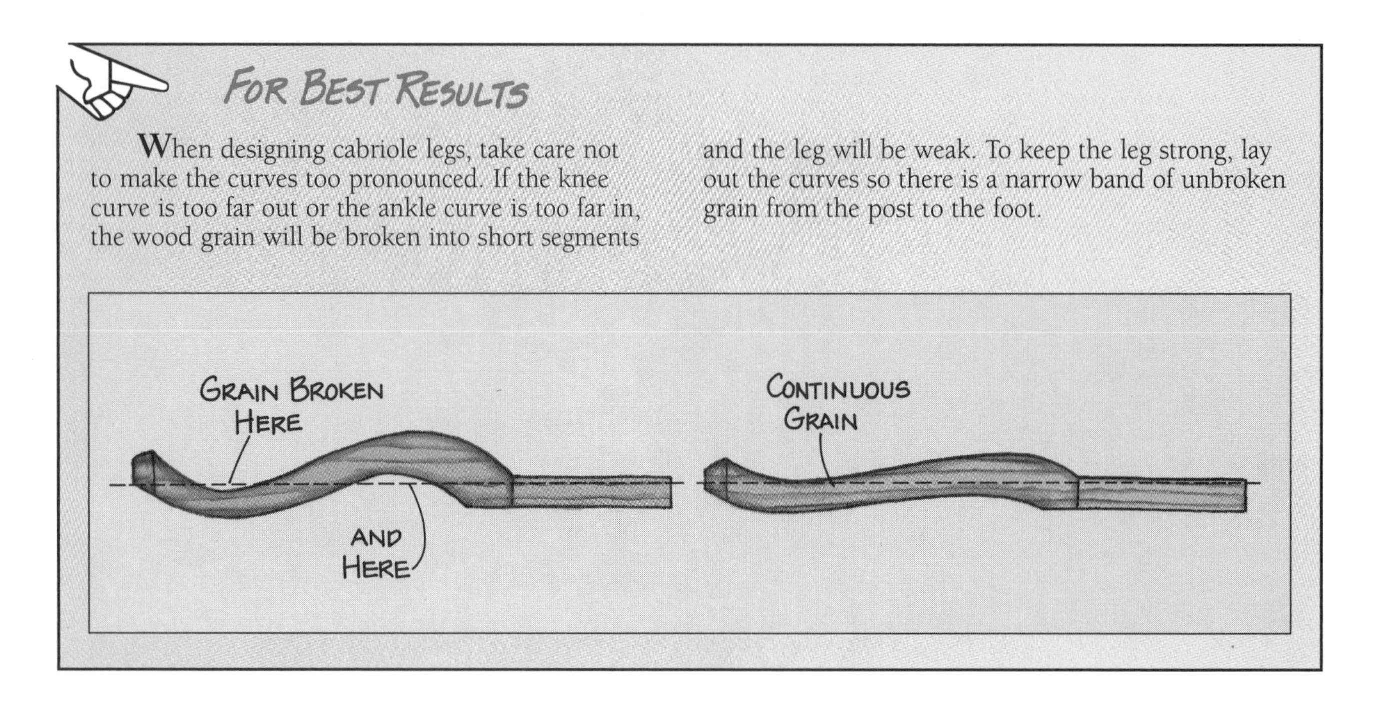

For Best Results

When designing cabriole legs, take care not to make the curves too pronounced. If the knee curve is too far out or the ankle curve is too far in, the wood grain will be broken into short segments and the leg will be weak. To keep the leg strong, lay out the curves so there is a narrow band of unbroken grain from the post to the foot.

DETAILING THE APRONS

Like the legs, the aprons can also be decorative. Often the bottom edges are molded, shaped, or cut with an ornamental profile. *(See Figure 2-28.)* On tables that are meant to be placed against a wall, only the front apron needs to be so treated; leave the side and back aprons plain.

2-28 Aprons may be decorative as well as functional. The bottom edge of the apron on the left has been cut with a band saw to create an ornamental profile. The one on the right has been routed to make a decorative bead.

3

Trestles and Pedestals

Although the leg-and-apron system is the most popular way to support a tabletop, trestles and pedestals have some advantages. Trestles are often easier to build than legs and aprons. And you can design them to be easily knocked down — join the rails to the trestles with wedged mortise-and-tenon joints, and remove the wedges to take the table apart. Trestle construction is also an ideal choice for long tables.

A pedestal is a good choice for a small table. It's strong, it's light, and it often takes up less space than legs and aprons. A pedestal also works well for a large round table. The assembly is less likely to interfere with the seating at a round table than legs and aprons.

Making Trestles

Trestles support a tabletop just as sawhorses support a plank — the top lies across them. The top portion of each trestle is often attached to a horizontal *batten.* The batten serves two purposes: It's used as a cleat to attach the trestle to the top, and it braces the top, preventing it from cupping.

Each table requires a set of two or more trestles. The trestles are joined with one or more horizontal *rails* or stretchers. The rails perform the same function for the trestles that aprons do for the legs — they keep them from racking.

TRESTLE DESIGNS

There are three common trestle designs (SEE FIGURE 3-1):

- A *slab* trestle, made from a single wide plank
- A *frame* trestle, consisting of two horizontal rails and one or more vertical stiles or posts
- A *sawbuck* or X-frame trestle, made from two crossed legs

TRESTLE JOINERY

The parts of a frame trestle are usually assembled with mortise-and-tenon joints. (SEE FIGURE 3-2.) Sawbucks are often made with lap joints. (SEE FIGURE 3-3.)

Traditionally, the trestles are joined to the rails with *tusk* mortise-and-tenon joints. This joint is made much like an ordinary through mortise-and-tenon joint, with several important additions. First of all, the tenon extends through the trestle and protrudes from the other side. The tenon itself is mortised for a wedge or *tusk,* and the mortise is located so the tusk draws the trestle tight against the shoulders of the tenon. (SEE FIGURES 3-4 THROUGH 3-7.)

3-1* Trestles support a tabletop** much the way sawhorses support a plank. Although there are many shapes and styles, most trestles are variations of three different designs — the ***slab trestle (1), the ***frame*** trestle (2), and the ***sawbuck*** trestle (3).

For Best Results

Although you can align the tusk in a tusk mortise-and-tenon in any direction, it's best to position it vertically so it drops into its mortise. As the wood expands and contracts with the seasons, gravity will pull the tusk down and tighten the joint.

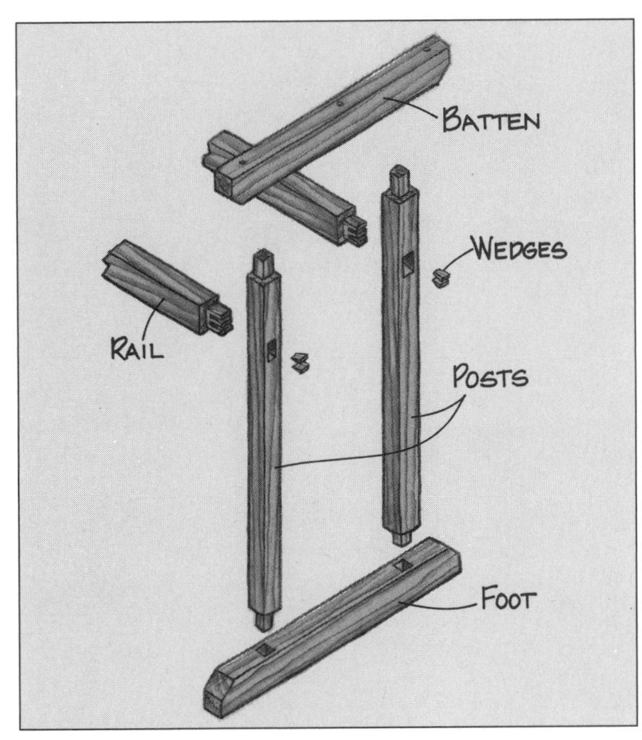

3-2 The members of a frame trestle are often joined with ordinary mortise-and-tenon joints. The top rail (or *batten*) and the bottom rail *(foot)* are mortised to accept the tenons on the ends of the stiles *(posts)*.

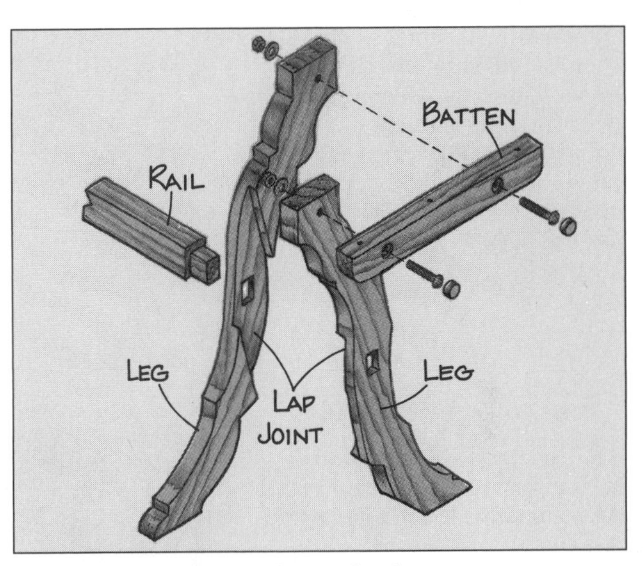

3-3 The crossed legs of a sawbuck trestle are sometimes joined with lap joints. Often, the top ends of the legs are attached to a horizontal batten, which in turn is attached to the tabletop.

3-4 When joining trestles and rails with tusk mortise-and-tenon joints, each tenon should extend through its mortise and protrude from the other side. Make a second mortise in the tenon itself to accommodate a wedge or *tusk*. Locate this tusk mortise so the tusk will draw the trestle tight against the shoulders of the tenon. There's no need to glue this joint; the tusk secures the parts. Should you want to knock the assembly down, drive the tusk out of the tenon and remove the tenon from the mortise.

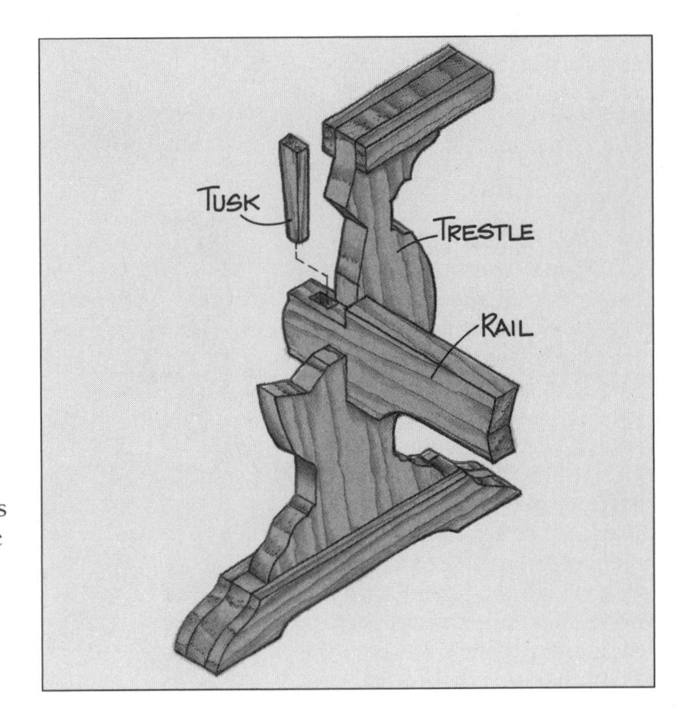

3-5 The trick to making a tusk mortise-and-tenon joint is locating the tusk mortise in the tenon. To do this, first cut the mortise in the trestle, then make a tenon in the end of a rail to fit it. Try for a slip fit — the tenon should slip through the mortise with little slop. It should not be tight. Press the tenon into the mortise so the shoulders are snug against the trestle. Mark the cheeks of the tenon even with the outside surface of the trestle.

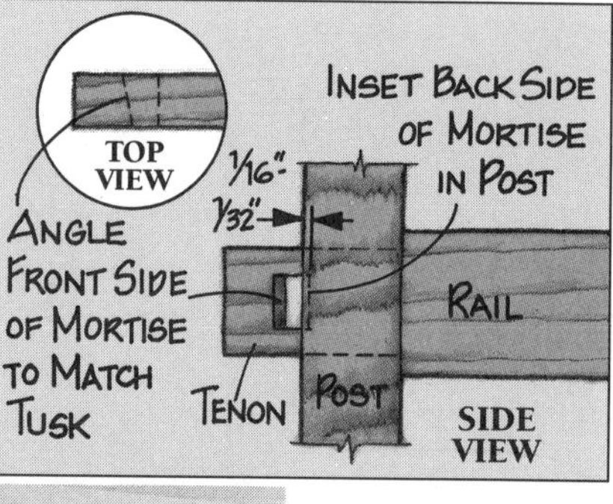

3-6 The back side of the tusk mortise (closest to the tenon shoulders) should be slightly *inside* the trestle mortise. Measure back 1/32 to 1/16 inch from the marks you made on the tenon. The front side must be angled to match the tusk. Make this angle fairly shallow, no more than 15 degrees from the back side. If it's too steep, the tusk will work loose. Remove as much waste as you can from the mortise with a drill bit, then clean up the inside surfaces with a chisel. As you work, occasionally insert the tusk into the tusk mortise to check the fit.

3-7 The weakest point of a tusk mortise-and-tenon joint is the end of the tenon. If you drive the tusk too tight or there's too much pressure from racking, the wood grain on the end of the tenon will split. There are two ways to prevent this. First, you can make the tenon longer — there should be at least 1 inch of solid wood from the tusk mortise to the tenon end to provide sufficient strength. Second, drill a hole through the tenon, across the wood grain and perpendicular to the tusk mortise. Glue a dowel in this hole to reinforce the tenon.

Making Pedestals

A pedestal is a single *post* with three or more *feet* joined to it near the bottom. The top of the post is usually attached to a horizontal brace or batten, and this is fastened to the tabletop.

PEDESTAL DESIGNS

Pedestal posts are usually turned round; but square, hexagonal, and octagonal posts are also common. Small posts are usually made of solid wood, but large ones may be hollow to save weight and materials. (See Figure 3-8.)

Pedestal feet also come in many sizes and shapes. The most common design is S-shaped or *serpent* feet, but they may also be straight or semicircular. Semicircular legs are also called *saber* legs and *spider* legs, depending on which way the curve faces. (See Figure 3-9.)

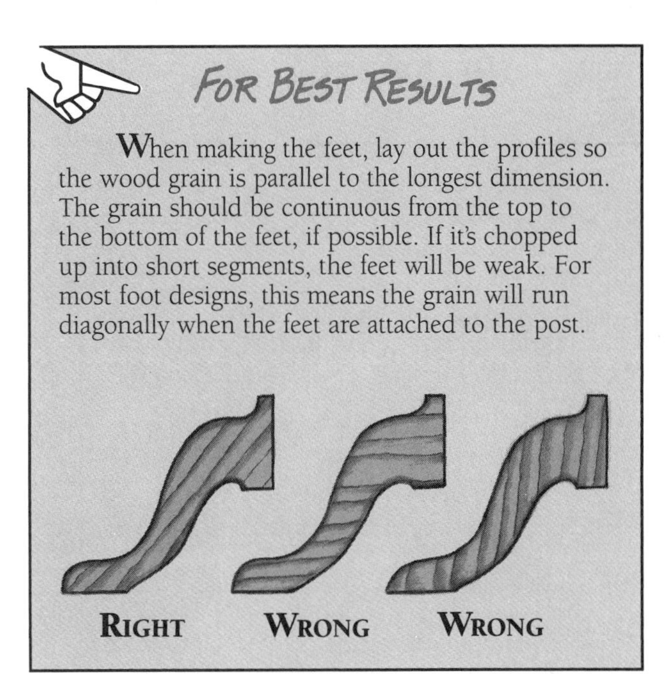

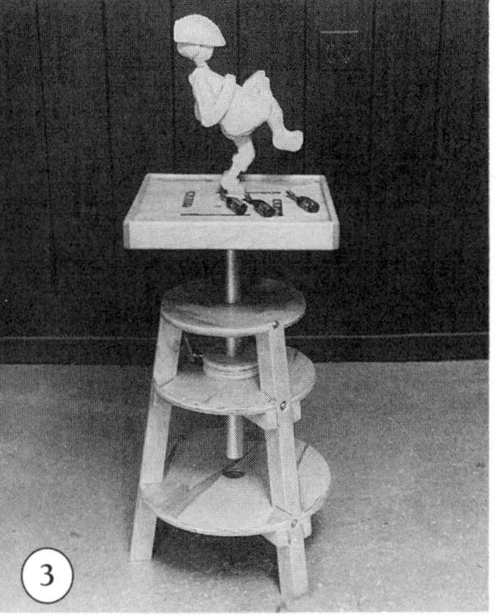

3-8 Pedestal tables come in all shapes and sizes, and the pedestals can be made in many ways. The large dining table (1) is supported by a massive pedestal with a hollow post. The middle section of the post is turned, while the top and bottom are octagonal. The pedestal of the traditional candlestand (2) has a solid post and has been turned round. The pedestal on the work stand (3) has an *adjustable* metal post — it can be raised and lowered to change the height of the work surface.

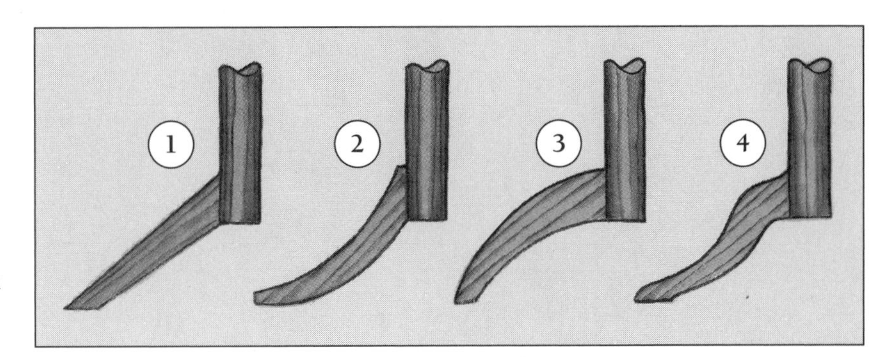

3-9 You can cut pedestal feet to many shapes. The four most common are ***straight*** (1), ***saber*** (2), ***spider*** (3), and ***serpent*** (4).

HOLLOW POST JOINERY

How you join the parts of a pedestal depends on whether the post is hollow or solid. If it's a large pedestal with a hollow post, make the post by gluing several strips of wood edge to edge to form a hexagonal or octagonal column. *(SEE FIGURES 3-10 AND 3-11.)* You may turn this hollow column on a lathe to make it round, or leave the sides flat. *(SEE FIGURE 3-12.)* If the column is round where the legs are attached, cope the ends of the legs to fit it. *(SEE FIGURE 3-13.)*

Although you can use traditional joinery, the easiest way to secure the feet to a hollow post is with lag screws or hanger bolts. If using lag screws, drive them through the post from the inside, and into the feet. If using hanger bolts, drive the screw ends into the feet and insert the bolt ends in the post. *(SEE FIGURE 3-14.)*

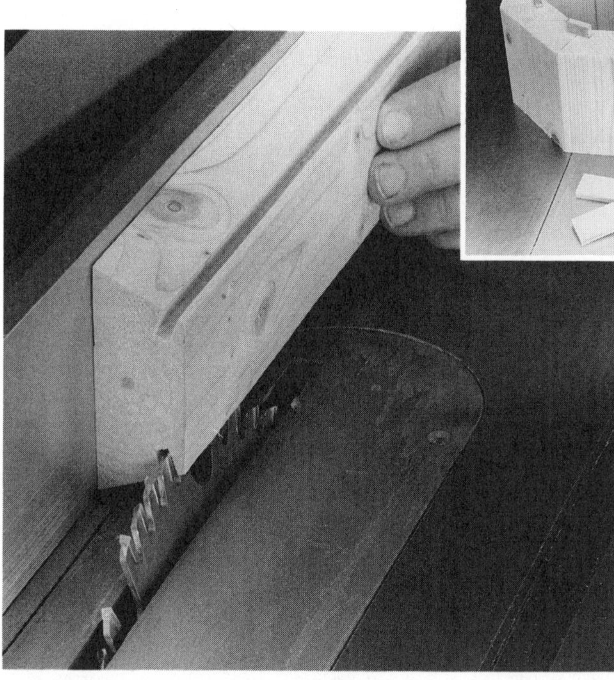

***3-10* To make a large hollow post,** glue strips of stock edge to edge to form a hexagonal or octagonal column. For extra strength, join the strip with plywood splines, as shown. If making a hexagon, rip the edges with the blade tilted to 30 degrees; for an octagon, the blade should be at 22½ degrees. Before cutting the good stock, rip a test strip, then cut it into six or eight short lengths. Assemble these pieces in a ring; they should fit together with no gaps. If any of the edge joints gaps toward the inside, the angle is too large — reduce it slightly. If any joint gaps to the outside, the angle is too small — increase it. **Note:** If you plan to turn the pedestal, make the strips from *thick* stock. Position the splines as close to the inside surfaces as is practical.

***3-11* When you've zeroed in on** the correct angle, rip the strips from the good stock. Glue them together in a column, securing the assembly with band clamps until the glue dries.

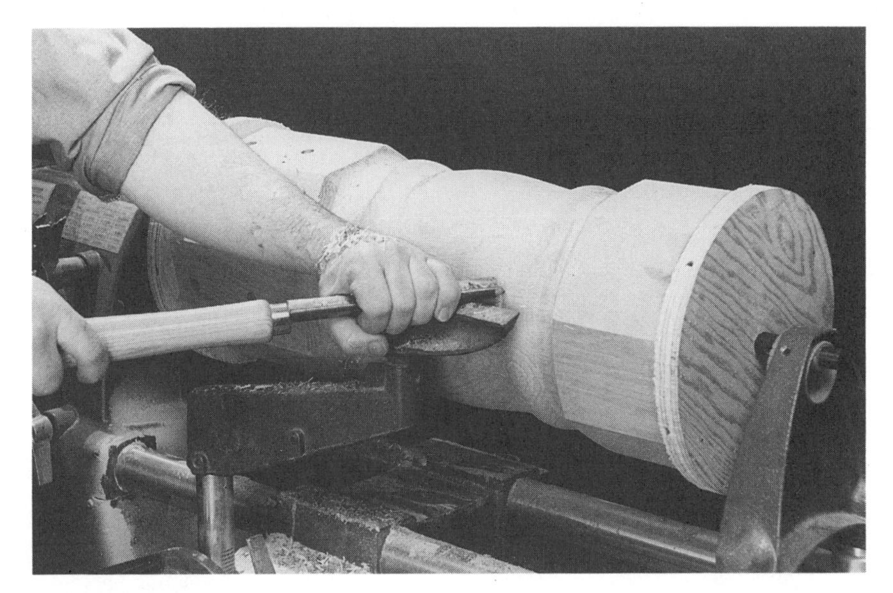

3-12 **If you wish to turn a hollow** post, cut two discs from scraps of plywood. The diameter of the discs should be slightly larger than the column. Carefully center the discs on the ends of the column, then secure them with screws or nails. Mount this assembly on a lathe, imbedding the centers in the discs. Turn the assembly at slow speed. **Warning:** Let the glue that holds the column together dry for *at least* 24 hours before turning it. Otherwise, the strips may fly apart on the lathe.

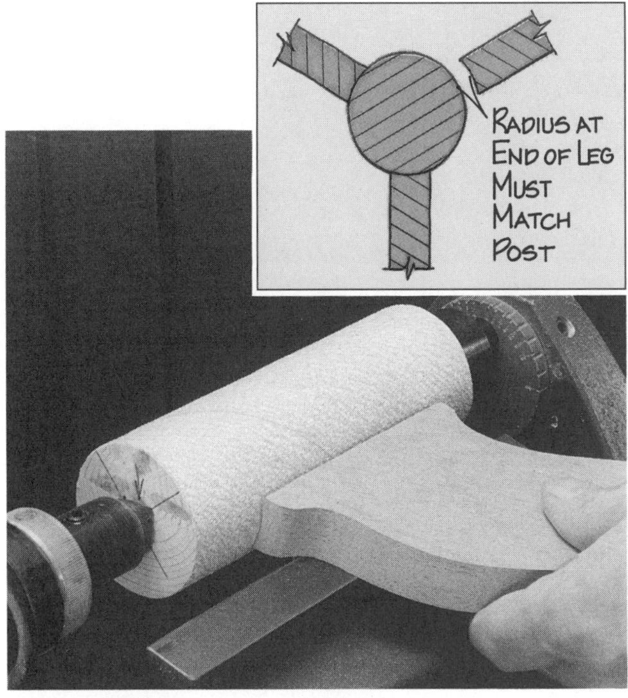

3-13 **If you turn a post round,** you must cut *hollows* or concave curves the same diameter as the post in the ends of the legs where they join it. Otherwise, they won't fit flush against the post. One of the easiest ways to make these hollows is with a drum sander the same diameter as the post. Turn a scrap on the lathe and adhere a coarse (50-grit) cloth-backed sanding belt to it with spray adhesive. Use this to sand the hollows in the ends of the legs.

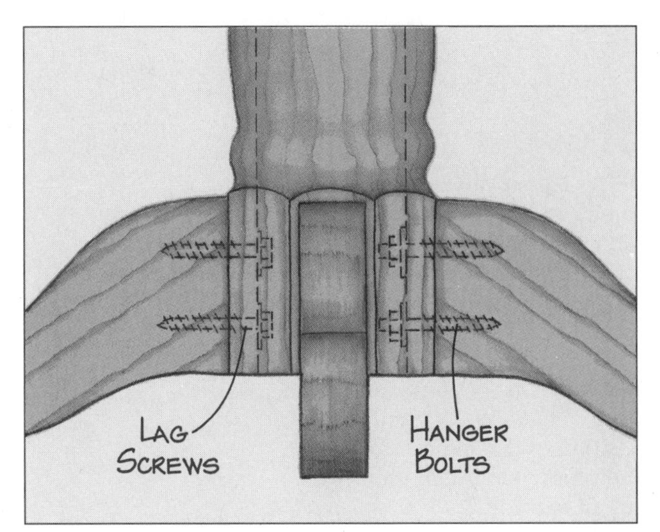

3-14 **One of the easiest ways to** attach the legs to a hollow post is to use lag screws or hanger bolts. If you don't plan to take the table apart, use lag screws — drive them through the post from the inside and into the ends of the legs. If you think you might want to knock the table down someday, either to move or to store it, use hanger bolts. Drive the screw ends of the bolts into the ends of the legs. Drill holes in the post, insert the bolt ends in the holes, and secure the legs with nuts and washers on the inside of the post.

SOLID POST JOINERY

Make smaller, solid posts from turning blocks or leg stock. For round posts, turn the stock on a lathe. For hexagonal and octagonal posts, straighten and square the post as you would a table leg, then rip the angled sides on a table saw.

Traditionally, feet are joined to solid posts with sliding dovetails. Cut dovetail slots in the bottom end of the post and dovetail tenons in the ends of the legs. Slide the tenons into the slots. *(SEE FIGURES 3-15 THROUGH 3-18.)* Or, you can use *keyed grooves* instead.

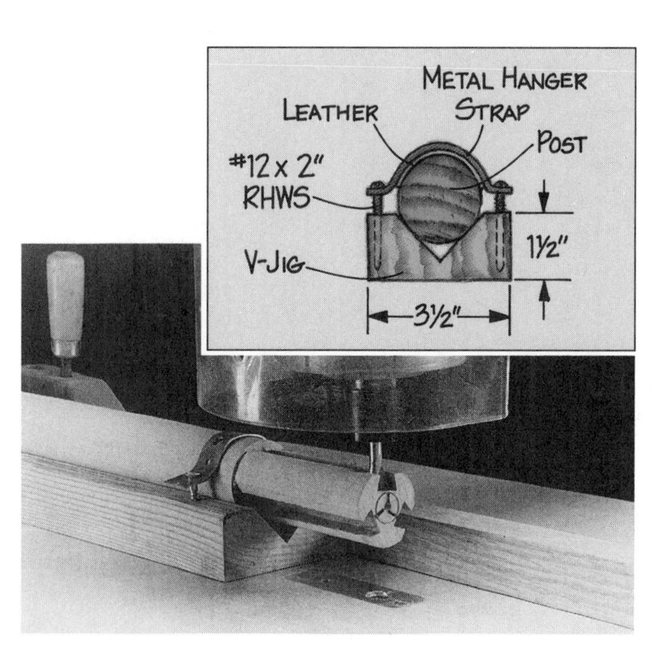

3-15 **To cut dovetail slots in a** round post, use an overarm router (shown) or an overhead routing jig and a dovetail bit. Mount the post in a V-jig and secure it with straps and roundhead wood screws. Using a fence to guide the V-jig, rout the first slot. Turn off the router, loosen the strap, rotate the post until it's in position to make the second slot, and repeat. Continue until you have cut all the slots.

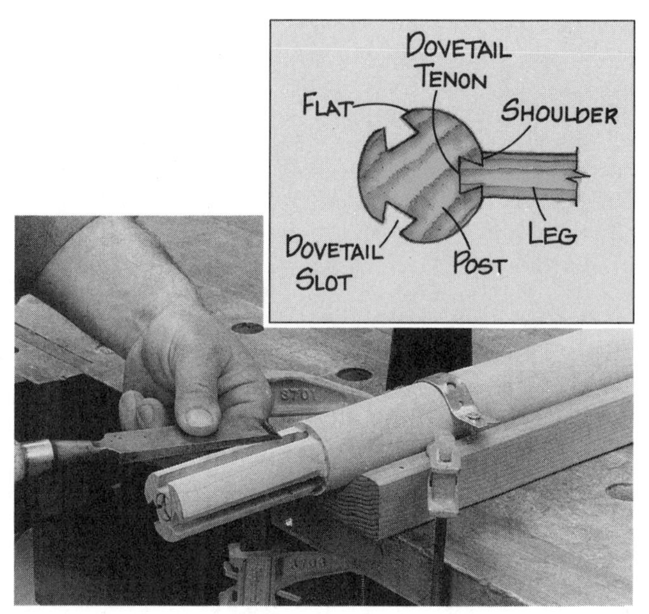

3-16 **Because you must use the** same bit to make the dovetail tenons as you used to make the slots, the tenons will have square shoulders. For them to fit flush, you must cut a flat area on the top of each slot. Remove the dovetail bit from the router and replace it with a wide straight bit. Rout the flats with the same setup you used to make the slots. Square off the upper ends of the flats with a chisel.

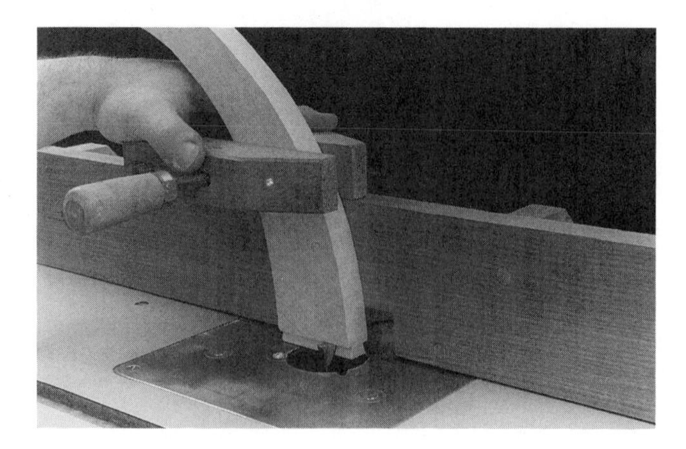

3-17 **Cut the dovetail tenons in** the ends of the legs, using a table-mounted router and the same bit you used to make the slots. Make each tenon in two passes. Rout one face of the leg, turn it around, and rout the other. Use a hand screw as shown to help hold the leg at the proper angle as you rout.

Rout grooves in the posts; glue the legs in the grooves; then drill dowel holes in the bottom end of the assembled pedestal. Position the holes so the dowels will serve as "keys" to keep the legs from pulling out of the post. (*See Figures 3-19 through 3-21.*)

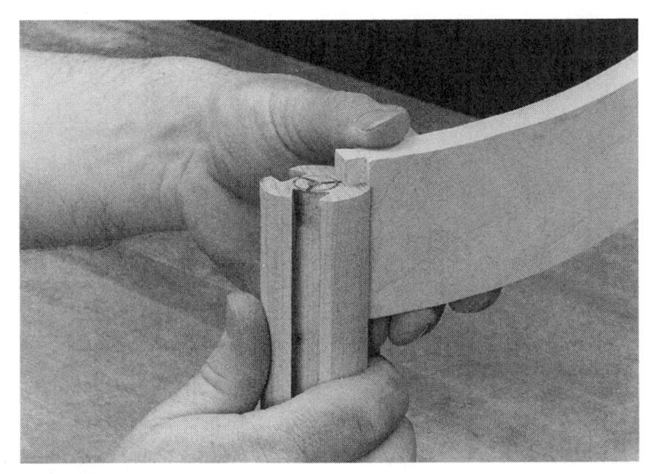

3-18 **Slide each tenon into its slot** to test the fit. It should be snug, but not too tight. It's a good idea to rout one or more test pieces in scrap stock to fine-tune your setup *before* routing the tenons in the legs.

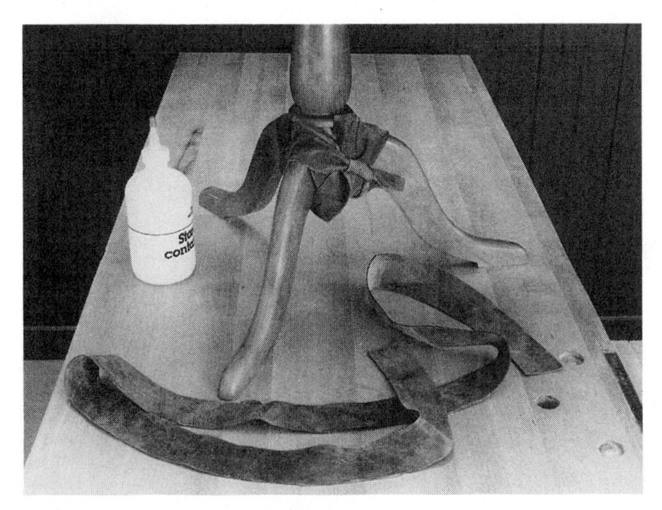

3-20 **Glue the legs in the post.** This assembly can be tricky; there's no commercial clamp commonly available that will hold the legs in the grooves as the glue dries. However, you can make one from bungee cords or strips of inner tube. Wrap the elastic material around the post, going over and under the legs, as shown.

3-19 **As an alternative to sliding** dovetails, you can attach legs to a post with *keyed grooves*. These are just as strong, but a lot simpler to make. First, rout straight-sided grooves in the post with an overarm router and a straight bit. The grooves must be as wide as the legs are thick. Square the blind ends of the grooves with a chisel.

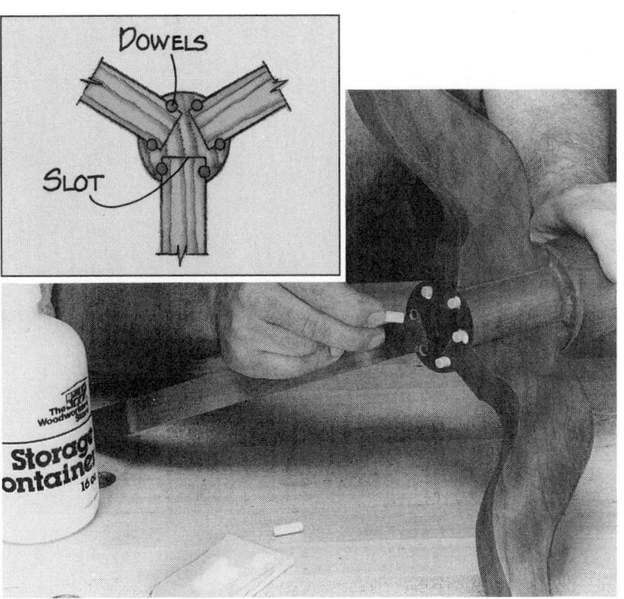

3-21 **Drill small dowel holes in** the bottom of the assembly, straddling the seams between the faces of the legs and the sides of the grooves. Glue dowels in these holes and cut them flush with the bottom end of the post. These dowels will serve as "keys," keeping the legs from pulling out of the grooves.

Tip-and-Turn Tables

A *tip-and-turn* table is a pedestal table on which the tabletop tips and turns. It was originally intended for serving food or drink. The top turned to provide easy access. When the meal was over and the table was no longer needed, the top tipped up so the table could be stored against a wall.

The device that enables the top to move so freely is called a *birdcage*. It's not really a cage, but an open box consisting of a top, a bottom, and four dowels or spindles. The tabletop is attached to the birdcage top with a hinge or pivots so it can be tilted horizontal or vertical.

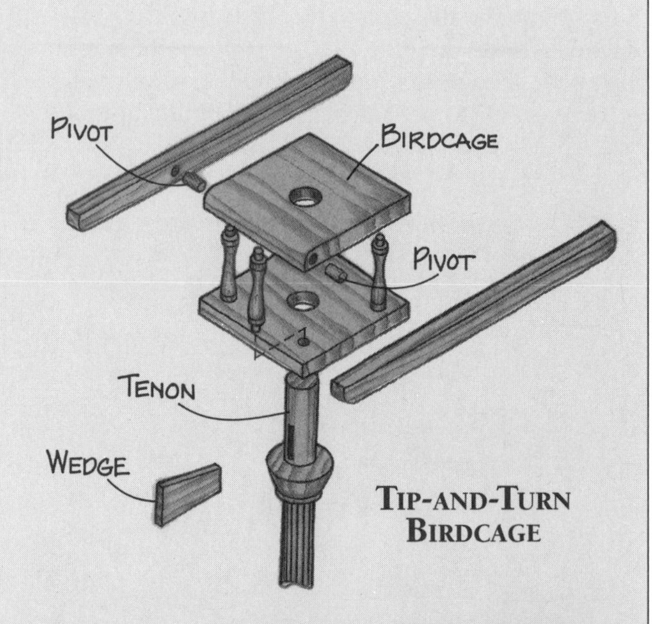

Tip-and-Turn Birdcage

1 **When making the pedestal** post, turn a large, round tenon in the top end. This tenon should be as long as the birdcage is tall. Drill both the top and the bottom of the birdcage to fit over this tenon.

2 **Mortise the tenon to accept a** slender wedge. Insert the wedge in the mortise to secure the birdcage to the pedestal. This prevents the top from coming loose, but it will leave it free to tip and turn.

4

TABLETOPS

There is more to making a single-slab tabletop than meets the eye, especially if you glue up the slab from several smaller boards. It isn't a simple matter of arranging the boards so they look attractive. You must also consider the moisture content of the wood, the orientation of the wood grain, and the type of grain at the adjoining edges. Otherwise, the slabs may split, cup, or develop *steps* — visible lines at the glue joints where the surfaces are no longer flush.

The same is true of table leaves. You must not only take care when gluing them up, but also consider how they join the tabletop and whether they fold or extend. Folding tabletops often require special joinery, while extending tops need special hardware.

When fastening tabletops to their supporting assemblies, you must allow for expansion and contraction. All wood shrinks and swells with changes in humidity, but the problem is compounded for tabletops because they are so much wider than other furniture parts. Consequently, you must employ special joinery that allows them to move.

MAKING SLAB TOPS AND LEAVES

Although 24-inch-wide boards were once common in America, it's rare to find them nowadays. And when you do find them, you should think twice about using them for a tabletop. Extremely wide planks are not stable, and they're sometimes prone to checking and cupping. For these reasons, most contemporary slab tops are made by gluing several narrow boards edge to edge to make a wide plank.

GLUING STOCK EDGE TO EDGE

At first glance, it's a simple technique: Joint the edges of the boards straight; arrange them so the wood grain of each board matches the adjoining board as well as possible; then glue them together. However, there is more going on here than meets the eye. To avoid some common pitfalls, you must consider how the wood moves.

Wood moves in three planes — *longitudinal* (parallel to the wood grain), *tangential* (tangent to the growth rings), and *radial* (across the growth rings). Longitudinal movement is negligible; the wood is almost completely stable along the grain. But tangential and radial movement is substantial. Furthermore, *tangential movement is twice that of radial movement* in most wood species. It's this difference that you must remember when gluing up tabletops. *(SEE FIGURE 4-1.)*

A typical plain-sawn board shows both the tangential and radial planes on its face — tangential near the center, radial close to the edges. Because the different areas of the board expand and contract at different rates, plain-sawn wood has a tendency to cup in the opposite direction of the growth rings. Quarter-sawn wood, on the other hand, shows only the radial plane on its face. It moves less than a plain-sawn board and has little tendency to cup. *(SEE FIGURE 4-2.)*

When gluing plain-sawn stock edge to edge, there are two useful ways to orient the boards. You can *alternate the growth rings,* turning every other one up and those in between down. When the individual boards move, they will cup in opposite directions. This will create a washboard effect, but overall the assembly will remain flat. This technique is best used for table leaves and *unsupported* tops — wide boards that will not be braced by aprons, battens, or cleats.

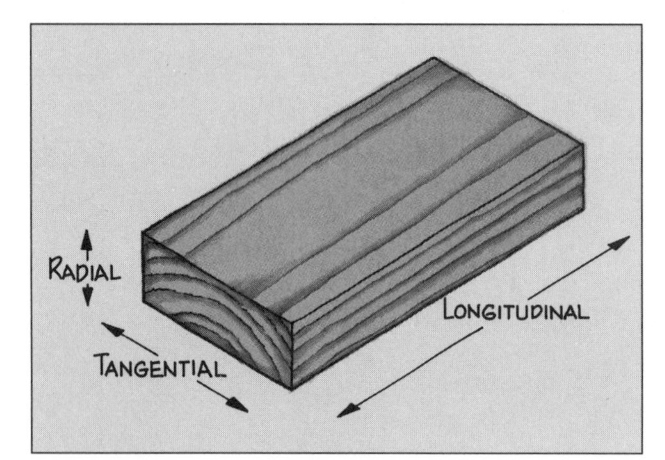

4-1 Wood moves in three planes — *longitudinal, tangential,* and *radial.* It is fairly stable longitudinally (parallel to the wood grain) and will only shrink or swell .001 percent of its length. However, wood is unstable radially and tangentially. Furthermore, the movement tangent to the growth rings is about twice that of the radial movement across them. Radial movement averages 4 percent, and tangential movement averages 8 percent.

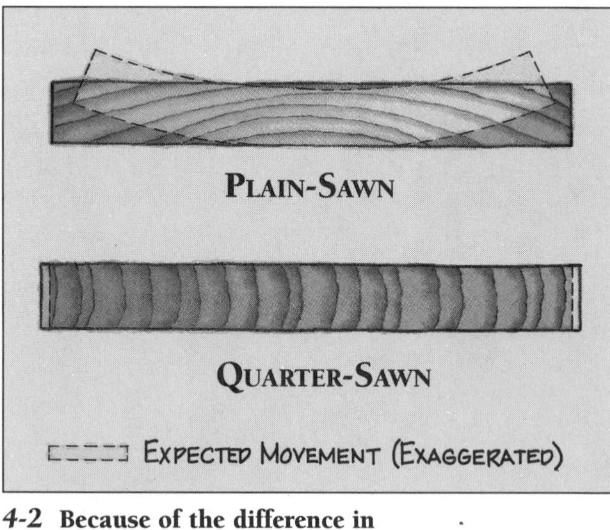

4-2 Because of the difference in movement between the tangential and radial planes, plain-sawn boards have a tendency to cup against the growth rings as they lose moisture. Quarter-sawn boards have no such tendency, and they expand and contract less than plain-sawn stock. If you need a tabletop or leaf to remain flat and move as little as possible, quarter-sawn stock is your best choice.

Or, you can *turn the growth rings up*. The individual boards will all cup in the same direction and the assembly will tend to rise in the center. This is best for *supported* tabletops. You can control the cupping by attaching the center of the assembly to the supporting members with a few screws. *(SEE FIGURE 4-3.)*

FOR YOUR INFORMATION

Turning the growth rings up also exposes the maximum amount of *heartwood* — the more colorful, innermost part of the tree.

Of course, none of this applies when gluing up quarter-sawn wood. Since this stock has little tendency to cup, it matters little whether the annual rings face left or right.

When you need an especially stable tabletop, you can turn plain-sawn lumber into quarter-sawn by reorienting the growth rings. Rip the plain-sawn lumber into narrow strips, then rotate each strip so the annual rings face either left or right. *(SEE FIGURE 4-4.)* Butcherblock and workbench tops are made in this manner.

You must also give some thought to the orientation of the growth rings if you wish to avoid *steps*. These are minuscule but abrupt changes in the surface level from one board to another in a glued-up assembly. They show up as lines at the glue joints, and they detract from the appearance of the tabletop. There is a common misconception that steps are caused from improper gluing procedures. Instead, they are usually the result of gluing a tangential edge to a radial edge. The two boards shrink and swell at different rates, and a step develops. *(SEE FIGURE 4-5.)*

To avoid this, orient the boards so you glue tangential edges to tangential edges and radial edges to radial edges. The easiest way to do this is to cut the strips for a tabletop from a single long board, then "fold" the edges in on one another, as if you were folding a carpenter's rule. *(SEE FIGURE 4-6.)*

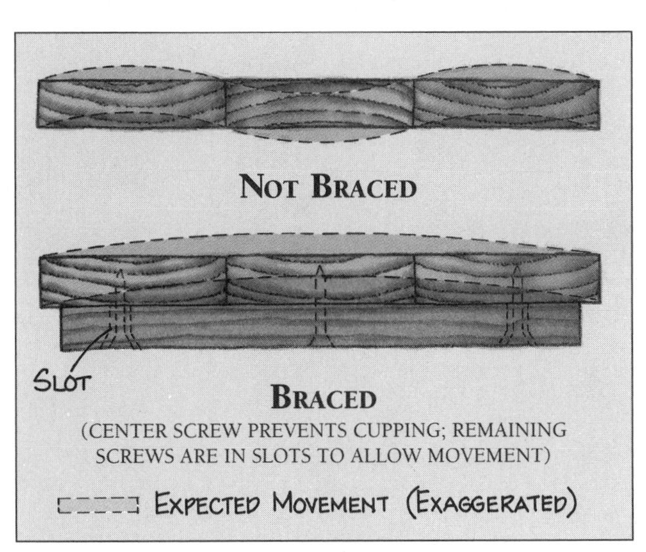

4-3 When gluing stock edge to edge, the best way to orient the growth rings depends on how you will use the assembly. For an *unsupported* tabletop or table leaf, alternate the growth rings. The individual boards may cup, but the glued-up assembly will remain relatively flat. For a tabletop that will be supported by aprons or battens, turn the growth rings to face *up*. Prevent the assembly from cupping by attaching the center portion to the supports with a few screws.

4-4 Butcherblock tabletops and workbench tops are designed for maximum stability. They're assembled from narrow strips of wood, and each strip is turned so the annual rings face right or left. The radial plane of each strip is aligned with the width of the tabletop, making the top as stable as possible. The tangential plane — the most unstable dimension — is aligned with the thickness, where it least affects the stability.

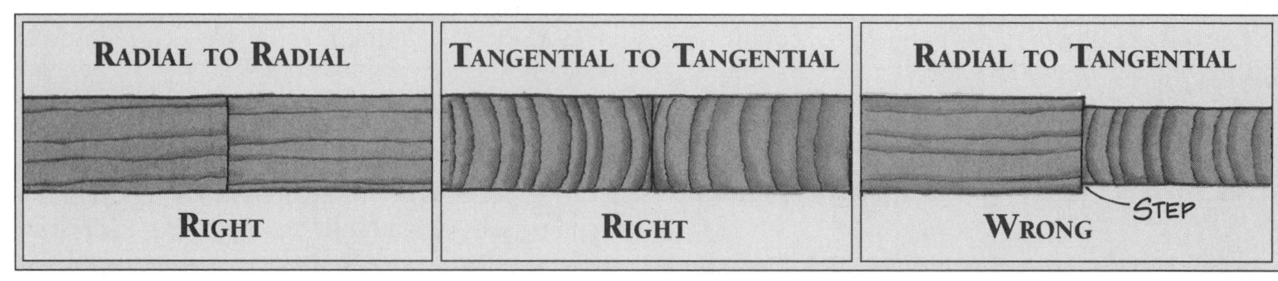

4-5 If you glue a tangential edge to a radial edge, the two boards will expand and contract at different rates. The glue, like any plastic, will creep under the stress, allowing a small *step* to develop. This shows up as an unsightly line at the seam between the boards. To avoid steps, carefully match the grain when deciding which edges to glue together. Note: Steps may also develop if the boards don't have the same moisture content. Make sure the boards rest in your shop for two or more weeks before joining them.

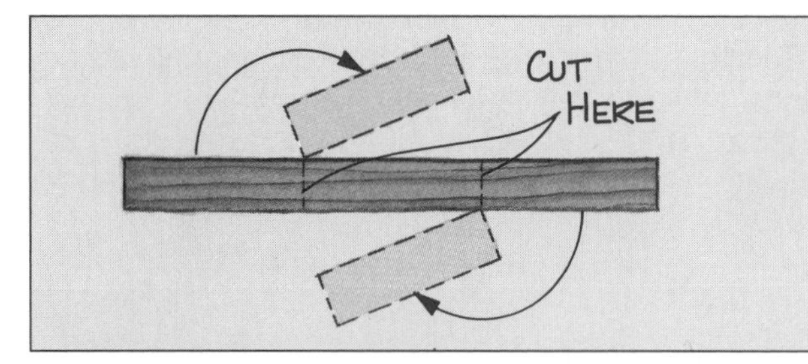

4-6 If possible, cut the pieces for a tabletop from a single long board. "Fold" the pieces like a carpenter's rule, joining the like edges. This technique has three advantages. First, it helps you to match the grain on the edges, preventing the assembled tabletop from developing steps. Second, the grain will seem continuous because the pattern on the edges will be similar — it may be almost impossible to see the edge joints. And third, the color will be even because all the pieces are from the same board.

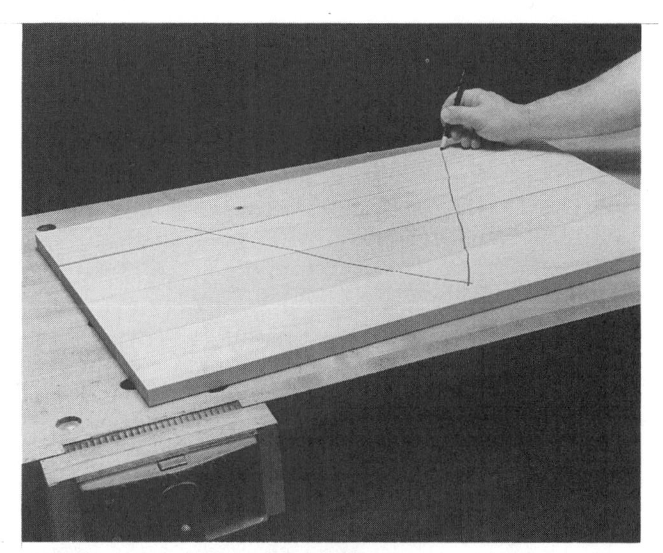

4-7 Once you've arranged the boards as they will be joined, mark a large "V" through the faces, on one side only. This will help you to glue the boards together in the proper order after you've jointed the edges.

Steps may also plague you if the boards don't have the same moisture content — the higher the moisture content, the more the board will shrink as it dries. To prevent this, acclimate the boards to your shop environment by letting them "shop-dry" for two weeks or more before gluing them together. Once you have decided how to orient the wood grain and what edges to glue together, arrange the boards in order and mark a large "V" across them. *(SEE FIGURE 4-7.)* Joint the edges perfectly straight.

Note: Some woodworkers recommend making *sprung* edge joints by cutting the edges slightly concave. This requires you to apply extra clamping pressure to draw the boards together, which supposedly pinches the ends of the boards together and keeps them from splitting or checking. In fact, the extra pressure crushes the wood fibers near the ends of the boards, weakens the joints, and *increases* the likelihood that the joints will split.

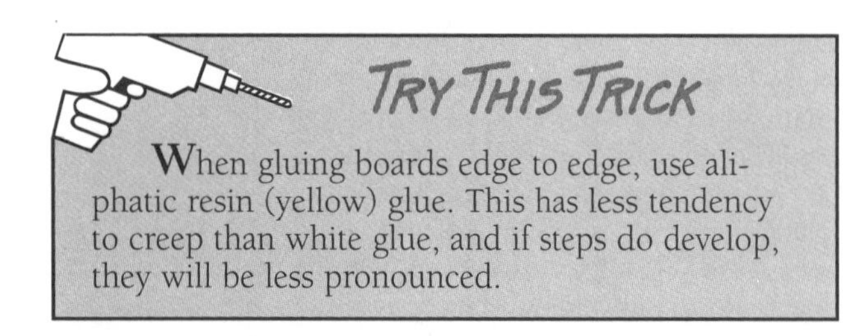

When gluing boards edge to edge, use aliphatic resin (yellow) glue. This has less tendency to creep than white glue, and if steps do develop, they will be less pronounced.

TRY THIS TRICK

To check that the jointer is cutting a straight surface, select a wood scrap that's 2 or 3 feet long and joint about 2 inches of it. Shade the jointed area with a pencil, turn the board around, and joint the entire edge. If the jointer is cutting straight, the knives will just kiss the pencil marks, blurring them but not removing them completely. If the knives remove the marks or miss them completely, either the outfeed table or the knives are set at the wrong height.

Glue the boards edge to edge, aligning the surfaces flush as you tighten the clamps. Under ordinary circumstances, the glue will be sufficient to hold the boards together. You shouldn't need to make tongue-and-groove joints or glue joints to increase the gluing surface, nor should you need splines or biscuits for reinforcement. However, these alternatives are helpful if you have trouble aligning the boards. (SEE FIGURE 4-8.)

Let the glue dry for *at least* 24 hours before you plane, scrape, or sand the edge joints. Although the glue may set up in less than an hour and harden sufficiently to remove the clamps, it doesn't achieve full strength for the better part of a day. Machine the assembly too soon, and it may come apart. If you use a water-based glue (such as yellow glue), you must also allow enough time for the water to evaporate. The water causes the wood to swell at the adjoining edges. If you plane the surface while the wood is still wet, there will be a noticeable depression along the joint when the wood dries and shrinks. (SEE FIGURE 4-9.)

4-8 **Although an ordinary edge** joint, glued together, should be sufficiently strong for most tabletops, a glue joint (shown) and similar joinery is sometimes useful to help align the boards. This ensures that the faces will be flush when the glue dries, and it cuts down on the amount of scraping and sanding you must do to true up the assembly.

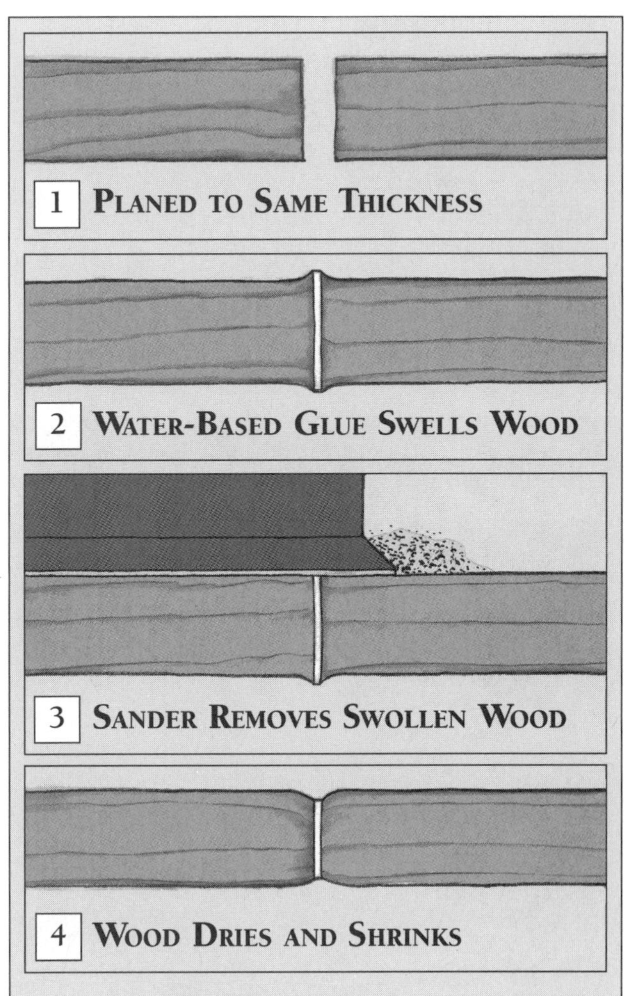

4-9 **If you plane lumber to uni-**form thickness (1) and then glue the pieces together with aliphatic resin (yellow) glue or another water-based glue, the water will cause the wood near the edges to swell slightly (2). If you then sand, scrape, or plane off the swollen wood (3), a depression will appear in the area around the seam when the wood dries and shrinks (4). Instead, wait for the wood to dry before sanding.

CUTTING SHAPES AND PROFILES

After gluing up the slab and smoothing the edge joints, trim the ends and edges to make it rectangular. Or, if you wish, cut the stock to a decorative shape. Tabletops can be almost any shape you can cut with a band saw or saber saw. *(SEE FIGURE 4-10.)*

You may also wish to rout or shape a profile in the edges of the tabletop. Profiles ease the hard corners and arrises of the top, making them look softer and adding decorative detail. They may also make the table more comfortable to use — the sharp arris won't dig into your wrists. Simple profiles work best; complex shapes are too fragile and quickly become chipped or broken. Here are five common table edge profiles *(SEE FIGURE 4-11):*

- *Roundover* — one arris (usually the top) is rounded to create a quarter-round shape
- *Bead* — both the top and bottom arrises are rounded to the same radius to create a half-round shape
- *Thumbnail* — both the top and bottom arrises are rounded, but to different radii
- *Ogee* — one arris is cut to an "S" shape; the other is sometimes rounded
- *Chamfer* — one arris (usually the bottom) is cut at an angle

***4-10* Tabletops can be cut to** almost any shape. This unique design is called a *porringer* table, named after a traditional English children's bowl with an oversize handle. The large, rounded corners on the table echo the handle on the porringer.

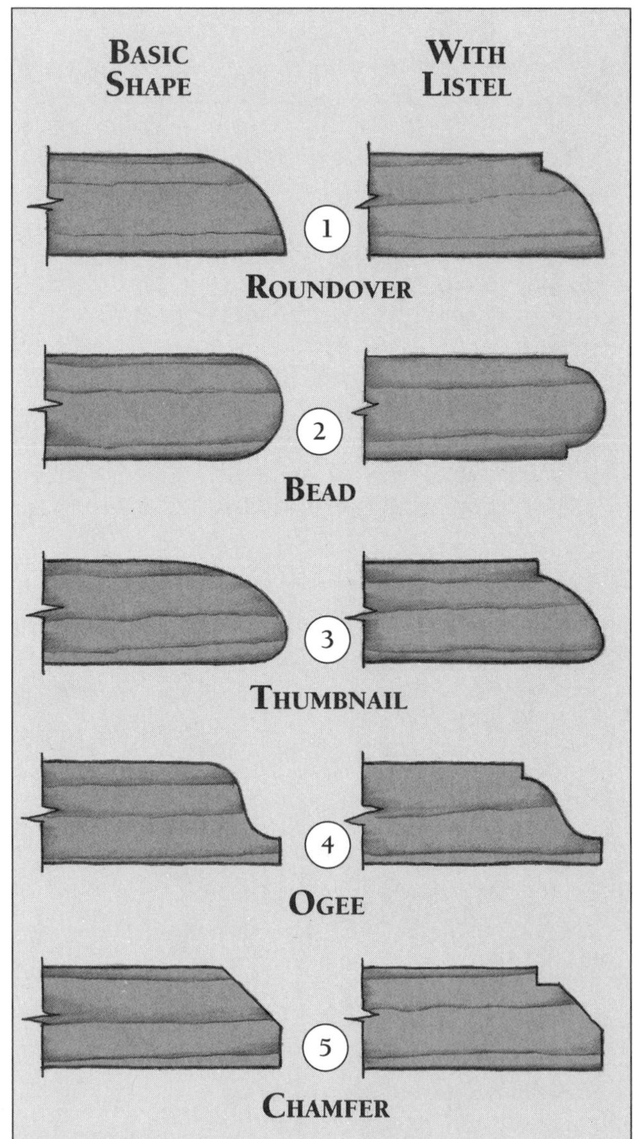

4-11* Shown are five common** profiles you can rout in the edge of a tabletop — ***roundover (1), ***bead*** (2), ***thumbnail*** (3), ***ogee*** (4), and ***chamfer*** (5). Each of these profiles can be cut with a small step or *listel* to add decorative detail.

Routing Round Tabletops

Although you can cut a round shape with a band saw or a saber saw, it can be made more accurately by *routing*. Routing creates a *fair curve* — a perfectly round circumference without any flat spots or changes in the radius.

Routing a circle is a straightforward technique. Attach the router to a beam and drive a nail or screw through the beam to serve as a pivot. Then swing the router around the pivot. This circle-routing jig offers two refinements. There's no need to put a screw or nail hole in the tabletop; the pivot is a separate assembly that's secured with carpet tape. And the beam has an adjustable collar so you can adjust the jig to rout any radius between 6 and 24 inches.

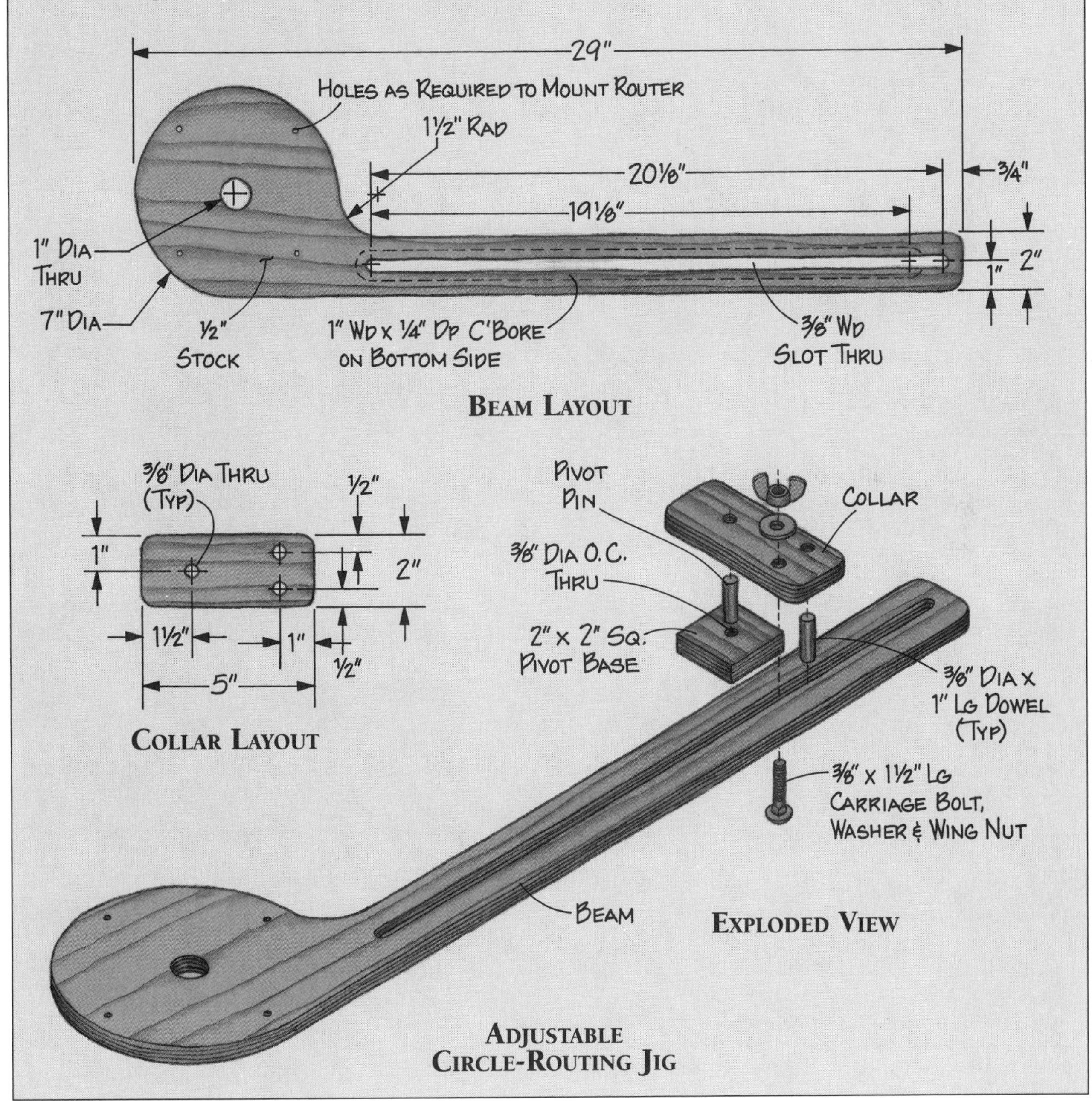

Adjustable Circle-Routing Jig

(continued) ▷

Routing Round Tabletops — continued

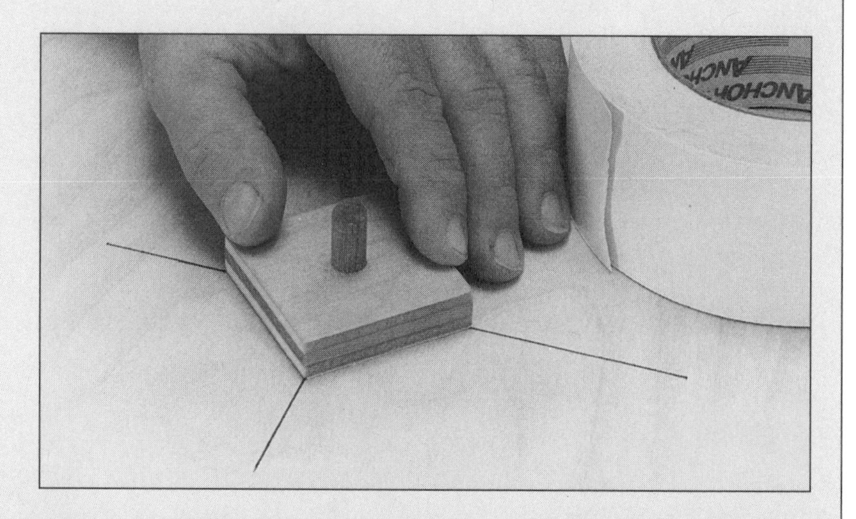

1 To mount the pivot, first mark the center of the table on the stock. Measure the radius of the circle out from the center and mark that, too. Draw two intersecting lines, 90 degrees from one another, that cross at the center. Position the pivot so the corners of the square pivot base line up with the crossed lines on the stock.

2 Mount a straight bit in the router, and mount the router on the beam. Place the movable collar that rides up and down the beam over the pivot. Loosen the wing nut that locks the collar in place, and position the router so the *inside* of the straight bit (the side closest to the pivot) is even with the radius mark. Tighten the wing nut to lock the collar in place. Swing the router past the radius mark several times to check that you've correctly positioned the collar.

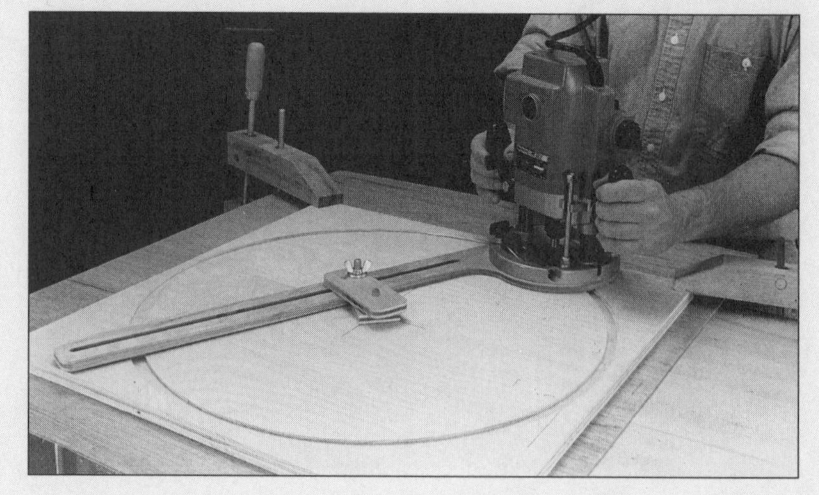

3 Adjust the depth of cut so the straight bit cuts no more than ⅛ inch deep. Turn on the router and swing it around the pivot, cutting a shallow circular groove. Turn off the router, lower the straight bit another ⅛ inch, and make another pass. Repeat until you cut through the stock.

Tops for Folding Tables

A folding tabletop consists of a fixed slab with one or more leaves hinged to it. In most folding tables, the leaves fold *down,* from horizontal to vertical. These are often called *drop leaves.*

MAKING RULE JOINTS

When drop-leaf tables first appeared around the fourteenth century, the leaves were attached to the fixed top with ordinary butt hinges, much as a lid is attached to a chest. The adjoining edges were jointed straight; when a leaf was up, they simply butted together. Several hundred years later, cabinetmakers began to cut mating shapes in the adjoining edges.

For a short time, at the end of the seventeenth century, the most popular shape was a half-round bead and matching flute. This quickly gave way to a quarter-round bead and cove, or *rule joint.* (*See Figure 4-12.*) In a rule joint, the hinge pins must be offset, requiring special *drop-leaf hinges.* This combination of joinery and hardware has remained the traditional method of attaching drop leaves to tabletops.

To make a rule joint, cut the mating shapes in the adjoining edges with a router or a shaper. Make the bead in the fixed top, and the cove in the drop leaf. (*See Figure 4-13.*) Mortise the underside of the top and the leaf for hinges, positioning the pins at the center of the radius for the bead. (*See Figure 4-14.*)

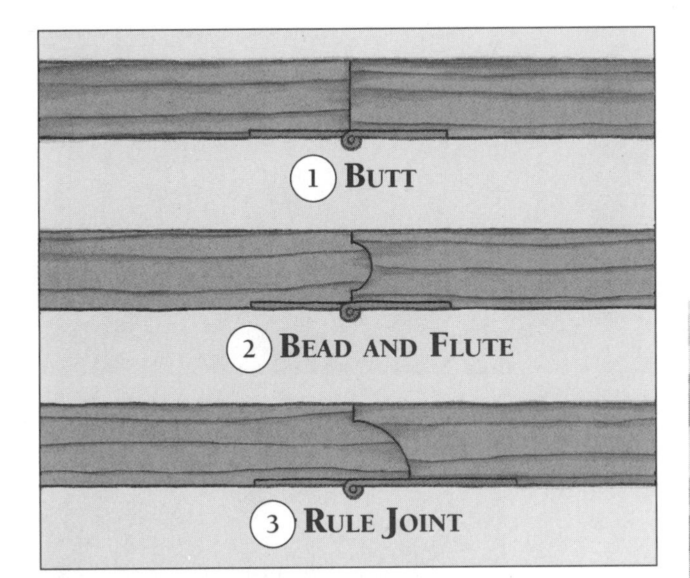

4-12 The adjoining edges of the first drop-leaf tables were jointed straight, and the pins of the butt hinges were centered directly below the joint. When the leaves were up, the edges simply butted together (1). Later, cabinetmakers began to cut matching half-round beads and flutes. The hinge pins stayed where they were before — directly below the joint. When the leaf was up, the bead and flute fit together (2). This evolved to the quarter-round bead and cove, or *rule joint* (3). For the shapes to mate when the leaf was up, the hinge pin had to be offset. Cabinetmakers modified the butt hinge, making one side longer than the other to create the *drop-leaf hinge.*

4-13 To make a rule joint, you need a set of matched cutters for your router or shaper. Cut the quarter-round bead in the adjoining edge of the fixed top, and the cove in the drop leaf. When cutting each shape, leave a small flat near the top surface of the board. This flat area must be the same thickness on both parts.

Install the hinges, joining the parts. When the drop leaf is up, the bead and cove should mate. When down, the edge of the leaf should stay close to the top — there should be very little gap between the two. *(SEE FIGURE 4-15.)*

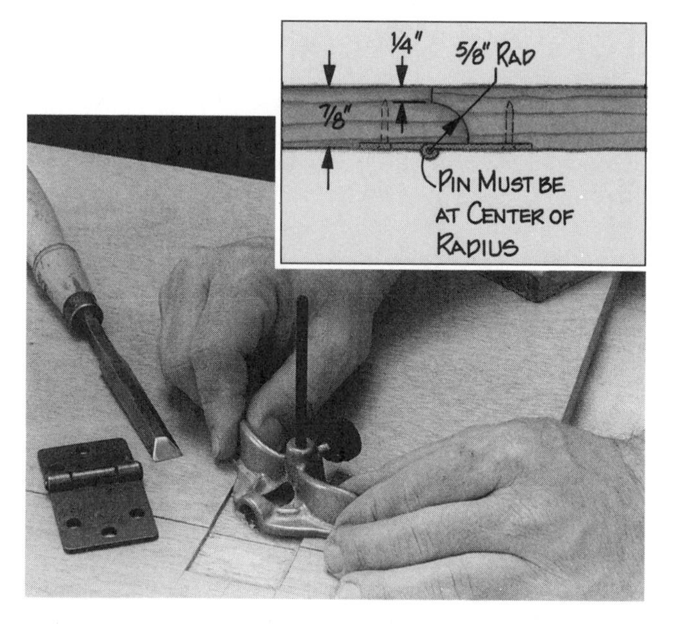

4-14 The trick to making a rule joint is not so much in shaping the edges as in installing the drop-leaf hinges. Each hinge must be set in a mortise in the underside of the fixed top and drop leaf so the pin is at the center of the arc described by the mating cove and bead. Fasten the long side of the hinge to the drop leaf and the short side to the fixed top.

4-15 When the folding tabletop is assembled, the bead will show when the drop leaf is down (vertical). When it's up, the rule joint will close and the surfaces will be flush.

SUPPORTING DROP LEAVES

You must support a drop leaf when it's horizontal. How you provide this support often depends on the size of the leaf. You can support small drop leaves with pull-out slides or swing-out braces. *(SEE FIGURES 4-16 AND 4-17.)* Larger leaves require something more substantial, such as a gateleg or swing leg. *(SEE FIGURES 4-18 AND 4-19.)*

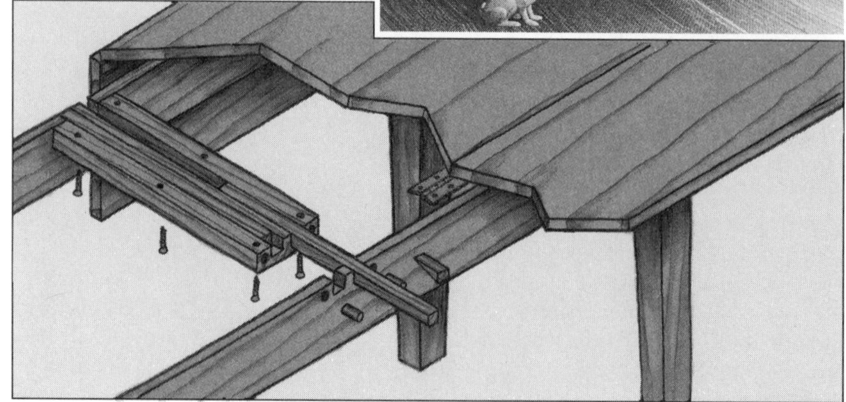

4-16 The drop leaves on this harvest table are short enough to be supported by pull-out slides. The slides store under the fixed top when the leaves are down.

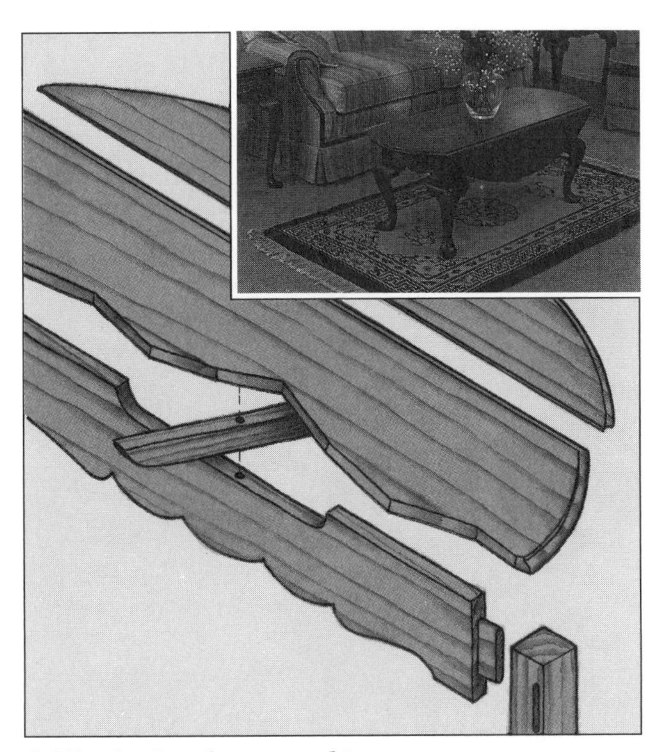

4-17 The drop leaves on this coffee table are supported by braces that swing out from the aprons. The braces were cut from the aprons, then fastened back in place with long roundhead wood screws. The screws serve as pivots. When the leaves fold down, the braces swing back parallel to the aprons.

4-18 The large, heavy leaves of this oval dining table are supported by swing legs — legs that swing out when the leaves are horizontal. When the leaves fold down, the legs swing back against the aprons. **Note:** Gateleg tables have a similar mechanism. The difference is that gatelegs have aprons at the tops *and* rails near the bottoms, while swing legs have aprons only.

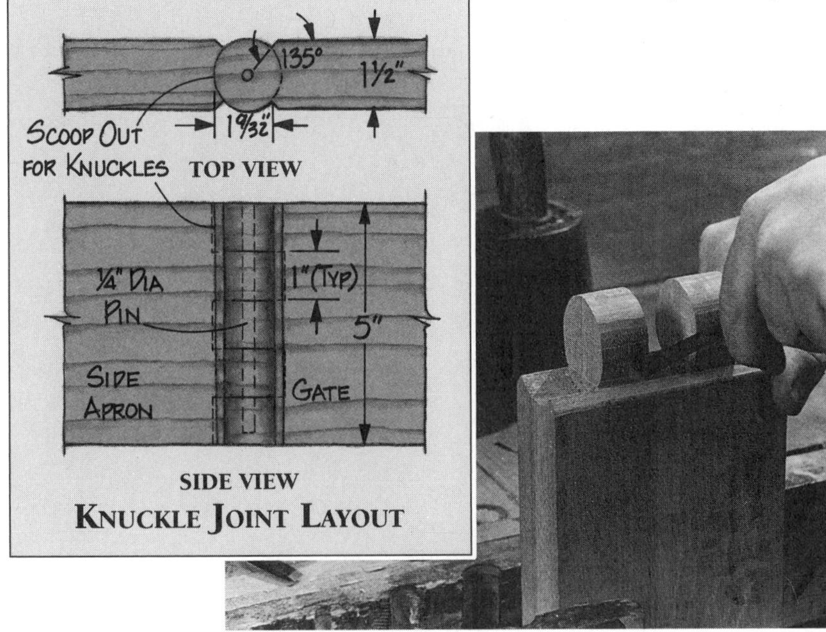

4-19 Traditionally, the aprons of swing-leg tables are hinged with *knuckle joints* to allow the legs to swing out. At first glance, a knuckle joint looks like a pivoting finger joint, but it's a little more complex. The "knuckles" are flat areas at the base of the fingers, and the spaces between the fingers are scooped out slightly. This arrangement limits the travel of the swing leg. When it's 90 degrees from the apron, the knuckles come together and stop it directly under the center of the drop leaf.

Installing Butler's Tray Hinges

A few folding tables are designed so the leaves fold up. A traditional butler's table is made in this manner — the leaves of this portable table fold up vertically, helping to keep whatever's on the table from sliding off while the table is carried from one place to another. Like a dropleaf table, a butler's table requires special hinges and joinery.

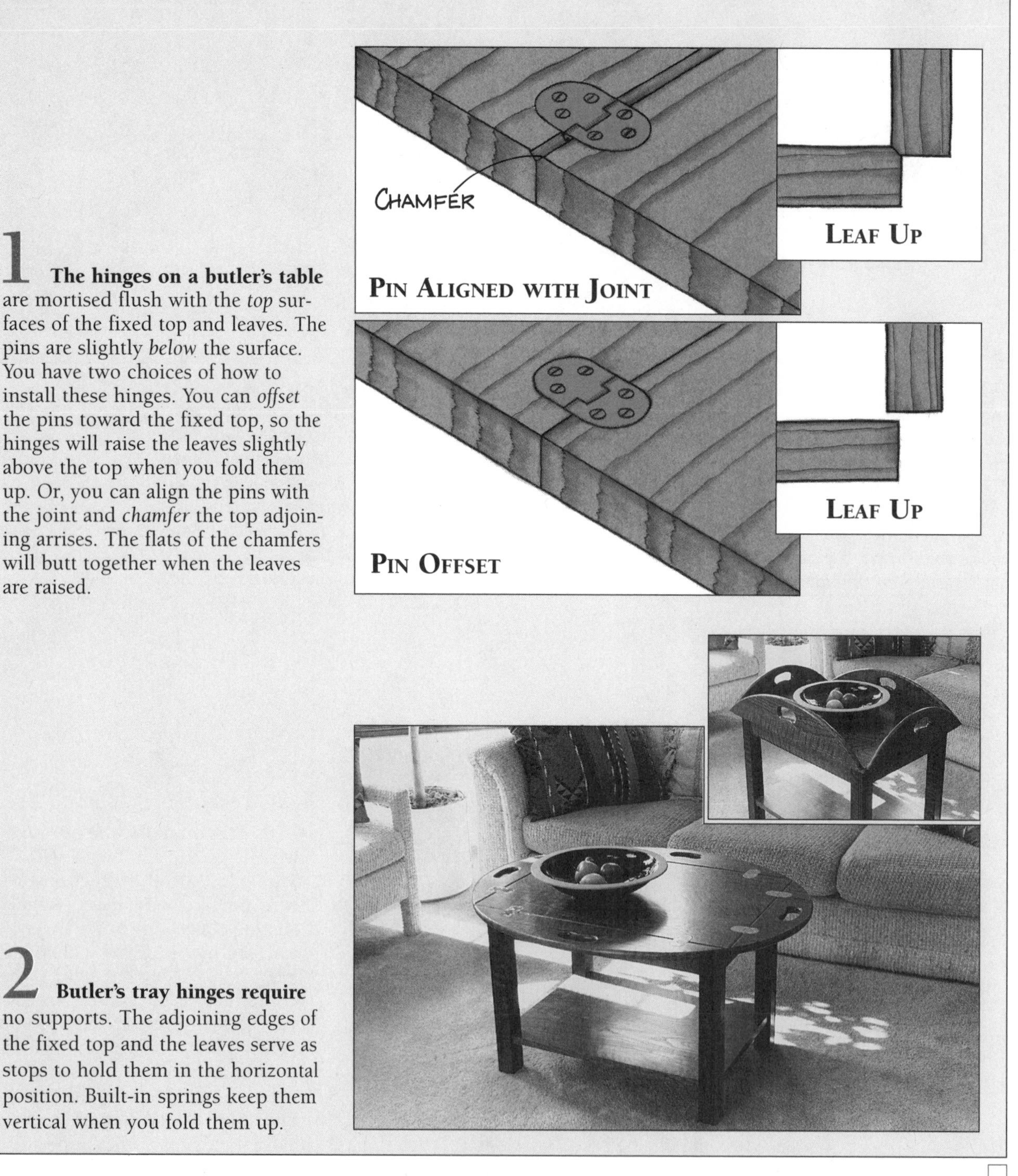

1 The hinges on a butler's table are mortised flush with the *top* surfaces of the fixed top and leaves. The pins are slightly *below* the surface. You have two choices of how to install these hinges. You can *offset* the pins toward the fixed top, so the hinges will raise the leaves slightly above the top when you fold them up. Or, you can align the pins with the joint and *chamfer* the top adjoining arrises. The flats of the chamfers will butt together when the leaves are raised.

2 Butler's tray hinges require no supports. The adjoining edges of the fixed top and the leaves serve as stops to hold them in the horizontal position. Built-in springs keep them vertical when you fold them up.

Tops for Extension Tables

INSTALLING EXTENSION SLIDES

On an extension table, the top is usually split into two halves. The halves are joined by *extension slides,* wooden or metal braces that telescope as you pull them apart. This allows you to make the table longer when you need more space — pull the top halves apart and place leaves between them. *(See Figures 4-20 and 4-21.)*

4-20 The top of an extension table is cut in two, and the halves are joined with wooden or metal slides. There are two types of slides, and the kind you need depends on how the table is supported. Ordinary *extension slides* (shown) are designed for tables that are supported by legs and aprons or trestles. One end of each slide is attached to one half of the tabletop; the other end is attached to the other half.

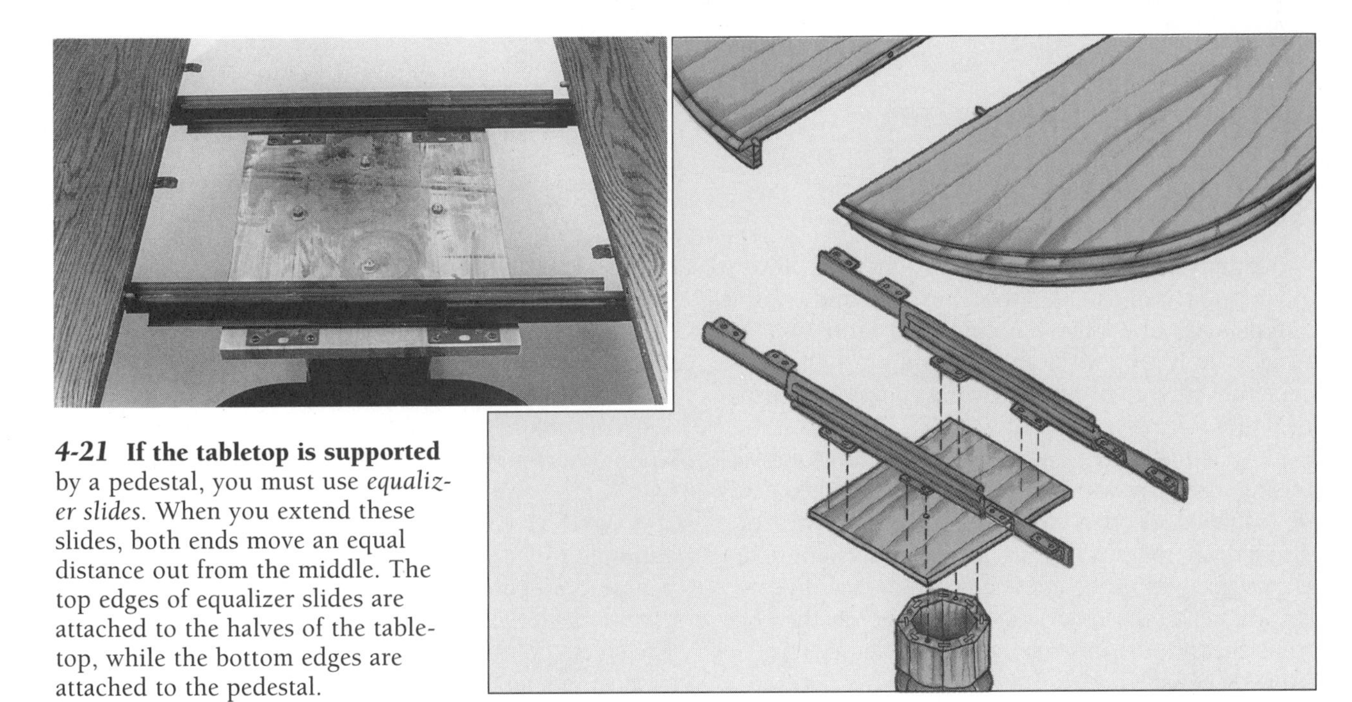

4-21 If the tabletop is supported by a pedestal, you must use *equalizer slides.* When you extend these slides, both ends move an equal distance out from the middle. The top edges of equalizer slides are attached to the halves of the tabletop, while the bottom edges are attached to the pedestal.

ALIGNING TOPS AND LEAVES

Extension tables also require special hardware to help align the tabletop halves and the leaves. Tabletop *eveners* and *table pins* keep the surfaces flush. (SEE FIGURE 4-22.)

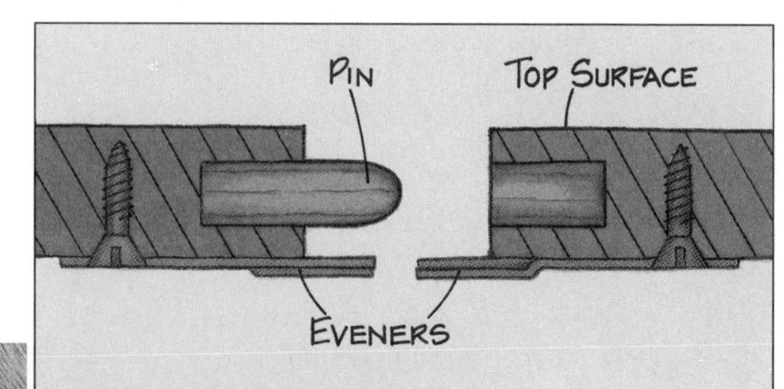

4-22 Extension tabletops and leaves are aligned with *table pins* and *eveners* — these can be used separately or in combination with each other. The pins are tapered dowels and are installed with a doweling jig. Drill matching holes in the adjoining edges, then glue the fat ends of the pins in one edge. The eveners are interlocking metal tabs that simply screw to the underside of the adjoining wooden parts.

ATTACHING TABLETOPS

ALLOWING FOR EXPANSION AND CONTRACTION

No matter what type of tabletop you make or how you support it or finish it, it will expand and contract with changes in relative humidity. You cannot attach it rigidly to its aprons or battens; you must allow for some movement. There are several common methods for doing this.

Clips and fasteners — Fasten the top to its supporting assembly with *clips* or *tabletop fasteners.* Clips are L-shaped wooden blocks you can make yourself; fasteners are the metal store-bought equivalent. Cut narrow grooves in the aprons or battens and insert the tongues of these devices in them. Screw the clips or fasteners to the underside of the tabletop. (SEE FIGURES 4-23 AND 4-24.)

TRY THIS TRICK

If you have a biscuit joiner, use it to cut slots for tabletop fasteners. Make one semicircular slot near the top edge of the apron for each fastener.

Cleats and battens — *Cleats* are slender strips of wood that fasten to both the aprons *and* the tabletop with screws, joining the two. *Battens* are somewhat larger and have enough strength to brace a tabletop and hold it flat. They are used with trestles and pedestals and are installed similarly to cleats. Fasten them to *both* the tabletop and its supporting assembly. The screw holes are slotted or oversize to allow for expansion and contraction. (SEE FIGURE 4-25.)

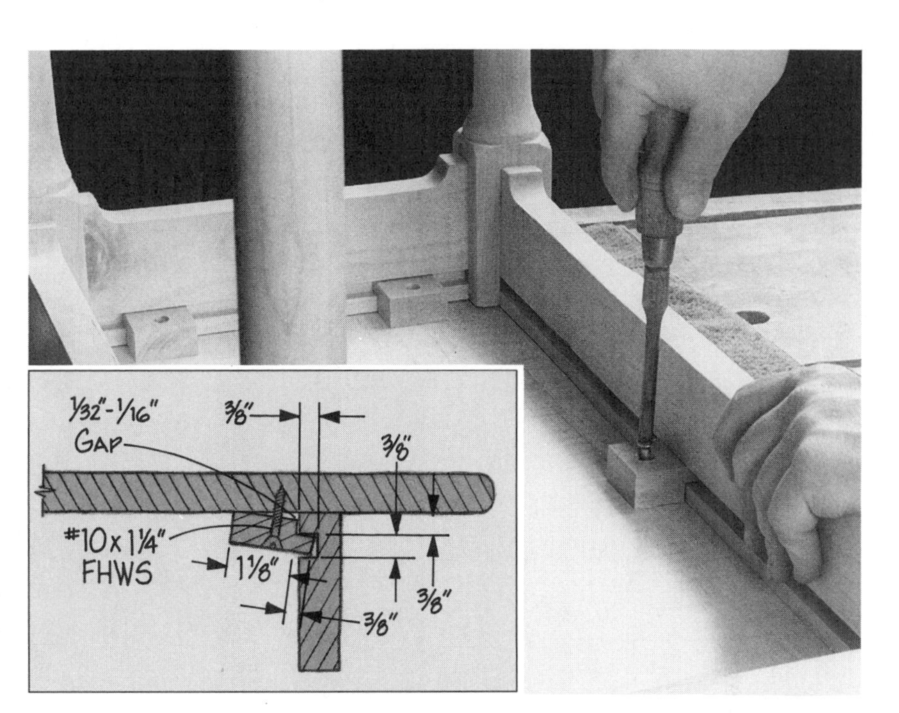

4-23 You can fasten tabletops with shop-made wooden *clips.* A clip is a small block of wood with a rabbet cut in one arris, creating a short tongue. To install the clips, cut grooves in the inside faces of the battens or those aprons that run perpendicular to the grain direction of the tabletop. The grooves must be wide enough to accommodate the tongues. Insert the tongues in the grooves, then screw the clips to the underside of the tabletop. As the top expands and contracts, the clips will slide sideways in the grooves. **Note:** Don't install clips in the aprons that run the same direction as the grain in the tabletop — they will restrict the wood movement.

4-24 *Tabletop fasteners* are the commercially made equivalent of clips. Cut a narrow groove or saw kerf in the aprons or battens, then insert one end of these Z-shaped metal brackets in them. Fasten the other end to the tabletop with screws. **Note:** Once again, just fasten those aprons that run perpendicular to the wood grain of the tabletop.

4-25 *Cleats* (left) are sometimes used to attach tabletops to leg-and-apron assemblies. Screw the cleats to the inside surfaces of the aprons and the underside of the top. In this example, the screw holes used to attach the cleats to the top are slotted, and the slots run perpendicular to the grain direction of the top. As the top expands and contracts, the screws move back and forth in their slots. ***Battens*** (right) are used in the same manner to attach tabletops to trestles or pedestals. The screw holes in these battens are oversize — slightly larger in diameter than the shafts of the screws. Like the slotted holes, this arrangement allows the top to expand and contract.

Screw pockets — If you don't have room for clips, fasteners, cleats, or battens under your table, you can make *screw pockets* — angled holes for screws. Make the shaft holes in the screw pockets slightly larger than the screw shafts to allow the tabletop to expand and contract. Screw pockets are generally used when attaching tabletops to leg-and-apron assemblies, but they may also be used with trestles. *(See Figures 4-26 through 4-28.)*

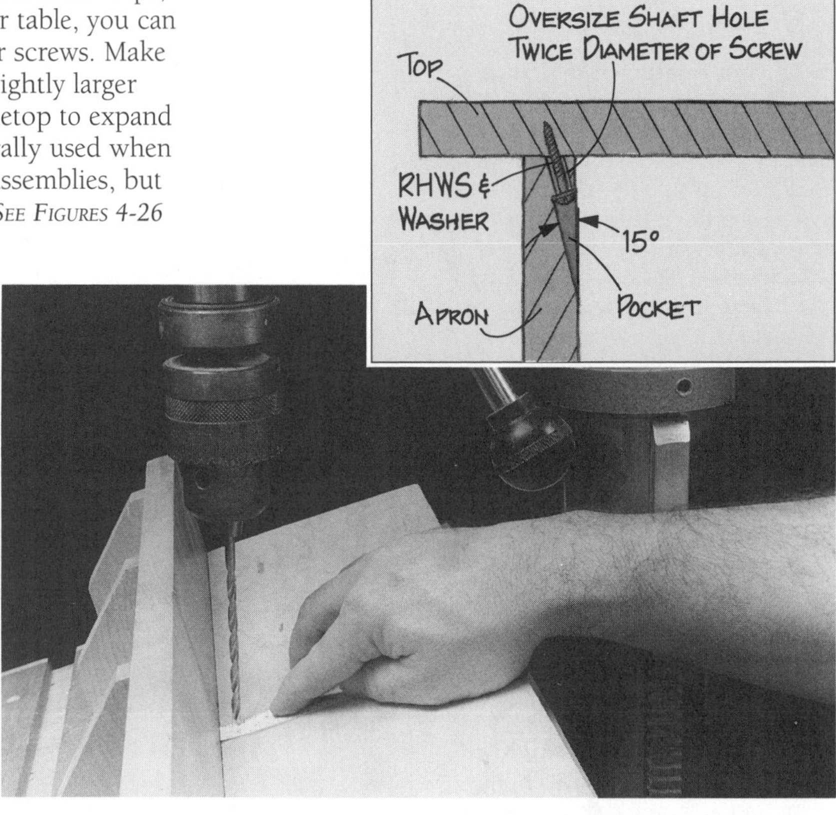

4-26 A *screw pocket* consists of a counterbore and an oversize shaft hole, both drilled at a slight angle. The pocket enters the inside surface of the apron and exits the top edge. To make a screw pocket, tilt the worktable of the drill press to 15 degrees. Mount the bit you will use to make the shaft hole in the drill press chuck and extend it until the tip touches the table. Clamp a fence to the table, a fraction of an inch away from the bit on the "down" side. **Note:** The distance between the fence and the tip of the bit should be equal to half the thickness of the apron.

4-27 Remove the shaft hole bit from the chuck and replace it with the counterbore bit. Place the apron on the worktable with the top edge down and the outside face against the fence. Clamp the apron to the fence to keep it from shifting as you work. Drill the counterbore in the inside face, stopping about ½ inch above the table. **Note:** Forstner bits work best for this task.

4-28 Remove the counterbore bit and replace it with the shaft hole bit. Do *not* loosen the clamp or move the apron. Drill the shaft hole in the center of the counterbore, down through the apron. The bit should exit the top edge approximately ⅜ inch from the outside face.

5

BUILDING A JOINED CHAIR

The joiner's chairmaking tradition dates back to medieval times, when there were no distinctions between carpenters and cabinetmakers. Woodworkers were called *joiners,* and according to historical tradition, these medieval joiners made houses through the summer and furniture through the winter. They relied on the same techniques for both endeavors. Thus, the frames of joined chairs are built like the frame of a medieval post-and-beam house — rectangular members assembled with mortise-and-tenon joints.

Over the centuries, joined chairs have evolved. Contemporary chairmakers use a variety of joints; dowels, loose tenons, and round mortises and tenons are often substituted for square mortises and tenons. And not all chair frame members are rectangular. The designs are sometimes a blend of the joiner's and turner's traditions, mixing round members with rectangular. But the joined chair frame remains the same: The front legs, back posts, and seat rails are all rectangular members where they join one another, and the front legs and back posts are mortised to accept tenons on the ends of the rails.

Photo courtesy of Israel Sack, Inc.

Joined Chair Construction

Joined chairs are strong constructions, designed not only to support the weight of their occupants but also to withstand constant racking. As shown in Figure 5-1, the major frame members are:

- The stiles, uprights, or *back posts,* which serve as the back legs and the vertical frame members for the chair back
- The *front legs,* which are sometimes extended to support an armrest
- The *seat rails* — front, back, and side — which tie the back posts and the front legs together and frame the seat

There may be many other parts as well:

- *Stretchers* and *rungs* to help keep the legs from racking
- *Corner blocks* to brace the seat frame and help attach the seat
- A *crest rail* to serve as the top horizontal frame member for the chair back
- A wide vertical *splat* to serve as the chair back; or narrow *slats* (either horizontal or vertical) to fill in the chair back
- A *shoe* or an *intermediate rail* to anchor the bottom of the splat or slats
- *Armrests* to support the elbows and forearms of the chair occupant
- *Arm supports* to support the armrests

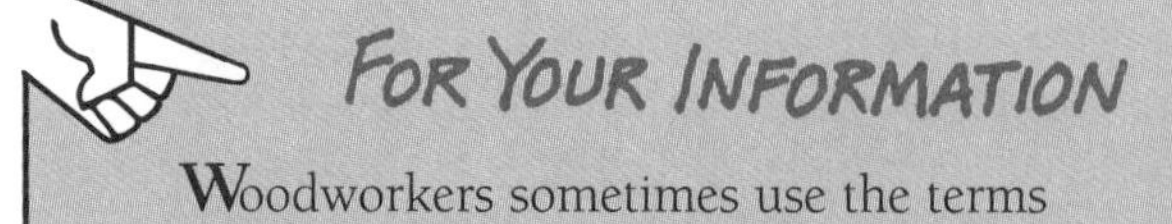

Woodworkers sometimes use the terms *stretcher, rung,* and *rail* interchangeably, when, in fact, they are different things. Stretchers are rectangular parts used to tie the legs together on joined chairs; rungs are turned round and used for the same purpose. Rails may be rectangular or round, and they support the seats.

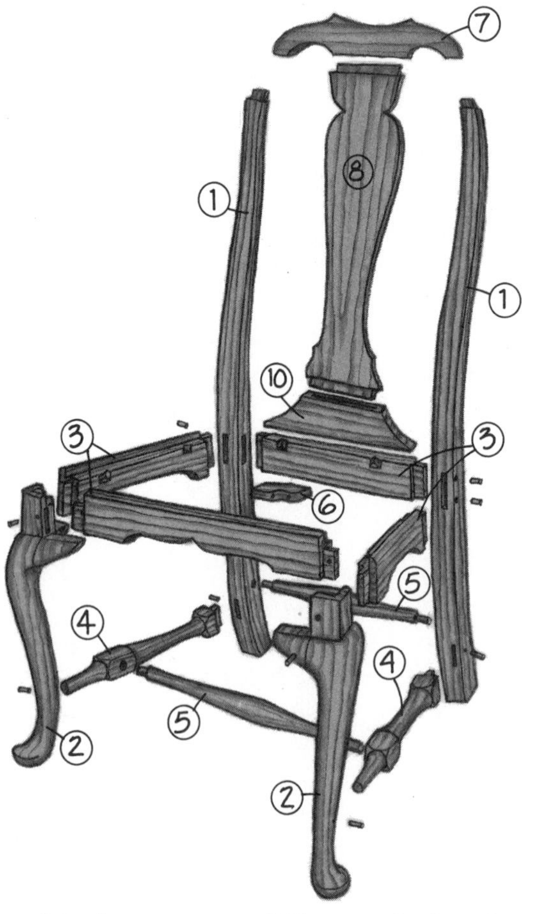

5-1 While there are many different designs for a joined chair, they all have a similar framework. The major frame members are the ***back posts*** (1), the *front legs* (2), and the *seat rails* (3). Additionally, there may be *stretchers* (4) and *rungs* (5), *corner blocks* (6), a *crest rail* (7), a *splat* (8), *slats* (9), a *shoe* (10), an *intermediate rail* (11), *armrests* (12), and *arm supports* (13).

Traditionally, these parts are joined with mortises and tenons, since a mortise-and-tenon joint best withstands racking. However, you may substitute dowel joints or loose tenon joints, provided you don't compromise the overall strength and durability of the chair frame. (SEE FIGURE 5-2.)

Note: *Racking* is the type of stress produced in a joint when you push one member sideways, like a lever. It is the most damaging force that furniture designers must reckon with.

JOINING THE CHAIR FRAME MEMBERS

It's a simple matter to join rectangular members to make a rectangular frame, when all the corners are 90 degrees. Chair frames, unfortunately, are rarely rectangular. Seldom do the corners meet at 90 degrees; the angles are usually slightly greater or smaller. Consequently, you must use special joinery techniques.

When making mortise-and-tenon joints that join parts at an angle, the cardinal rule is to always *cut the tenon parallel to the wood grain.* You can cut the mortise and the tenon shoulders at almost any angle without affecting the strength of the joint, but if you cant the tenon at an angle, it will be weak. (SEE FIGURE 5-3.) The second rule is to lay out the mortise and tenon carefully before you cut them. The actual cutting is fairly simple, so long as you have clear guidelines to follow.

To make an angled mortise, one of the simplest methods is to drill a line of overlapping angled holes to remove most of the waste, then clean up the sides and the corners with a chisel. (SEE FIGURES 5-4 AND 5-5.)

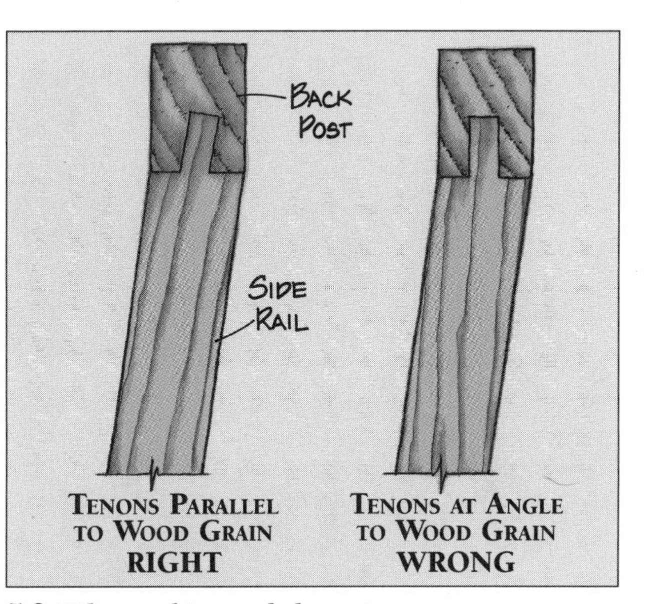

5-3 When making angled mortise-and-tenon joints, always cut the tenon parallel to the wood grain and angle the mortise. If you angle the tenon, the wood grain will be cut into short segments. This, in turn, will make the tenon weak.

5-2 Joined chair frames are traditionally assembled with square *mortise-and-tenon joints* (1), since these are strong and durable and withstand racking. However, you may substitute other joinery, provided the overall structure remains sound. ***Dowel joints*** (2) are acceptable for chairs that will see light duty or for the parts of chairs that don't require enormously strong joinery, such as children's chairs. If made properly, ***loose tenon joints*** (3) are as strong as mortises and tenons and are often easier to make. If you have several chairs to produce, loose tenon joints can save you time without sacrificing strength.

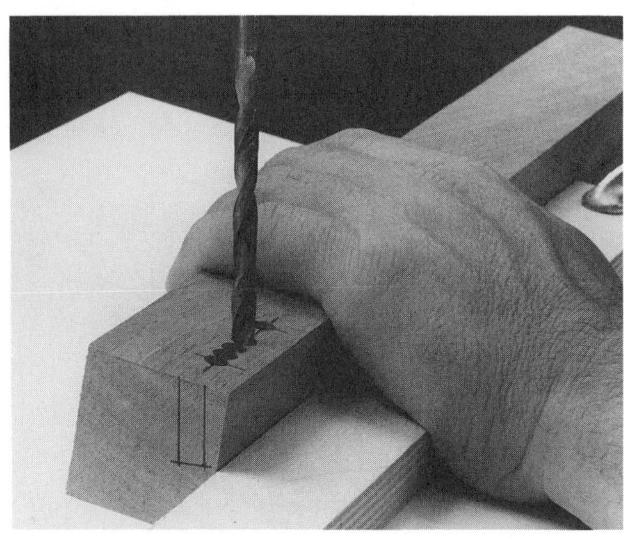

5-4 To rough out an angled mortise on a drill press, tilt the table to the angle required. Secure a fence to the table on the "down" side of the bit to help hold and guide the stock as you work. Then drill a line of overlapping angled holes. Drill the holes at the ends of the mortise first, then make the holes between them.

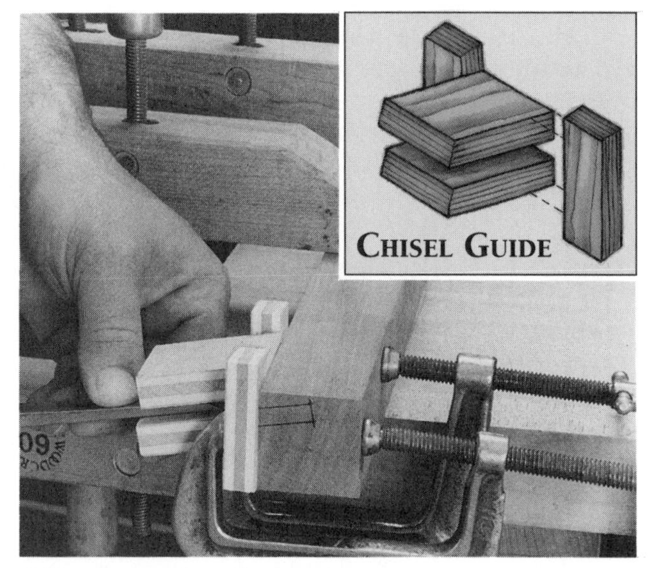

5-5 After drilling the overlapping holes, clean up the sides and the corners of the mortise with a chisel. The jig shown helps to guide the chisel at the proper angle. Clamp this jig to the surface of the workpiece over the mortise, and rest the flat back of the chisel against the guides as you cut.

However, this won't work for all the chair parts — particularly the back posts. The curved profiles of the back posts are usually cut *before* you make the angled mortises for the side rails, and this makes them difficult to position on a drill press. You can use a horizontal boring machine if you have one, or a horizontally mounted router. *(SEE FIGURE 5-6.)*

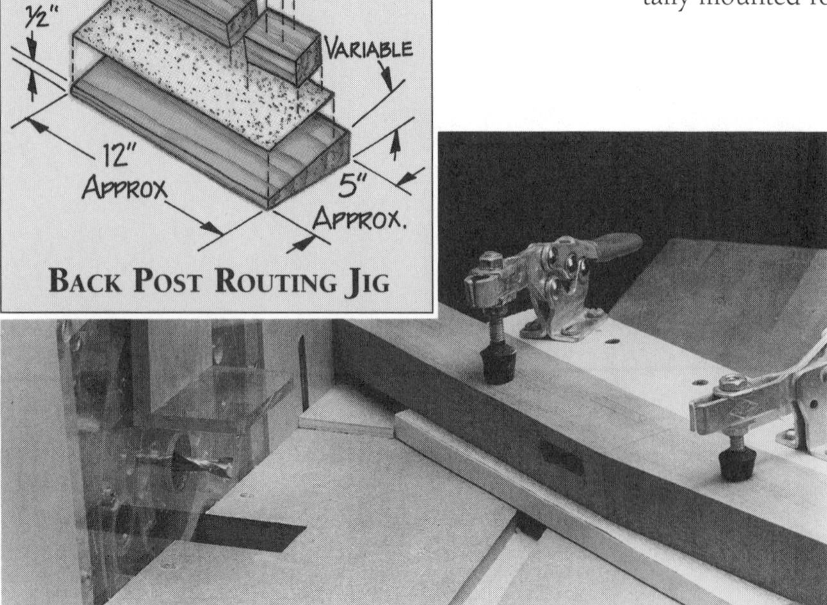

5-6 You can also use a horizontal router or "joint maker" and a straight bit to create angled mortises. Build the jig shown to hold the work at the proper angle to the router bit. Attach stops to the worktable to help guide the jig and limit the length of the mortise. To cut the mortise, plunge the work into the bit as you slide the jig back and forth. Take shallow cuts, going no more than ⅛ inch deep with each pass until the mortise is the desired depth.

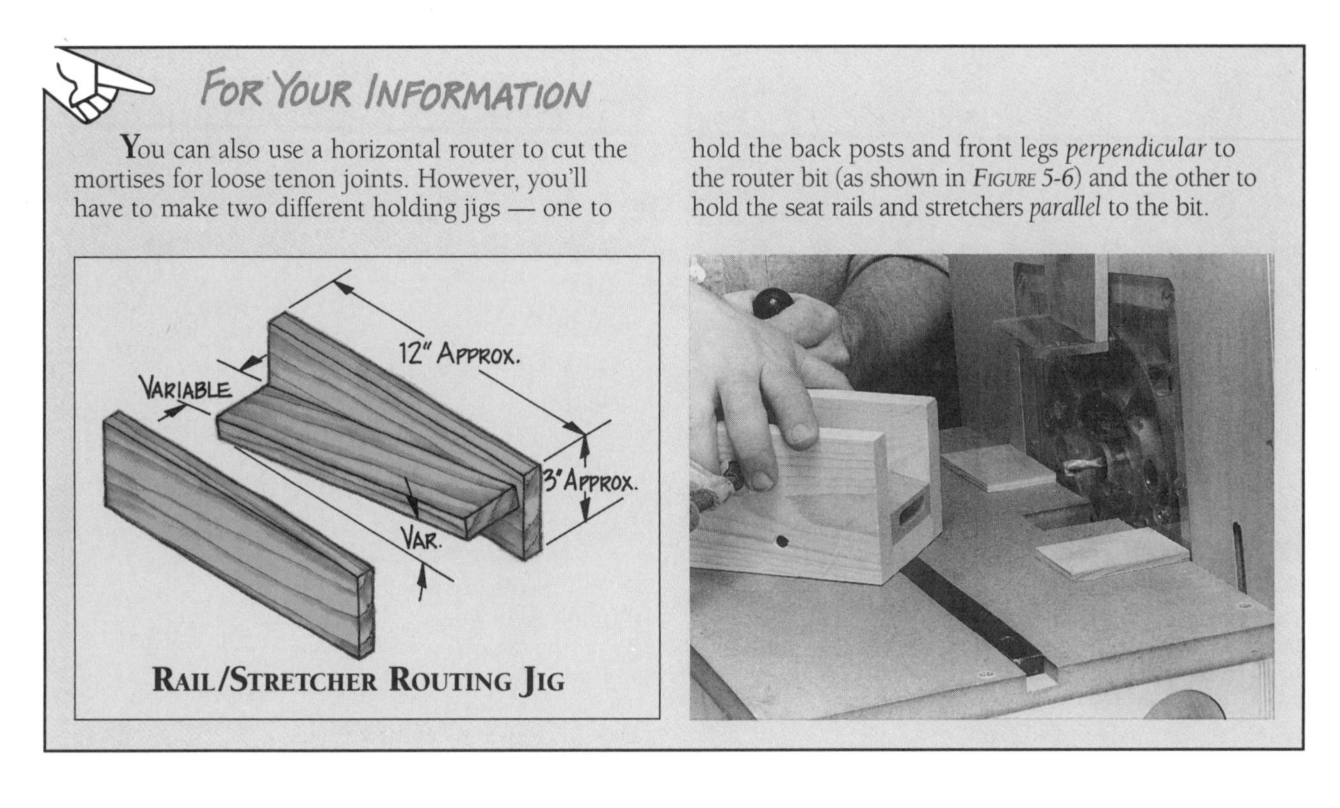

To make tenons with angled shoulders, many craftsmen prefer to cut the shoulders and the cheeks with a dovetail saw. You can also use a table saw, although you must change the angle of the blade and the miter gauge as you work. (SEE FIGURES 5-7 AND 5-8.) But even if you opt to use a power saw, you'll probably have to do a little handwork to clean up the tenons and fit them to their mortises. (SEE FIGURE 5-9.)

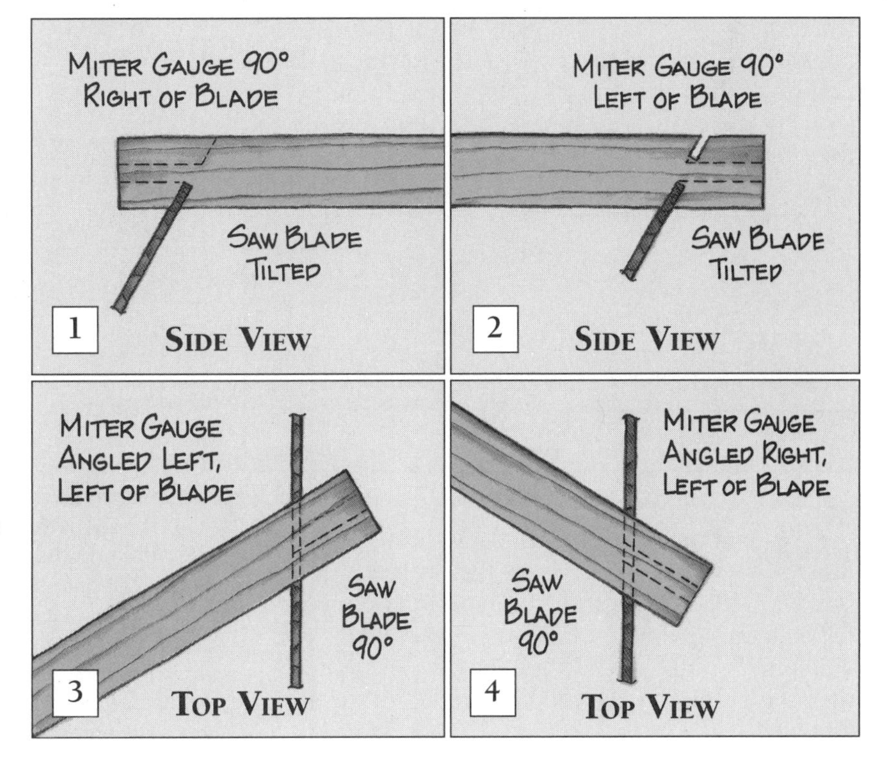

5-7 Cutting angled shoulders for a tenon on a table saw requires that you change the angle of the blade and the miter gauge as you work. (1) Tilt the blade to cut the side shoulders, and set the miter gauge square to the blade. (2) Move the miter gauge from one side of the blade to the other to cut both shoulders. (3) To cut the top and bottom shoulders, set the blade square to the table and turn the miter gauge the required number of degrees to the *left*. (4) Cut one shoulder, then change the miter gauge angle, turning it the same number of degrees to the *right*. Turn the wood over and cut the last shoulder.

***5-8* To cut the cheeks, use a** tenoning jig to hold the workpiece vertical as you push it past the saw blade. You will have to adjust the angle of the tenoning jig and the height of the blade to make all four cuts.

***5-9* You probably won't be able** to complete the cheeks and shoulders on the table saw. Likely, each tenon will require a small amount of handwork with a dovetail saw or a chisel before you can fit it to its mortise. **Note:** If the ends of the mortise are round, use a file to round over the top and bottom of the tenon to match.

ASSEMBLING THE CHAIR FRAME

Most chairmakers start with the back posts and the rear seat rail — these three parts are the foundation on which a chair is built. Lay out the joinery and the profiles of the parts. Cut the joinery, test fit the parts, then cut the profiles. Compare the results to your drawings.

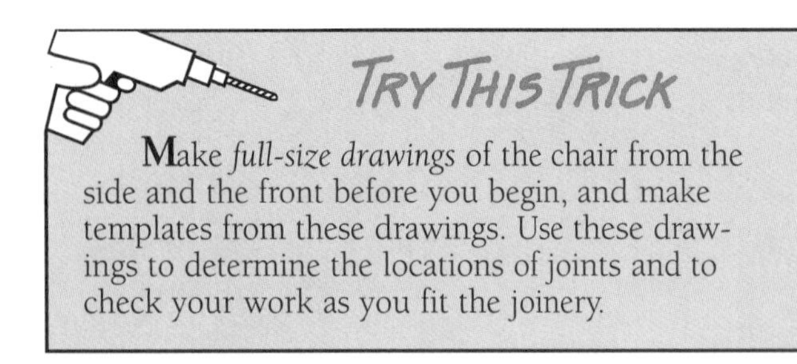

Make *full-size drawings* of the chair from the side and the front before you begin, and make templates from these drawings. Use these drawings to determine the locations of joints and to check your work as you fit the joinery.

Next, join the side seat rails to the back posts. Most posts are cut in an arc, so they appear to bend backward. Because of this, you must sand or plane a flat area on the front surface of the posts where you will join the rails. *(SEE FIGURE 5-10.)* Cut the joinery, then the profiles. Again compare the results to the drawings.

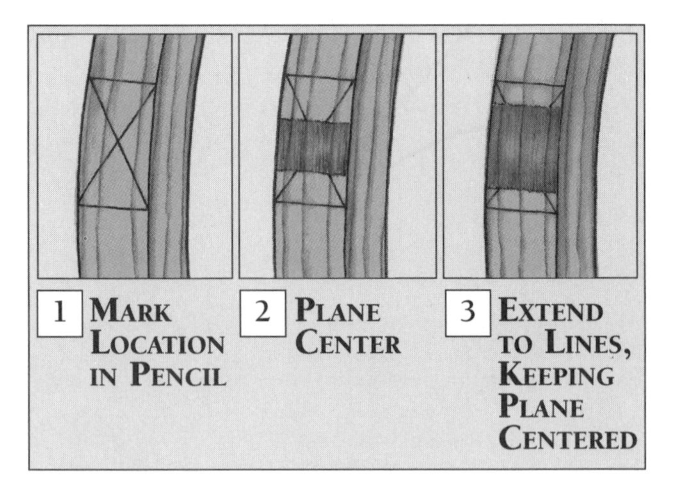

***5-10* To create a flat area on the** convex surface of a back post, (1) mark the top and bottom of the flat. Then scribe diagonals from the left end of one mark to the right end of the other, making an "X" over the area. (2) Plane the area with a block plane or sand it on a disc sander, using the diagonals to check your progress. They should disappear evenly. (3) Stop when the diagonals are gone completely.

Join the front legs and front seat rail to the assembly, following the same procedure: Cut the joinery, cut the profiles, and compare the results to the drawings. Do the same for the stretchers, the chair back, and the armrests, in that order. It's important to check your progress against the drawings at each step to make sure the chair design evolves as planned. If an angled joint is off by just a degree or two and you don't catch it before proceeding, you can waste hours of work.

FOR BEST RESULTS

Because of the way in which the mortises and tenons are angled, it's often easier to assemble the chair frame members in a different order than that in which you cut the joints. Glue the left and right halves of the chair frame together first, then join the halves with the front and back seat rails and other parts that run horizontally from side to side.

5-11 **There are often several** mortises in each of the back posts, the crest rail, and the intermediate rail to accommodate the parts of the chair back. When this is the case, it speeds things up to make a routing template for these mortises. Select a scrap of plywood a little larger than the chair part, and cut slots in it to guide the router. The template shown is made for the back posts of a chair with horizontal slats. Because the mortises in these posts must be *mirror images* of each other, the template is *reversible.* One surface faces up when cutting the left post, and the other surface is up for the right post. Move the blocks that help position the back posts from one side of the template to the other.

JOINED CHAIR BACKS

Two of the most common chair back designs are shown in *FIGURE 5-1* — a single *splat* and multiple *slats.* The splat rests in mortises in the crest rail and a shoe, while the slats are mortised into the crest rail and intermediate rail.

MORTISING FOR SPLATS AND SLATS

Generally, the mortises and tenons for the parts of the chair back are straight — you don't have to worry about cutting angled mortises or tenons with angled shoulders. Sometimes there are no tenons to cut at all; the splat or slats simply rest in mortises.

If you have just a few mortises to make, use the same methods as before — drill lines of overlapping holes or rout the mortise with a straight bit. However, if there are many mortises or you are making several chairs, you may want to make a *mortising template.* Clamp this template to the part you wish to mortise, then follow the template with a guide collar as you rout the mortises. *(SEE FIGURES 5-11 AND 5-12.)*

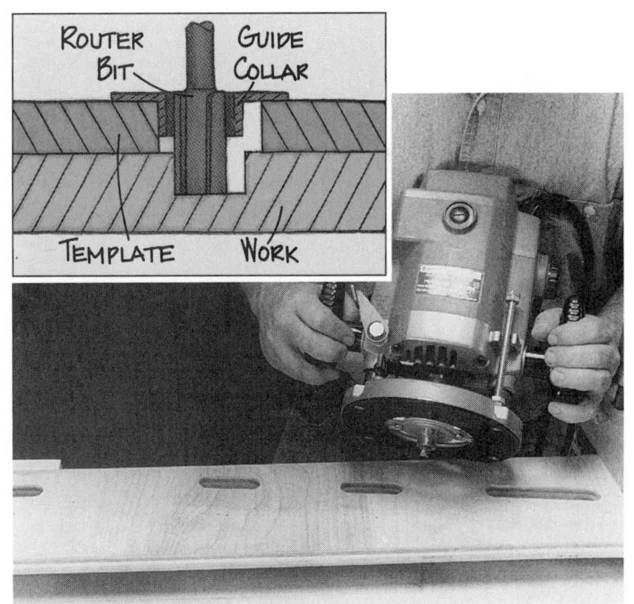

5-12 **To use the template, mount** a guide collar on the base of the router and a straight bit in the chuck. The guide collar rides inside the slots in the template, guiding the router as the bit cuts the mortise. Make each mortise in several passes, cutting about ⅛ inch deeper with each pass until you reach the desired depth.

CUTTING CURVED PARTS

Crest rails, intermediate rails, splats, and slats are often gently curved. Make these curves the same way you created the profiles of the posts, legs, and seat rails — cut them with a band saw, saber saw, or coping saw. Whenever possible, cut the joinery in the parts *before* cutting the curves.

Occasionally, these curves must be bent rather than cut. Bend the wood if the parts are thin or if the curve would otherwise divide the wood grain into short segments and weaken the part. Refer to "Bending Chair Parts" on page 83 for information on how to bend wood.

JOINED CHAIR SEATS

INSTALLING THE SEAT

The seat on a joined chair is usually a *slip seat* — a separate piece that slips into the chair frame between the seat rails. This makes it easy to replace or repair the seat when it becomes worn. Slip seats are supported in one of three ways (SEE FIGURES 5-13 AND 5-14):

- The seat rests inside ***rabbets*** in the seat rails. Usually, just the front and side rails are rabbeted, and a strip of wood — a ***ledger*** — is applied to the back rail to support the back of the seat.
- The seat rests on the ***corner blocks***. This construction method is sometimes used when the rails are too thin to rabbet.
- The seat itself is rabbeted and rests on the ***seat rails***. This method, too, is used when the rails are thin.

Secure a slip seat to its chair frame by driving screws up through the corner block or rails. You may also use clips or tabletop fasteners, attaching the seat to the chair rails much as you'd attach a tabletop to its aprons. Cut grooves or saw kerfs in the inside faces of the seat rails, and insert the tongues of the clips or fasteners in them. Screw the clips or fasteners to the underside of the seat. *(SEE FIGURE 5-14.)*

You can make the seat out of a solid slab of wood. Or, you might make a frame and stretch leather, cane, or some other material over it. Most joined chair seats, however, are *upholstered* — a wooden frame or piece of plywood covered with padding and cloth.

UPHOLSTERING A CHAIR SEAT

The first step in upholstering a seat is to ease the top outside edges of the wooden frame or plywood base. Round over or chamfer the perimeter so the sharp arrises won't dig into your thighs when you sit. *(SEE FIGURE 5-15.)*

Upholstery is applied in layers. If you are upholstering a wooden frame, the first layer should be the *webbing* — a thick, strong material stretched over the frame members. *(SEE FIGURE 5-16.)* If you are upholstering a piece of plywood, you can start with the next layer, the *padding*. Use animal hair, cotton or dacron batting, or foam rubber for padding; the material should be sufficiently thick and resilient to make the seat comfortable. *(SEE FIGURE 5-17.)*

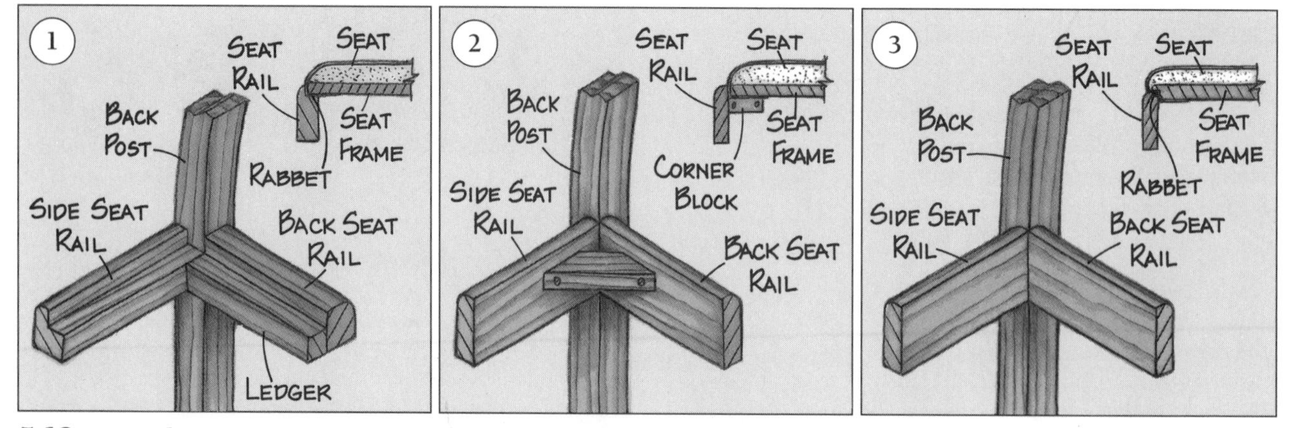

5-13 Most slip seats rest in *rabbets* (1) in the inside surfaces of the seat rails. However, when the rails are too thin to rabbet, they may instead rest on the ***corner blocks*** (2) or the ***seat rails*** (3). If they rest on the rails, the edges of the seats are usually rabbeted to keep them from sliding around.

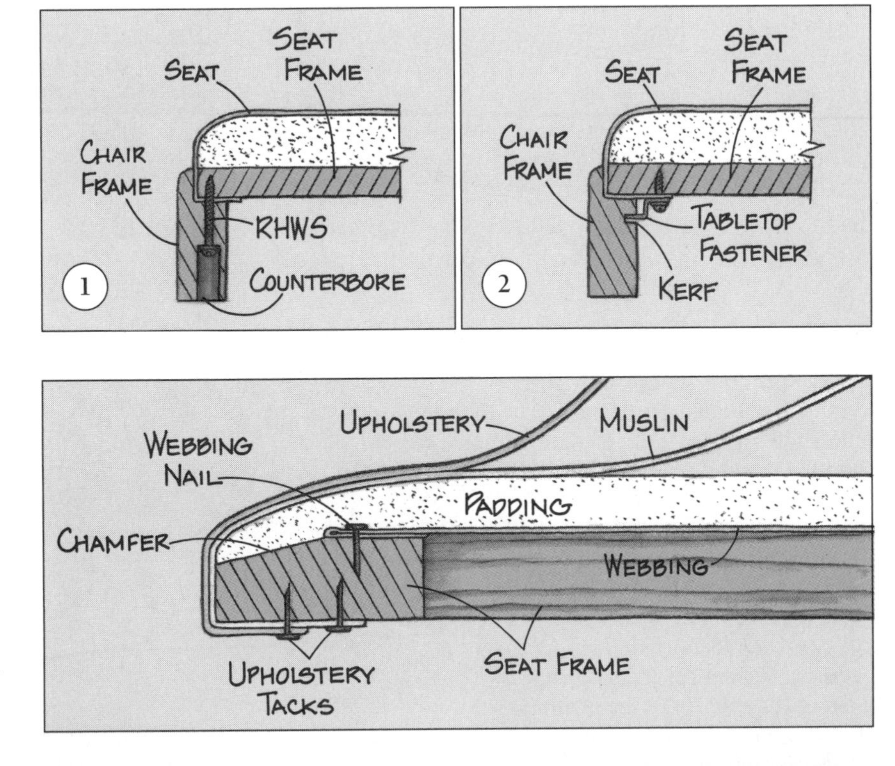

5-14 To secure a slip seat in a chair frame, drive ***screws*** (1) up through the corner blocks or seat rails. Or, use ***tabletop fasteners*** (2) and attach the seat to the rails much as you'd attach a tabletop to its aprons.

5-15 To upholster a seat, first ease the edges of the frame or base with a chamfer or a quarter-round bead. Some upholsterers prefer to use an *edge roll* — a piece of cloth rolled around a cord — to cushion the edges. Both methods keep the sharp arrises from digging into your thighs. Apply the upholstery in layers — ***webbing*** (if needed), ***padding***, ***muslin***, and finally the ***upholstery material***.

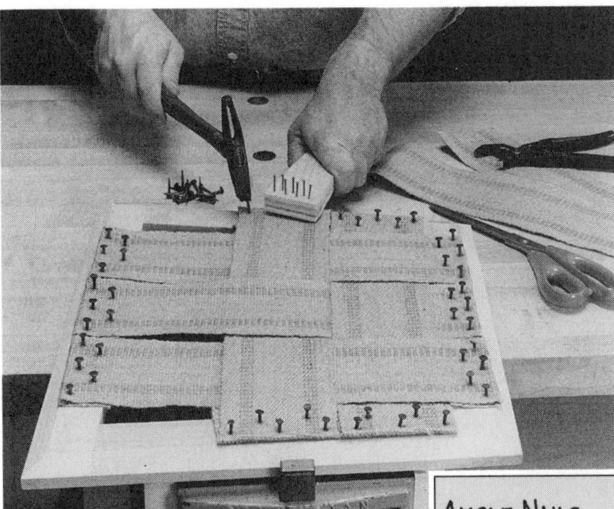

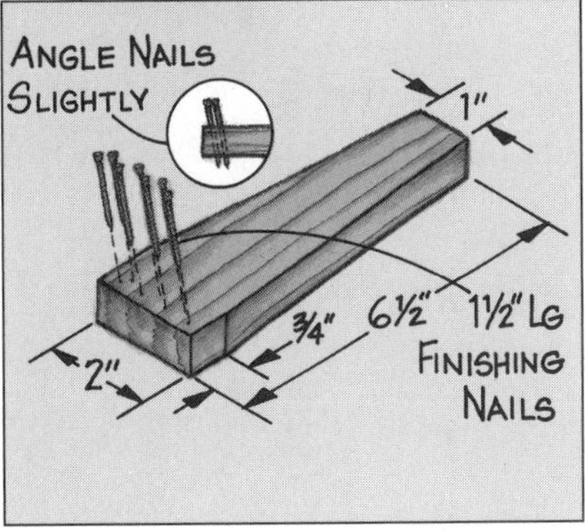

5-16 If you're upholstering a wooden frame, stretch stiff, durable webbing material over the members to support the padding. For strength, fold under the edges of the webbing and stagger the fasteners, as shown. Attach the front-to-back strips with webbing nails; pulling them taut across the frame. Repeat for the side-to-side strips, weaving them over and under the front-to-back strips. Make a handle with angled nails to help pull the webbing.

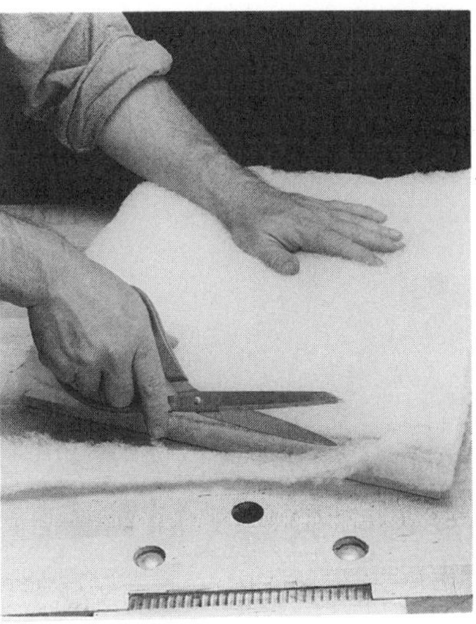

5-17 Arrange the padding on top of the webbing (or plywood). The depth and density of the padding should be as even as possible, although you can thin it out a little at the edges. It should be at least 1 to 1½ inches thick over most of the seat. If you're using horse hair or cotton batting, you may have to add to or shift the padding on the seat as you stretch the muslin over it to make the cushion as smooth as possible.

Hold the padding in place with a layer of *muslin* or *nylon*. (SEE FIGURE 5-18.) Then apply the decorative *upholstery material* over the muslin. (SEE FIGURE 5-19.) The webbing is usually fastened with webbing nails, and the muslin and upholstery with upholstery tacks.

Why use a double layer of muslin and upholstery material over the padding? Because this arrangement keeps the seat smooth. When you sit on the chair, the material slides over the muslin. If the upholstery material were in direct contact with the padding, the padding would be pulled this way and that, and the seat would soon become lumpy. Also, it will be easier to reupholster a chair when the upholstery material wears out — you won't have to reposition or replace the padding.

5-18 Spread a piece of muslin or nylon over the padding. Tuck it under the seat and hold it there with your hands while you carefully turn the seat over. Attach the center of the muslin's back edge to the seat frame or plywood base with upholstery tacks, then do the same for the front edge, stretching the muslin tight enough to smooth out the padding. Repeat for the side edges, tacking the muslin in the center. *Don't set the tacks yet!* Check that the muslin is smooth; if not, remove a tack, adjust the muslin, and fasten it in place again. Tack the edges, working out from the center of each edge and spacing the tacks about ¾ inch apart. Again, don't set the tacks — wait until you have completed all four edges, then check that the muslin is smooth. When you're satisfied it is, set all the tacks. Finally, pull the muslin taut over the corners, neatly fold the material, and tack the corner folds in place.

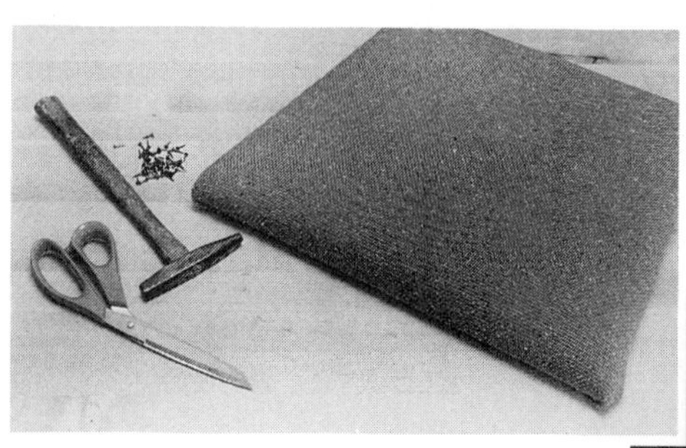

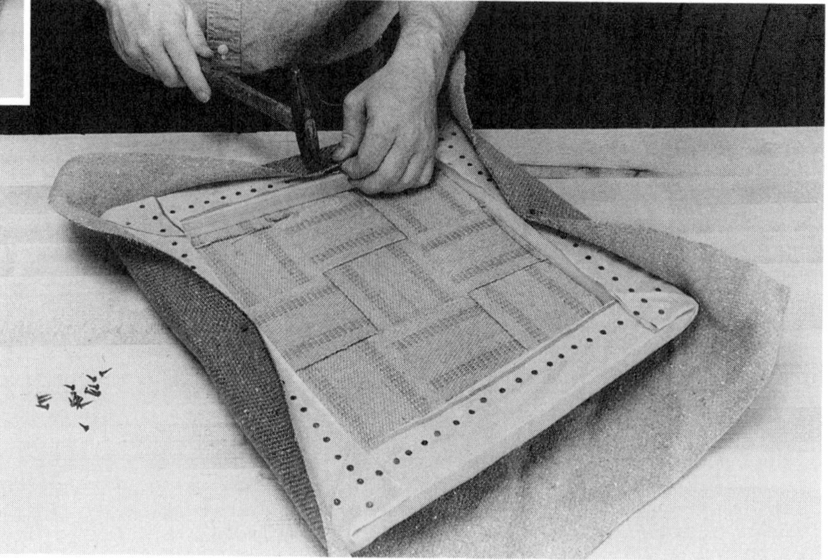

5-19 Attach the upholstery material over the muslin in exactly the same way you applied the muslin. Fasten the center of each edge first, then work out from the center points to the corners. Some upholsterers add a layer of cotton or dacron batting between the muslin and the upholstery material to make the seat more comfortable. When you've finished, slip the seat in the chair frame. Hold it in place with screws or tabletop fasteners.

CHAIR WOODS

Have you ever owned a store-bought chair with joints that came apart no matter how you glued or reinforced them? Chances are, the errant chair parts were made from the *wrong wood species.*

Wood selection is more important for chairs than for any other woodworking projects. The joinery is subjected to the worst kinds of stress; many surfaces suffer continual abrasion. The wood must be able to stand up to this punishment; otherwise, the chair will come apart and no amount of glue can ever fix it.

There are several important rules of thumb for selecting chair woods. Most importantly, use hard wood for parts that must withstand heavy loads, such as legs, posts, rails, and stretchers. Use lighter, softer woods for extremely thick parts such as chair seats and armrests. This will cut down on the weight of the chair without affecting the soundness of the structure. However, never join softwood to softwood in a chair — the joint won't last.

If you need to scoop or carve a chair part, make it from a wood that can be easily sculpted. This same kind of common sense applies to chair parts that must be bent — choose a wood that bends easily.

WOOD SPECIES	FRAME MEMBERS	SEAT (SOLID)	SCULPTED PARTS	BENT PARTS	OTHER PROPERTIES
Ash	Good	Poor	Okay	Good	Light but very durable
Beech	Good	Poor	Poor	Okay	Splits easily if turning slender parts
Birch	Good	Poor	Poor	Good	Very hard to carve
Cherry	Good	Okay	Okay	Poor	Better suited for joined chairs
Hickory	Good	Poor	Poor	Good	Extremely hard and durable
Mahogany	Okay	Good	Good	Okay	Better suited for joined chairs
Maple	Good	Okay	Okay	Good	Best all-round chair wood
Oak, Red	Good	Poor	Poor	Good	Very strong grain, better suited for painted chairs
Oak, White	Good	Poor	Poor	Good	Best choice for bent parts
Pine	Poor	Good	Good	Poor	Typically used for seats only
Poplar	Poor	Good	Good	Poor	Typically used for seats only
Walnut	Good	Okay	Good	Poor	Better suited for joined chairs

6

Building a Turned Chair

In the turner's tradition, the major parts of the chair frame (posts, legs, and rails) are turned round on a lathe. Only the seat, splats, and slats are made from flat boards or slabs of wood. It is an old, old design, and one that can be made with a few simple tools. Itinerant turners or *chair bodgers* once roamed Europe, each with a lathe, a drill, and an adze, making these chairs for the common folk.

It remained a common design for centuries — folks with the money to employ a cabinetmaker preferred the joined chair. But bodging eventually evolved into a skilled trade, and the turned chair evolved into an art form. By the late seventeenth century, the upper class was beginning to appreciate the merits of the graceful, comfortable *Windsor* chair.

Just how the turned chair earned this nickname is a matter of conjecture. One story has it that the Duke of Windsor was out duking around when he came upon a traveling bodger of unsurpassed skill turning out chairs for the peasants in his dukedom. The Duke had an eye for quality and promptly bought a set for his dining hall. At the very next ducal wingding, all the society types admired "Windsor's chairs" — and ran out to purchase their own.

TURNED CHAIR CONSTRUCTION

The forces that plague a joined chair all conspire against a turned chair as well. So, like a joined chair, a turned chair has to be a strong construction, designed to handle racking stress. It too is joined with mortises and tenons — but *round* mortises and tenons. (SEE FIGURE 6-1.)

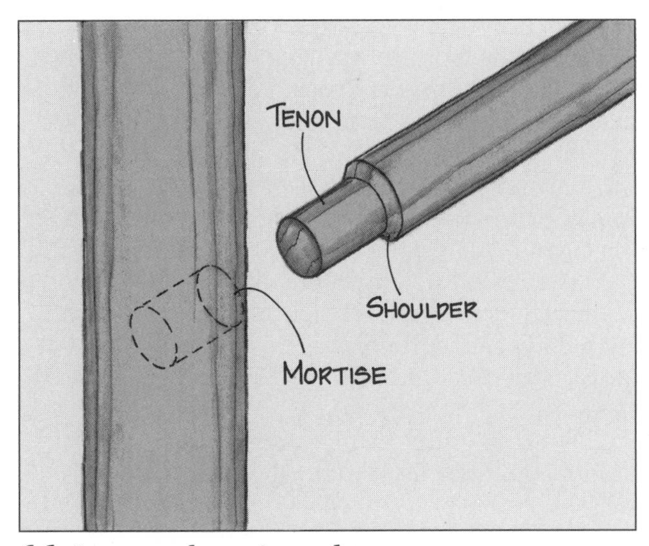

6-1 In a round mortise-and-tenon joint, the mortise is a round hole. The hole is stopped, usually; it does not continue through the part. The tenon is turned round to fit the hole, and it often has beveled shoulders.

TURNED CHAIR PARTS

There are two distinct types of turned chairs. A chair with a solid wood seat is called a ***slab-and-stick*** chair, while one with a framed seat is simply a ***stick*** chair. The parts of a stick chair are similar to a joined chair (SEE FIGURE 6-2):

- *Back posts* serve as the back legs and the vertical frame members for the back.
- *Front legs* support the front of the chair.
- *Seat rails* frame the seat and tie the legs and posts together.
- *Rungs* keep the legs from racking.

The parts of a slab-and-stick chair are slightly different:

- The *seat* is a shaped block of wood. If it's sculpted or scooped to fit the posterior, it's a *saddle seat*.
- Four *legs* support the seat.
- *Rungs* tie the legs together and keep them from racking.

There is a wide variety of back designs for turned chairs, especially for slab-and-stick chairs — when the back posts are optional, there is room for much more creativity. Depending on the design, the backs

6-2 On a stick chair, the *back posts* (1) serve as the back legs and the vertical support for the back. There are also ***front legs*** (2), ***seat rails*** (3), and ***rungs*** (4). The back is often made from horizontal ***slats*** (5) running between the posts. On a slab-and-stick chair, there is a solid wooden ***seat*** (6) supported by four ***legs*** (7). The legs are tied together with ***rungs*** (8). If there are ***back posts*** (9), they extend from the seat up. There may be a ***crest rail*** (10) tying the tops of the posts together, and ***spindles*** (11) running between the seat and the crest rail.

may include crest rails, intermediate rails, splats, hoops, bows, continuous arms, and many other parts. But most turned chair backs include one of the following:

- Horizontal *slats* run between the back posts. This arrangement is called a *ladderback.*
- Multiple vertical *spindles* run between the seat and another member, such as a crest rail.

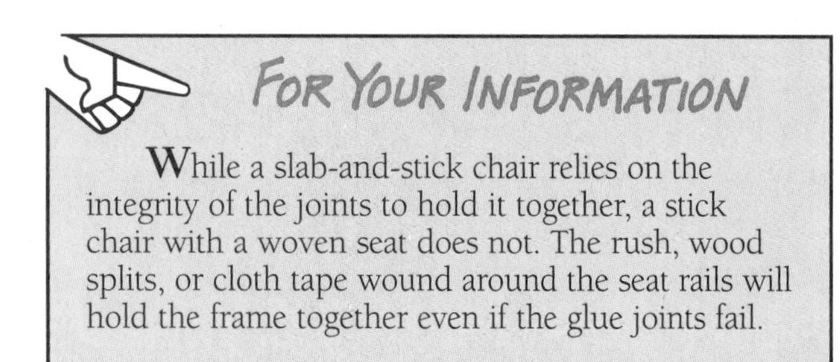

While a slab-and-stick chair relies on the integrity of the joints to hold it together, a stick chair with a woven seat does not. The rush, wood splits, or cloth tape wound around the seat rails will hold the frame together even if the glue joints fail.

JOINING TURNED CHAIR PARTS

When making round mortises and tenons, the procedure is often just the reverse of making a square mortise and tenon. Make the tenon first, then the mortise. This is because it's easier to make the tenons while you're turning the parts of the chair. Measure the diameter of the tenon with calipers or shop-made tenon gauge as you work. *(SEE FIGURES 6-3 THROUGH 6-6.)* **Note:** If the chair part has tenons *only,* you can turn the tenons and the shape at the same time. However, if it has tenons *and* mortises or mortises only, turn it to a rough cylinder and stop until after you've made the mortises. It's much easier to bore mortises in a cylinder than in an odd-shaped part.

Making the mortises is a simple matter of drilling stopped holes. There is a trick, however. You must mark the mortises accurately, locating both the *radial* and the *vertical* positions of each mortise. To mark the radial positions, make a *mortising collar* for each turned part and a *spindle-marking straightedge.* Transfer the radial marks on the collar to the circumference of each part, then extend these marks down the length of the cylinder with the straightedge. *(SEE FIGURES 6-7 AND 6-8.)* For the vertical positions, make a *story stick* for each set of mortises (front, side, back) and use this story stick to mark the mortise locations along the lines. *(SEE FIGURE 6-9.)* Rest the part in a V-jig and drill the mortises. *(SEE FIGURE 6-10.)*

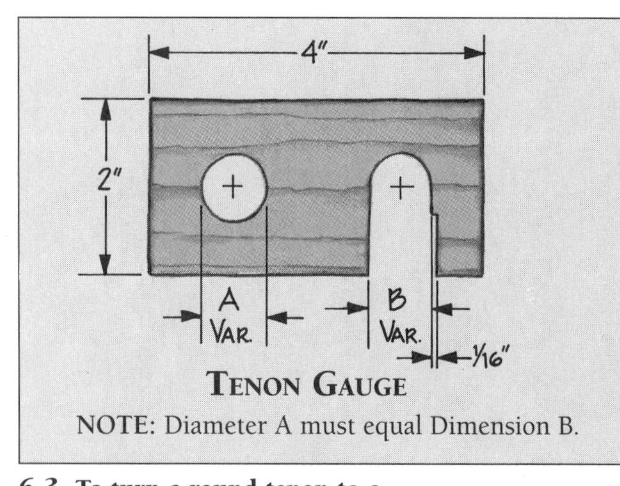

6-3 To turn a round tenon to a specific diameter requires patience and precision. You can simplify this chore by making a *tenon gauge* from a scrap of plywood. This gauge is a fixed caliper for a specific diameter, with a round mortise to test the fit of the tenon once it's turned. Note that the opening of the caliper is 1/16 inch wider than the desired diameter, and there is a 1/16-inch step placed just inside the opening, where the caliper closes down to the correct diameter.

You can also cut accurate tenons with a set of *tenon cutters.* Tilt your drill press table so it's vertical, and clamp a V-jig to it to hold the turning directly under the chuck. Mount the tenon cutter in the chuck and the turning stock in the V-jig, then cut the tenon to the proper length.

6-4 Turn the tenon, checking the work frequently with the tenon gauge as the diameter decreases. When the gauge slips over the work up to the step, you know you're close to the correct diameter. From this point, you must remove stock very slowly.

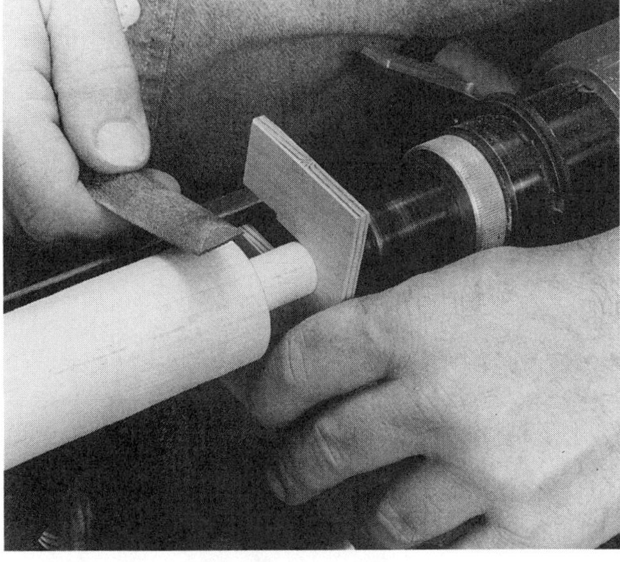

6-5 Remove a minute amount of stock and check the tenon with the gauge. Continue doing this until the gauge slips over the tenon past the step. At this point, the tenon should be the correct diameter. **Note:** Some craftsmen prefer to *sand* or *file* the tenon to its final diameter, rather than cutting it with a chisel. Both sandpaper and files remove stock very slowly. This decreases the risk that you might turn the tenon down past the desired diameter.

6-6 Turn off the lathe and dismount the chair part. Test fit the tenon in the round mortise in the gauge. If any further lathe work is required, mount the part back on the lathe. **Note:** Before removing the workpiece, mark it and a spur of the drive center so you can reposition the part on the lathe exactly as it was before you removed it.

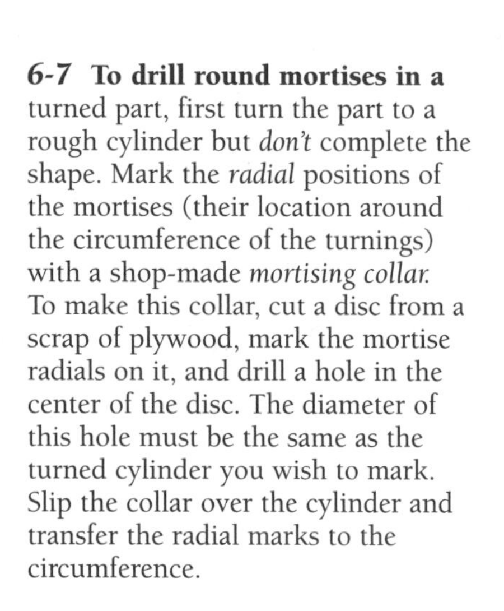

6-7 To drill round mortises in a turned part, first turn the part to a rough cylinder but *don't* complete the shape. Mark the *radial* positions of the mortises (their location around the circumference of the turnings) with a shop-made *mortising collar.* To make this collar, cut a disc from a scrap of plywood, mark the mortise radials on it, and drill a hole in the center of the disc. The diameter of this hole must be the same as the turned cylinder you wish to mark. Slip the collar over the cylinder and transfer the radial marks to the circumference.

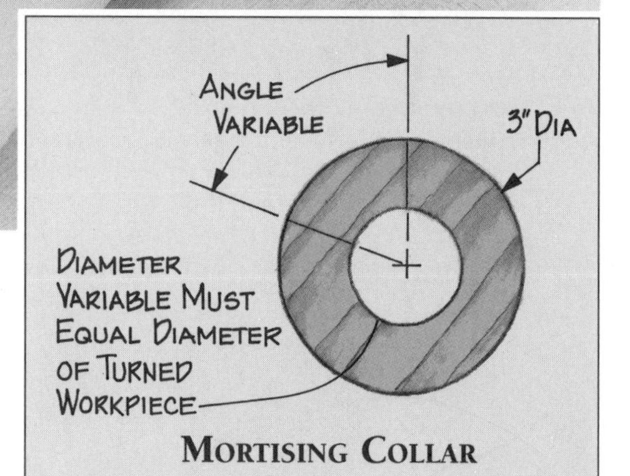

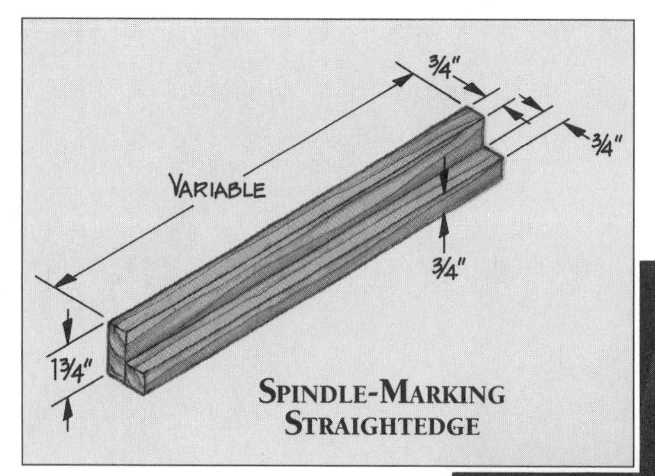

6-8 Extend the radial marks along the length of the cylinder. To do this, make a *spindle-marking straight-edge* by gluing two long, straight scraps together, edge to face, to form an L-shaped beam. Rest the turning in the inside corner of the straight-edge, align a mortise mark with one side of the jig, and draw a line down the turning. Repeat for each mark. **Note:** It helps to label the lines "side rungs," "back slats," and so on, to keep from mixing them up.

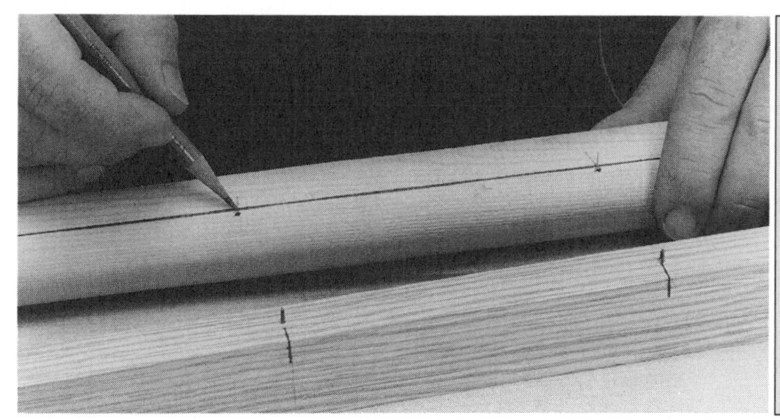

6-9 To mark the *vertical* positions of the round mortises on a turned chair part, make a story stick for each set of mortises — the front rung mortises on the front legs, the side rung mortises on the front legs and back posts, and the back rung mortises on the back posts. You may also wish to make another story stick for the mortises that hold the chair back parts in the back posts. Line up each story stick with the appropriate mortise line on each cylinder and make sure the bottom ends are flush. Transfer the mortise location for the story stick to the surface of the cylinder. **Note:** If you wish, you can make the story sticks with built-in scribes — drive brads partway into the edges of the sticks, then clip off the heads.

6-10 Cradle the cylinders in a V-jig to drill the round mortises. Clamp a fence to the drill press worktable to hold the jig so the point of the "V" is directly under the tip of the bit. Keep the V-jig pressed against the fence as you work. If you need to drill angled mortises, tilt the worktable left or right. When you've made all the mortises, mount the parts back on the lathe and complete the turned shapes.

JOINING LEGS TO SEATS

When making a slab-and-stick chair, you must join the legs to the seat with *angled* round mortises and tenons. You can cut the tenons on the ends of the legs as shown in FIGURES 6-3 THROUGH 6-6, but the mortises must be drilled at an angle.

Furthermore, the legs are *splayed;* that is, they are angled out from the seat to make the chair more stable. The front legs are splayed toward the front and side, while the back legs are splayed toward the back and side. Calculating the compound angle and the direction in which each leg is splayed can be a nightmare. Fortunately, you can build a *leg mortise drill guide* for boring the mortises at the correct angles without ever figuring those angles! This jig holds the seat above a board that represents the floor. Notches in this "floorboard" and holes in the corresponding "seatboard" (the board that holds the seat) guide the drill bit at the proper angles.

To make the jig, you must measure how far each leg is splayed to the front, back, or side. Consult your chair plans — although they vary considerably, almost all plans have a front view and side view that show you the *length* of each leg, how each leg is *angled* (when viewed from the front or side), and the *height* of the seat above the floor.

FOR YOUR INFORMATION

On most slab-and-stick chairs, the back legs are not angled as far to the sides as the front legs. This lets you walk around the back of the chair without tripping over the legs.

Using these measurements, draw triangles that represent the front and side views of one of the chair's front legs, and the same views of one back leg. The hypotenuse of each triangle should equal the length of the leg, while the vertical side of the triangle equals the seat height. The angle between these two lines should match the splay angle shown on the plans. To determine how far each leg splays, measure the base of each triangle. Use these splay measurements to lay out the *footprint* of the chair (where the feet touch the floor). *(SEE FIGURE 6-11.)*

Consult the drawings again to find the location of the leg mortises in the seat. (These should be shown on either the top view or the seat layout.) Using the footprint and the leg mortise locations, create the fixture shown in *FIGURE 6-12*. Fasten this fixture to the seat stock and use it to guide a spade bit as you bore the leg mortises. *(SEE FIGURE 6-13.)*

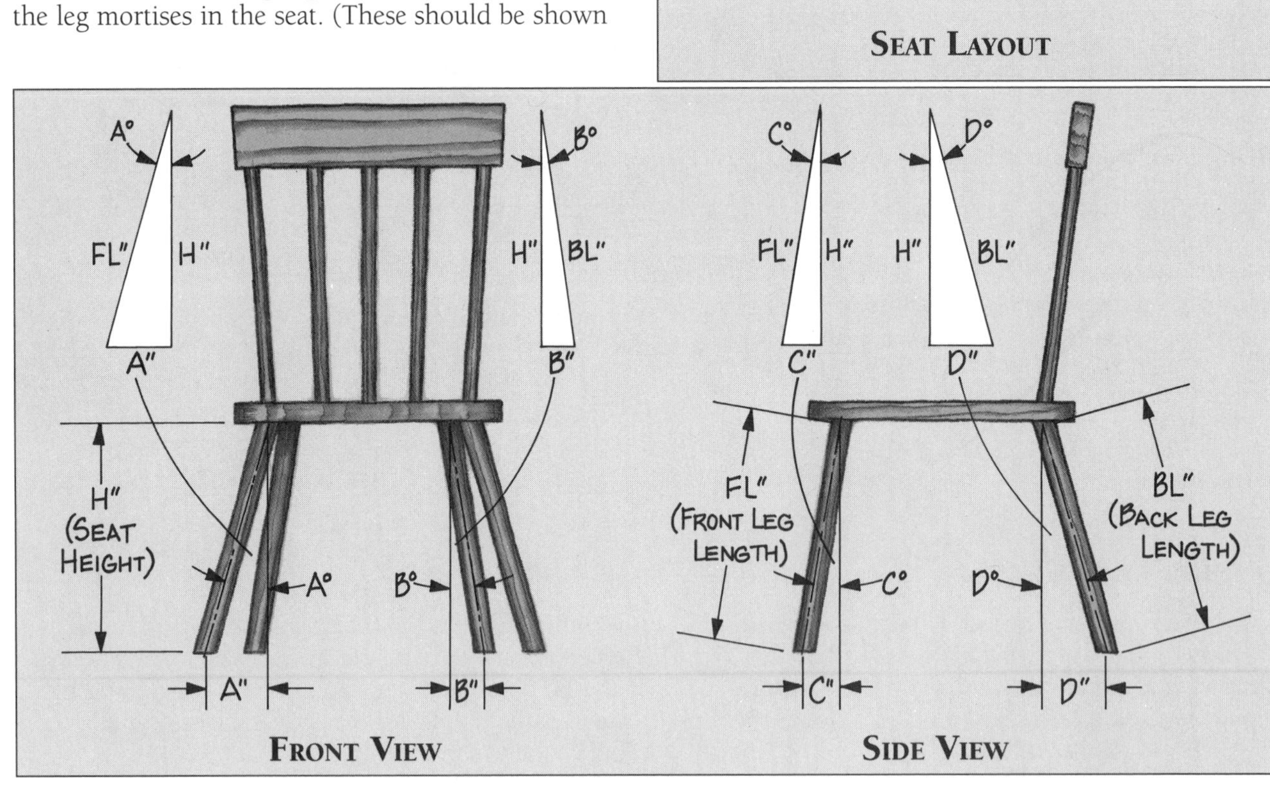

6-11 To drill the leg mortises, you must first lay out the *footprint* of the chair in relation to the seat. Consult the chair plans to find the leg lengths, leg angles, and seat height. Using these figures, draw four right triangles — one for a *front leg* viewed from the *front*, one for a *front leg* viewed from the *side*, one for a *back leg* from the *front*, and one for a *back leg* viewed from the *side*. On each triangle, the hypotenuse must equal the length of the leg, the vertical side must equal the seat height (as measured from the floor to the *underside* of the seat), and the angle between them must equal the angle shown on the front view or side view. Once you have drawn the triangles, measure their *bases* to find A, B, C, and D, as shown. Use these measurements to lay out the *footprint* of the chair (where the feet touch the floor) in relation to the seat.

For Your Information

If you're comfortable doing the math, you can also use simple geometry to determine the splay of each leg. For example, to find out how far the front legs splay toward the front (S), consult the side view for the front leg length (L) and the seat height (H). Plug these numbers into the all-purpose Pythagorean theorem to calculate the splay:

$$S^2 = L^2 - H^2$$

Or you can take a shortcut through trigonometry, using the front leg angle (A) and the seat height (H). Multiply the tangent of the leg angle by the seat height:

$$S = \tan(A) \times H$$

To find out how far the front leg splays toward the side, perform the same calculation, but use the numbers shown on the front view. Repeat for the back legs. **Note:** You can look up the tangents to angles in tables in most algebra and trigonometry books. Or, if you have a scientific calculator, punch in the angle and push the button marked "TAN."

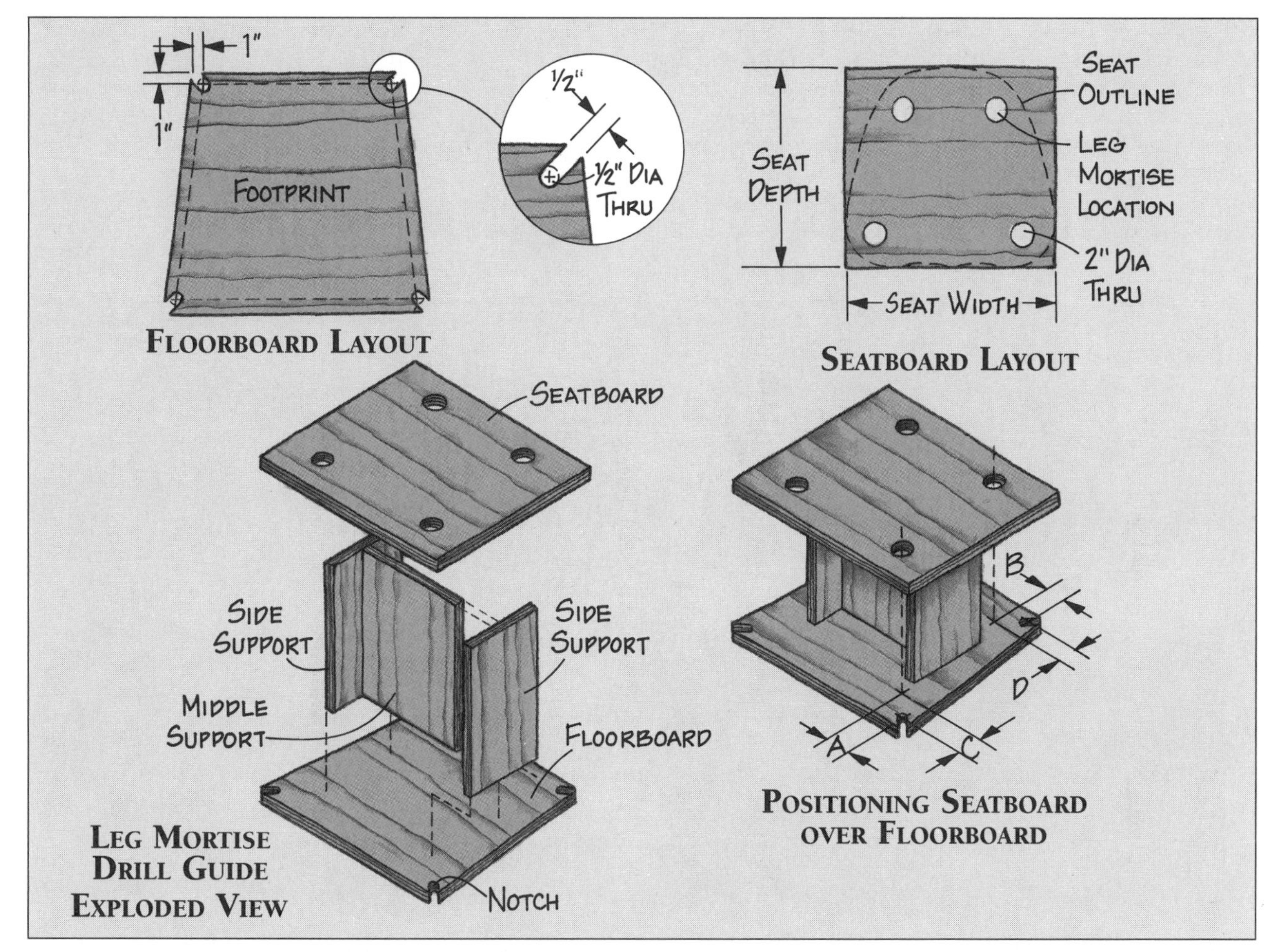

6-12 Once you have the footprint, you can make a simple jig to guide the drill bit as you bore the leg mortises. Cut two pieces of ¾-inch plywood — the *seatboard* and *floorboard.* The seatboard should be the same size as the seat, and the floorboard 2 inches wider and longer than the footprint. Lay out the seat and the location of the leg mortises on the seatboard, and drill 2-inch-diameter clearance holes at the mortise positions. On the floorboard, mark where the legs will meet the floor. Drill ½-inch-diameter holes at these marks, then open up the holes to the corners to make notches. Fasten the boards together so the distance from the *top* of the seatboard to the *top* of the floorboard is equal to the seat height. Use the front, back, and side splay measurements as shown to position the boards relative to one another. **Note:** If the plans show the seat is sloped, the seatboard should be sloped to the floorboard at that same angle.

6-13 Lay out the leg mortise location on the seat stock, then clamp the jig to the seat, centering the clearance holes in the seatboard over the mortise marks. (The seatboard shown has stops around the edges that automatically position it over the seat stock.) Mount a spade bit in a drill extension. Place the tip of the bit over a mortise mark on the seat stock, cradle the extension in the corresponding notch in the floorboard, and bore the mortise through the seat. Use light pressure to keep the extension in the notch as you work — this will hold the bit at the *precise* compound angle *and* direction needed. Repeat for the remaining mortises. **Note:** Depending on the height of the seat and the length of the spade bit, you may have to use two or more extensions.

Lathe Steadyrest

Turning long, slender chair parts can be tricky. Once the diameters have been reduced past a certain dimension, the parts will start to bow and whip on the lathe. To avoid this, apply just enough pressure to hold the stock firmly between the centers when you mount it on the lathe. When turning extremely long pieces, use a steadyrest to keep them running true. Some lathe manufacturers offer these as accessories, or you can make your own.

Mount the steadyrest to the lathe bed. Turn the center portion of the chair part first, and adjust the rollers of the steadyrest so they lightly contact the round surface. Then turn the right and left portions.

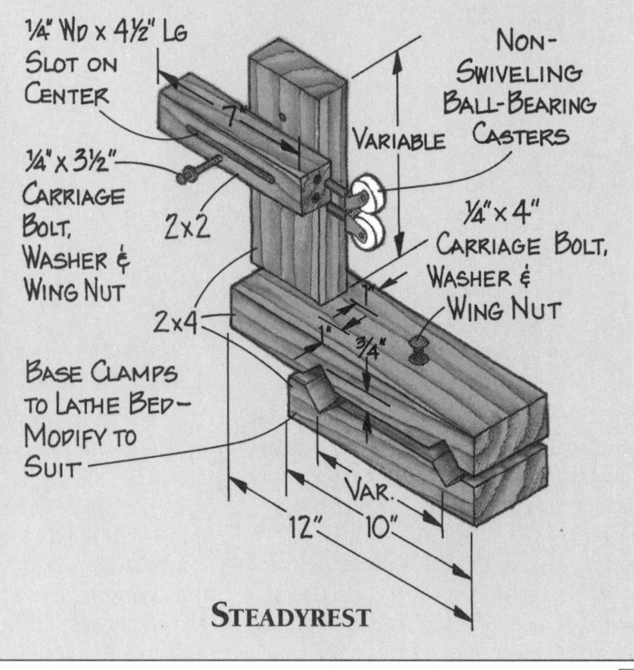

Steadyrest

Turned Chair Backs

MAKING A LADDERBACK

To make a ladderback for a turned chair, you must cut *slot* mortises in the back posts, then fit horizontal slats to the mortises. Mark these mortises in the same way you did the round mortises. Round the parts to make simple cylinders, but don't complete the shapes yet. Use a mortising collar and spindle-marking straightedge to find the radial positions, then mark the vertical positions with a story stick or measuring tape.

Mount the back posts in a V-jig and strap them down so they won't roll. (SEE FIGURE 6-14.) Cut the slots with a drill press and a chisel or rout them with an overhead router. (SEE FIGURES 6-15 AND 6-16.) There's usually no need to cut tenons on the ends of the slats to fit the mortises. On most ladderback chairs, the slats simply rest in the mortises. After cutting the mortises, replace the posts in the lathe and finish turning the shapes.

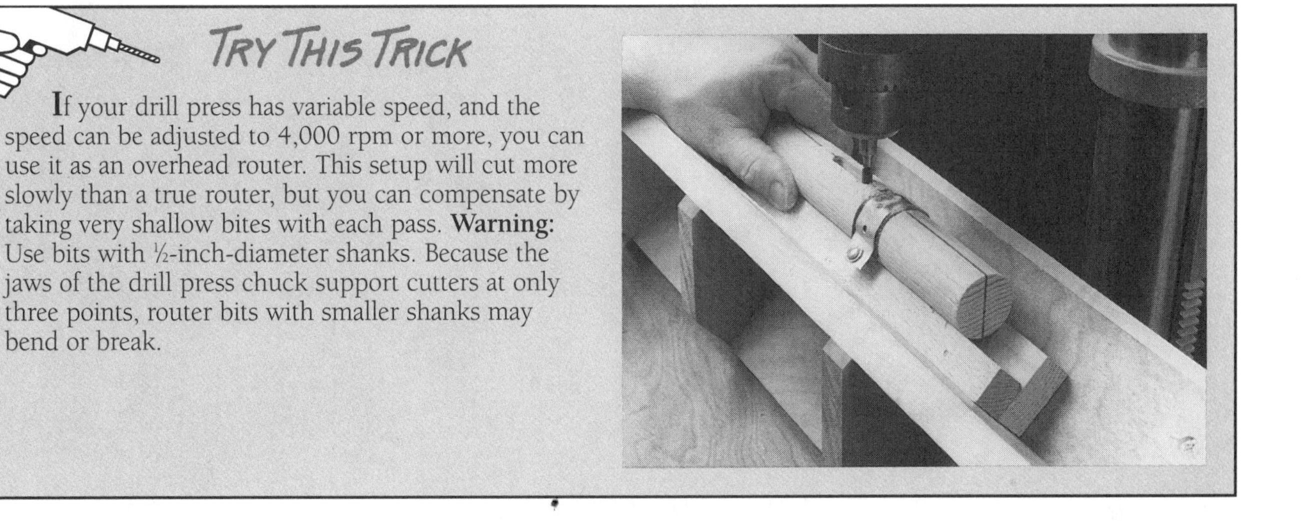

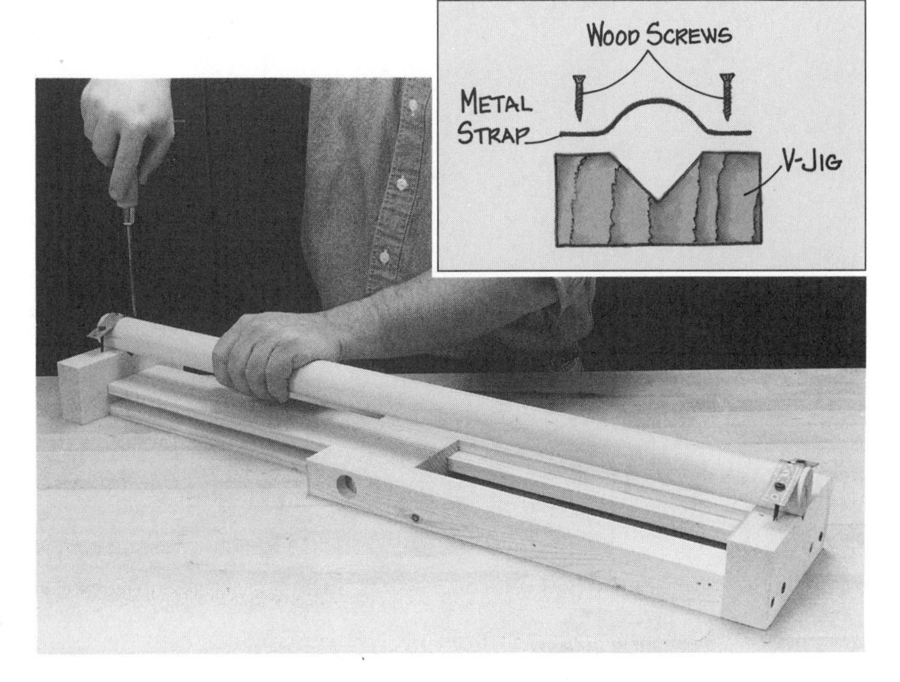

6-14 To make slot mortises in a turned chair part, you must fasten it in a V-jig so the turning won't roll. Cut short lengths of metal plumber's strap (flexible metal strap with predrilled holes). Bend the straps so they fit over the turning without quite touching the top of the V-jig. Rotate the turning so the marks for the mortises face up, then fasten the straps to the V-jig with wood screws. As you tighten the screws down, the straps will clamp the turning in the jig. **Note:** If you won't be turning the part again after mortising it, protect the surface by placing strips of leather, rubber, or cardboard between the wood and the metal straps.

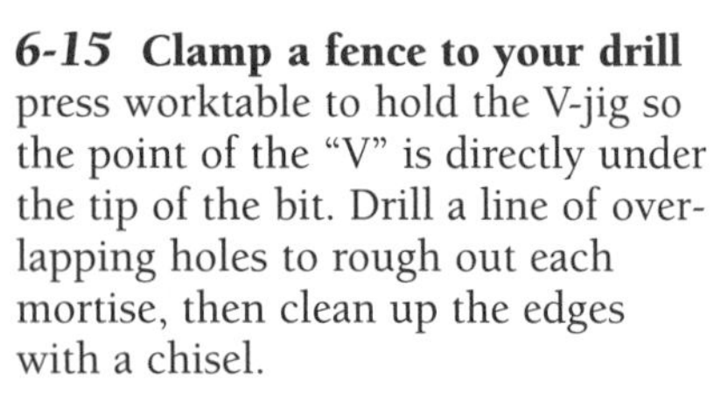

6-15 Clamp a fence to your drill press worktable to hold the V-jig so the point of the "V" is directly under the tip of the bit. Drill a line of overlapping holes to rough out each mortise, then clean up the edges with a chisel.

6-16 If you have an overarm router or an overhead routing jig (shown), you can rout the slot mortises. Use a fence to guide the V-jig, positioning the fence so the point of the "V" is directly under the center of the cutter. Rout each slot in several passes, cutting just ⅛ inch deeper with each pass.

MAKING A SPINDLE BACK

The spindles in spindle-back chairs fan out at many angles, and each spindle leans in a slightly different direction. This presents the same problem to a woodworker as the legs — every mortise must be drilled at a different angle or from a different direction. However, you can solve this problem exactly the same way you made the leg mortises — build a jig.

Make a *spindle mortise drill guide* using two sets of dimensions that you can find in the plans — the locations for the spindle mortises in the seat and those in the crest rail. Lay out the seat spindle mortises on one sheet of plywood and the crest rail spindle mortises on another. Cut a notch at each mortise mark and fasten the two pieces together so the distance between them is the same as the distance between the seat and the crest rail. *(See Figure 6-17.)* Clamp the seatboard to the seat stock and bore the spindle mortises in the seat, then clamp the crest rail board to the crest rail to drill them in the rail. *(See Figures 6-18 and 6-19.)*

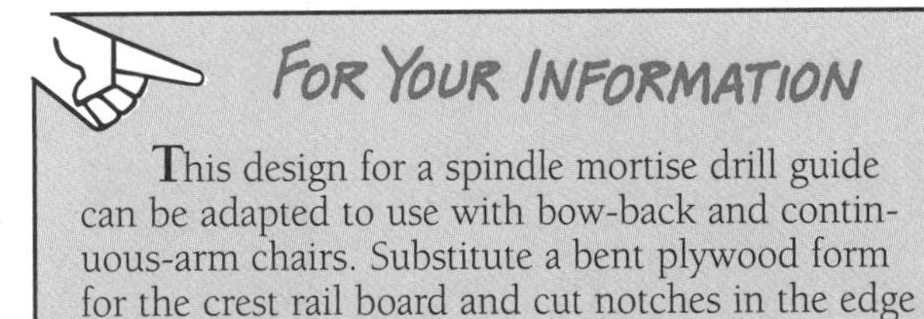

This design for a spindle mortise drill guide can be adapted to use with bow-back and continuous-arm chairs. Substitute a bent plywood form for the crest rail board and cut notches in the edge of the form. To drill the mortises in the bow or the continuous arm, clamp it to the plywood form.

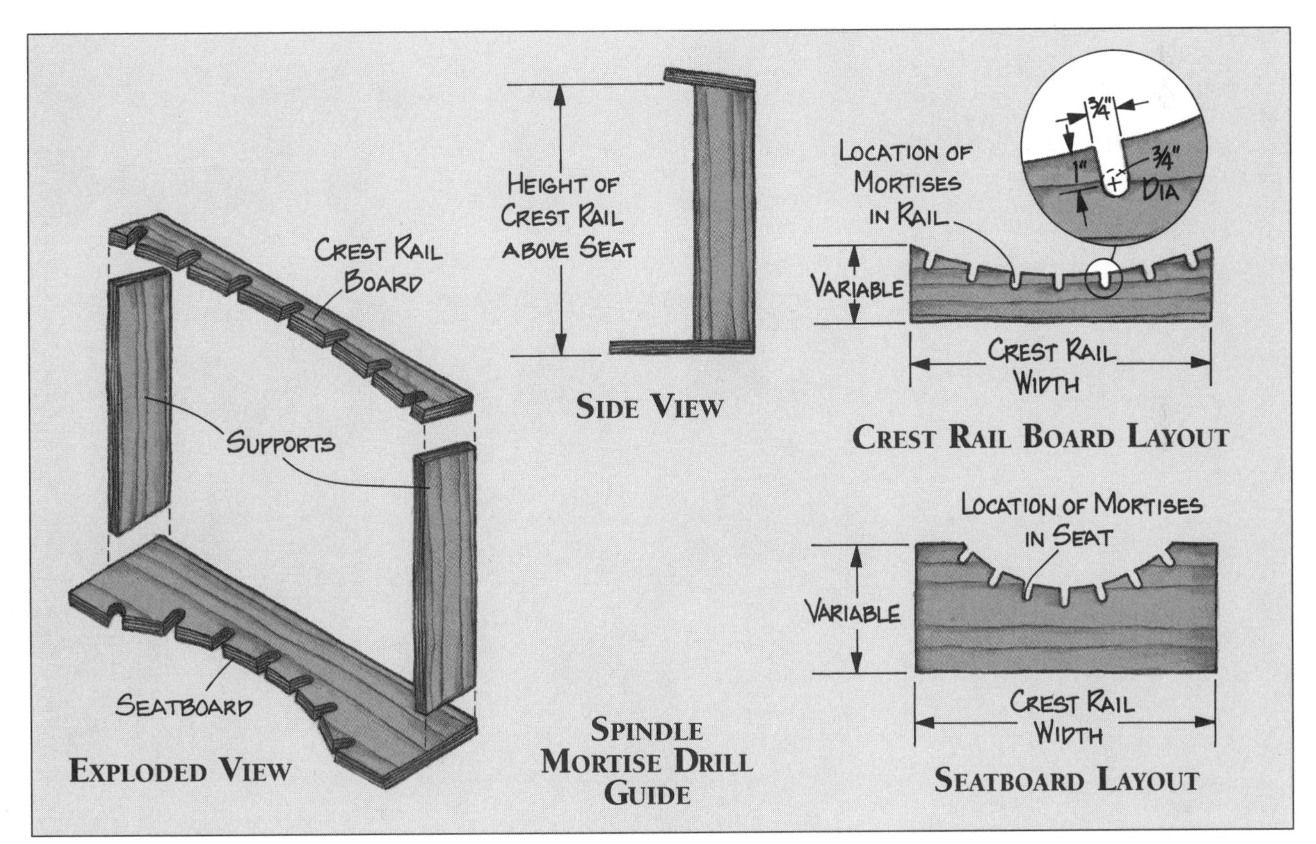

6-17 To drill the spindle mortises in the seat and crest rail, first make a *spindle mortise drill guide*. Lay out the location of the seat spindle mortises on one piece of plywood, and the crest rail mortises on another. On each piece of plywood, sketch an arc that follows the mortises and lies an inch in *front* of them, as shown. Cut the arcs on a band saw. At each mortise mark, drill a 3/4-inch-diameter clearance hole and open up the hole to the edge of the arc, creating a notch. Fasten the plywood pieces together so the distance between the *bottom* of the seatboard and the *bottom* of the crest rail board is equal to the distance between the top of the seat and the bottom of the crest rail. **Note:** The front face of most crest rails is parallel to the spindles, and the bottom edges are tilted in relation to the seat. The crest rail board must be tilted the same number of degrees in relation to the seatboard.

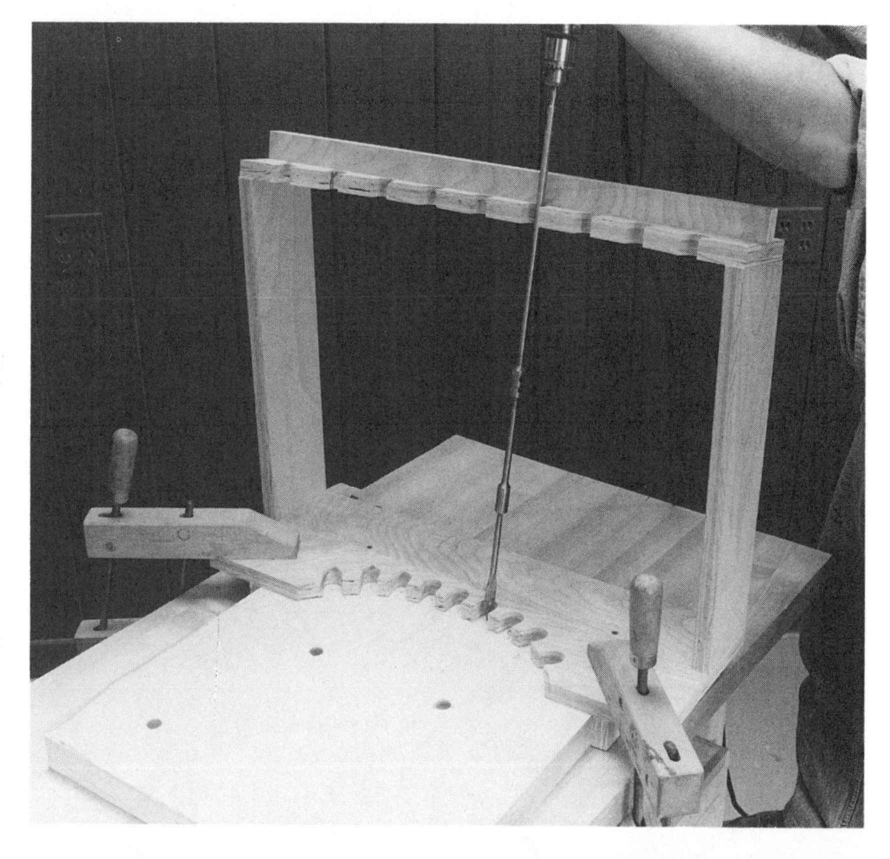

6-18 To use the spindle mortise drill guide, lay out the locations of the mortises on the top of the seat stock and the bottom edge of the crest rail stock. (*Don't* scoop the seat or cut the shape of the crest rail yet — the stock should be flat.) Mount a spade bit in a long extension, then mount the extension in a portable drill. (You may have to use two or more extensions, depending on the length of the spindles.) Clamp the seatboard to the seat, centering the notches over the mortise marks. Place the point of the bit on a mark, rest the extension in the corresponding crest rail notch, and bore the mortise. This jig will keep the bit at the *precise* angle and direction needed to drill the mortise. Repeat for all the seat mortises.

6-19 Use the same procedure to drill the spindle mortises in the crest rail, clamping the rail stock to the rail board. Again, position the notches over the mortise marks. Use light pressure to keep the extension in the proper notch as you work. After boring all the mortises, scoop the seat and cut the curve and the profile of the crest rail.

Bending Chair Parts

Slats, spindles, and the back posts of turned chairs are often bent. Although there's a lot of mystery surrounding wood bending, it's a simple procedure. Just apply moderate heat and press the wood in a bending form.

Wood is composed primarily of two substances — long *cellulose* fibers stuck together with gluelike *lignin.* If you heat the wood to about 200 degrees Fahrenheit, the lignin becomes *plasticized* (semi-liquid), but the cellulose remains rigid. The fibers will slide past one another, and the wood can be bent to a new shape. When it cools and the lignin hardens, the wood will hold that shape.

1 **The easiest way to heat short** pieces of wood is to boil them. Make a boiler from a length of metal guttering, rest it across two or three electric hot plates, and fill it with water. Float the wood you want to bend in the water; then heat the water to the boiling point.

2 **Let the wood boil until it's** pliable — this will take anywhere from 15 minutes to an hour or more, depending on the species and thickness of the wood. (Watch the boiler carefully; don't let the water evaporate away.) Remove the wood from the boiler with tongs, then *quickly* place it in a bending form and tighten the clamps. (Wear heavy gloves when you do this so you won't burn yourself.) Let the wood rest in the form for a week or more until it dries completely. **Note:** There's usually some *springback* when you take the wood out of the form; it doesn't completely conform to the form's shape. To compensate, make the curves in the form slightly more pronounced than those you want the wood to assume.

(continued) ▷

Bending Chair Parts — continued

3 For long parts that are bent in one spot (such as back posts), heat just that spot. Wrap a sopping wet towel around the spot you want to bend. Wrap a sheet of aluminum foil around that, and metal "muffler tape" (available at automotive stores) around the foil. The foil and the tape will hold in the moisture. Heat the muffler tape evenly with a heat gun. This, in turn, boils the water and heats the wood in the immediate area. After 30 minutes, clamp the post in a bending form. (If it's hard to bend, heat it a little longer.) Let it cool in the form, then take it out and remove the tape, foil, and towel. Replace it in the form and let it rest a week or more until it dries.

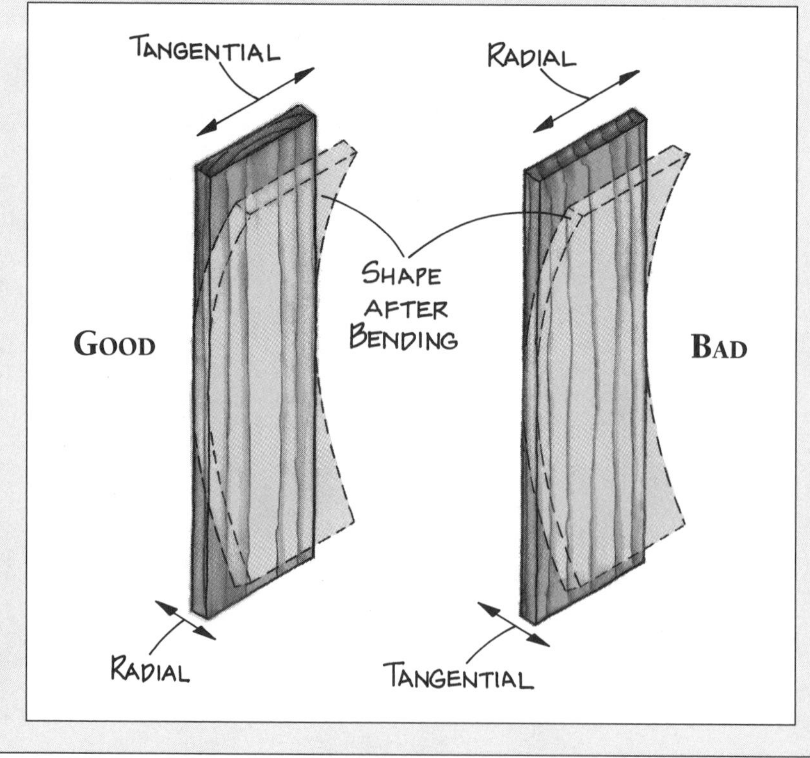

4 Always bend *tangential* grain, never radial. Make sure the tangential faces are against the sides of the bending form when you apply pressure. If you attempt to bend the radial grain, the wood may warp or twist unpredictably. There will also be a lot more springback.

Turned Chair Seats

As with joined chairs, there are several types of seats that you can make for a turned chair. The two most common are *saddle seats* and *woven seats*.

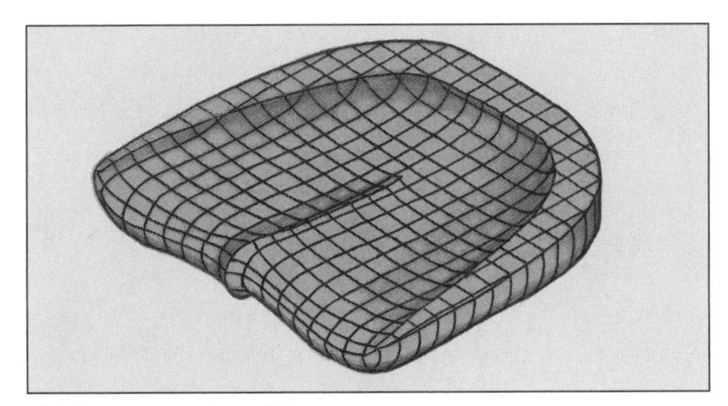

6-20 A typical saddle seat is scooped low toward the back and sides, sloping down from the front. The craftsman usually leaves a flat ridge at the back of the seat, where the spindles and back posts will be attached. There may also be a gentle crest carved in the center of the seat, running front to back, forming the "pommel" of the saddle.

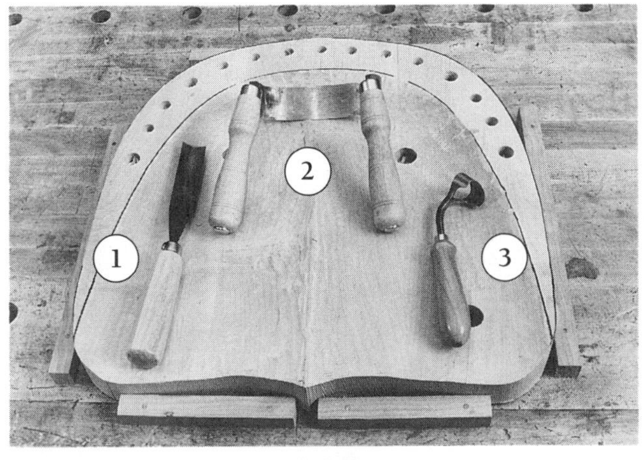

6-21 You can use several different tools to scoop a seat by hand. In addition to the traditional adze, you might also carve the shape with a ***bent gouge*** (1), a curved drawknife or ***inshave*** (2), or a ***scorp*** (3). Novice chairmakers usually find it easier to rough out the saddle with a gouge, then finish with a scorp. You can use an inshave for both the rough and finish work, but it takes practice to develop the knack.

SCOOPING A SADDLE SEAT

Saddle seats are scooped from a thick block of wood and shaped to fit your backside. *(See Figure 6-20.)* Old-time chairmakers once used an adze to scoop the seats, but contemporary craftsmen use a variety of tools and techniques.

To make the seat, first bore the round mortises for the legs and spindles, then cut the top profile of the seat. If you opt to scoop the seat by hand, there are several tools you might use — a bent gouge, an inshave, or a scorp. *(See Figure 6-21.)* If you prefer power tools, make a series of shallow cove cuts with a circular saw. *(See Figures 6-22 through 6-24.)* Finish with a random-orbit sander. *(See Figures 6-25 and 6-26.)* Finally, round over the bottom edge of the seat. *(See Figure 6-27.)*

6-22 If you prefer to work with power tools, use a hand-held circular saw to make a series of semicircular cove cuts. Use a triangular curve-cutting blade — this will give you more control. Hold the saw reversed, as shown, so that if the saw kicks back, it will kick out from your body.

6-23 To begin scooping with a circular saw, adjust the shoe so just 1/16 inch of the blade protrudes. Rest the saw on the front edge, or "nose," of the shoe with the back edge slightly above the stock. Turn on the saw and lower it until you feel the blade bite. Then move the saw sideways. **Warning:** Always cut toward the side of the saw where the shoe is the widest — usually there's more shoe on the right side of the saw to help guide the cut. If you work toward the side where the shoe is narrow, the saw may tip over.

6-24 With each pass of the saw, scoop just 1/32 to 1/16 inch deeper. As the carved portion of the seat becomes deeper, readjust the shoe so more and more of the blade shows. Don't try to cut the final seat shape; just rough it out.

6-25 Use a random-orbit disc sander to grind the final shape of the seat. It will grind away wood very quickly, yet leave a smooth surface. The disc on the sander fits the saddle shape perfectly. Start with a coarse grit — 50-grit — and work your way to 150-grit.

6-26 After shaping and smoothing the scooped portion of the seat, round over the front and side edges of the seat with the random-orbit sander. Once again, start with 50-grit and work your way to 150-grit. When you sit on the finished chair, you shouldn't contact any hard, square edges.

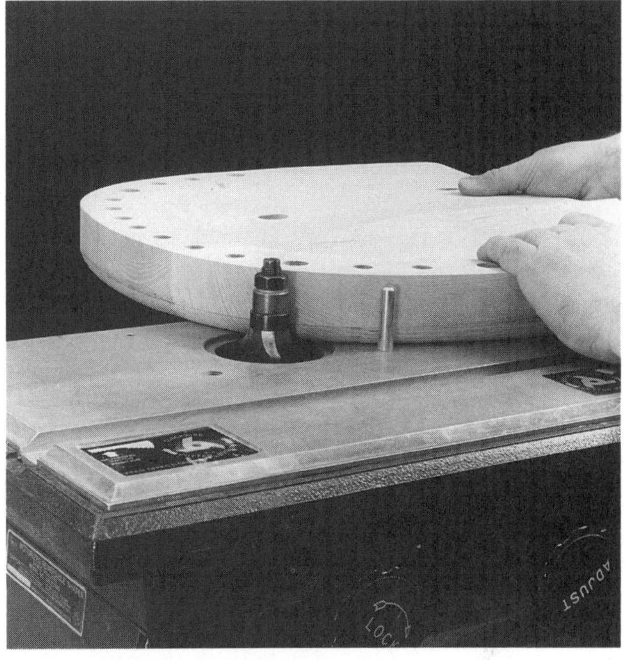

6-27 Finally, round the bottom edge of the seat, using a shaper or a table-mounted router and a quarter-round cutter. Sand the bottom surfaces smooth, too.

WEAVING A CHAIR SEAT

You can weave a chair seat from several different materials, but perhaps the easiest to use is *cloth tape*. The Shakers perfected the technique for weaving tape seats in the early nineteenth century and made this type of seat popular. Today there are many colors of cloth tape available in two different widths — ⅝ inch and 1 inch. The wider tape is easier to work with, especially if you're weaving a simple pattern. More complex patterns are best woven from narrower tape.

A typical chair requires about 30 yards of 1-inch tape. You'll also need about two dozen small upholstery tacks, a needle and thread, and a 1-inch-thick foam rubber pad to cushion the seat. Begin weaving with the *warp* — the front-to-back strands of tape. Wind these around the front and back rails, making a rectangle as wide as the back rail. Because the front rail is generally longer than the back, there will be open triangular spaces at the sides. Leave these; you'll fill them in later. *(SEE FIGURES 6-28 THROUGH 6-30.)* Stuff the foam rubber pad between the warp layers *(SEE FIGURE 6-31)*; then weave the *weft* — the side-to-side strands — into the warp. *(SEE FIGURES 6-32 THROUGH 6-37.)* Finally, fill in the triangular spaces. *(SEE FIGURES 6-38 AND 6-39.)*

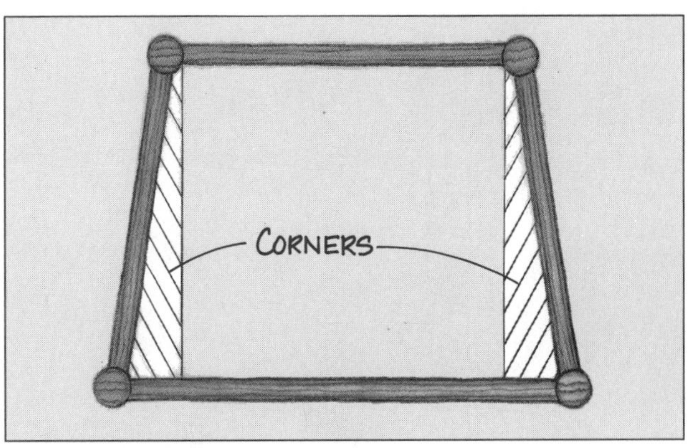

6-28 Because the front rails of chair seats are longer than the back rails, the seats will be trapezoid-shaped when you look at them from the top. The *warp* (front-to-back tapes) and the *weft* (side-to-side tapes) are square to one another, and the weaving forms a rectangle. When you impose this rectangle on top of a trapezoid, it leaves two "corners" on the sides. Find these corners with a square and mark them on the front seat rail. You must weave the rectangle first, then fill in the corners later.

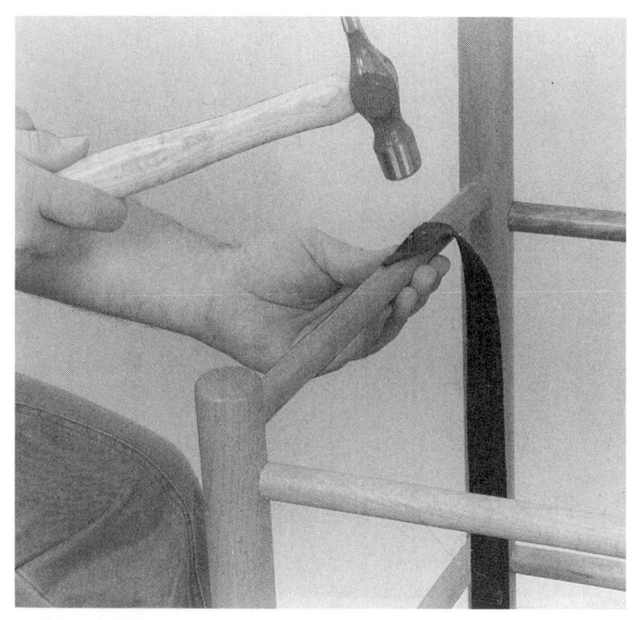

6-29 Begin by weaving the warp. If you're using two colors of tape, use the *darker* color for the warp. Because the warp covers the front seat rail, the dirt will show less. Tack the end of a roll of cloth tape to the left side seat rail, near the back seat rail.

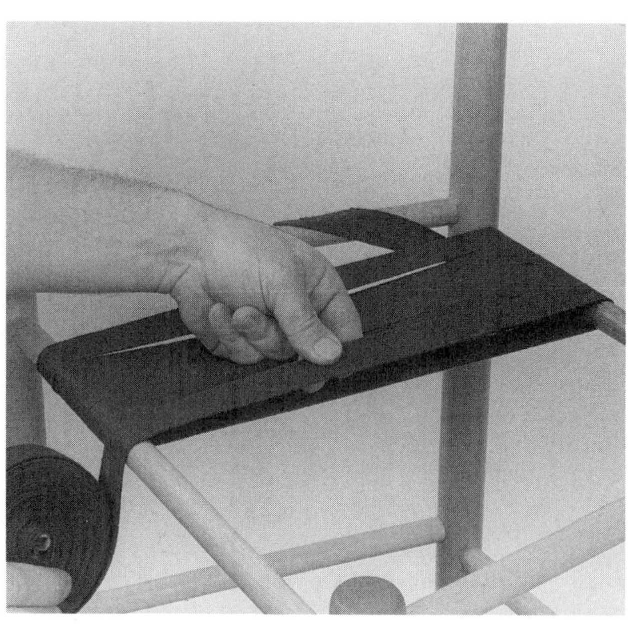

6-30 Stretch the warp tape under, then back over the back seat rail. Bring it forward, over, and under the front seat rail, then back under and over the back seat rail. Do *not* fill in the corners at this time; leave them open. Continue wrapping the tape onto the rail until you've covered the back seat rail. Tack the warp tape to the right side seat rail and cut it off.

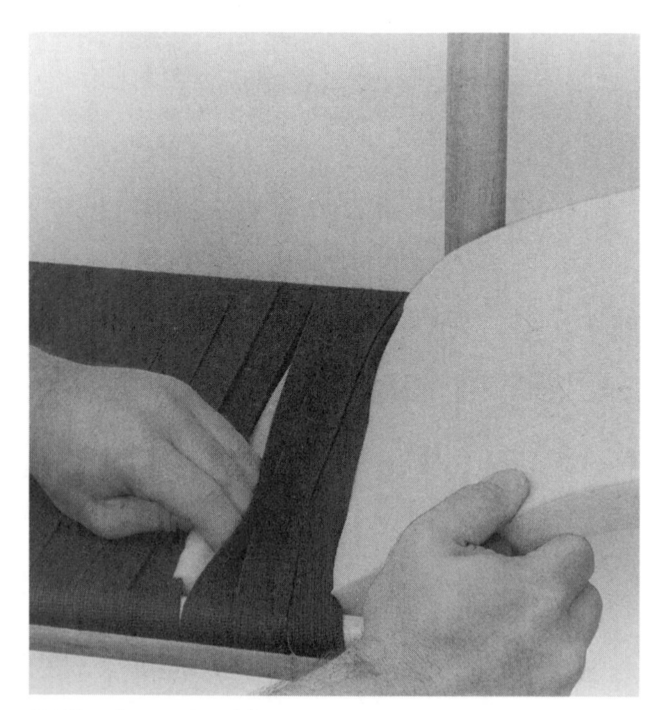

6-31 The top and bottom warp layers will have a space between them. Cut a 1-inch-thick foam rubber pad to the trapezoid shape of the seat and stuff it into this space.

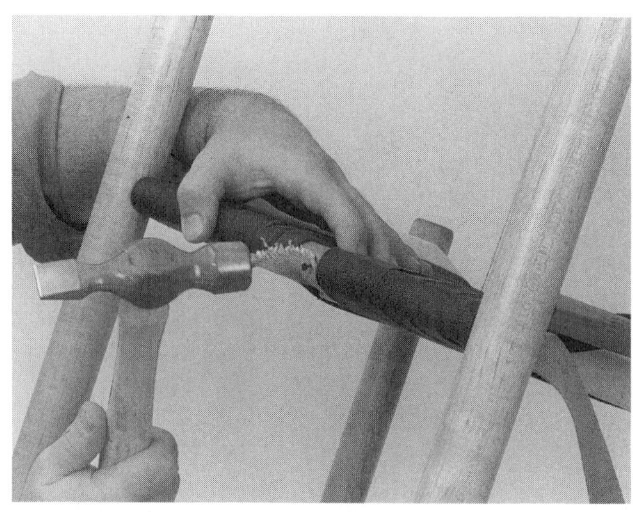

6-32 Next, weave the weft into the warp. Insert the end of a roll of weft tape into the space between the top and bottom warp, near the back seat rail. Temporarily spread apart the warp on the back seat rail and tack the end of the tape to the rail near the left back post.

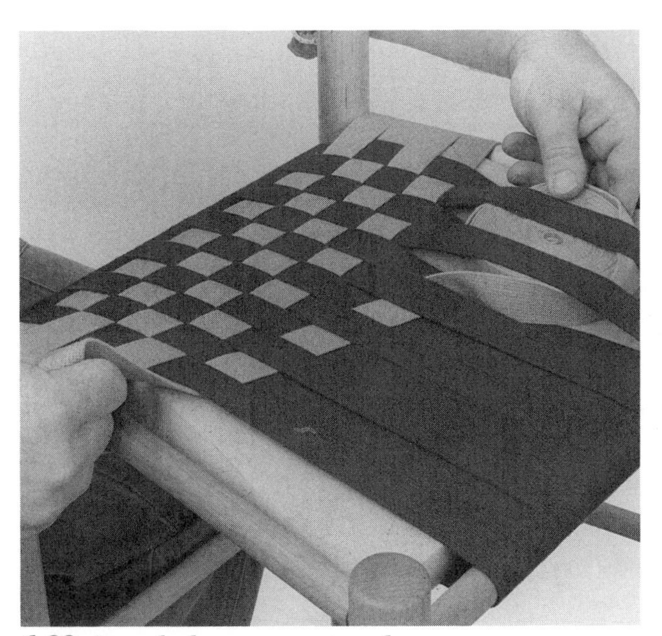

6-33 Stretch the warp tape under the left side seat rail, bring it over the seat rail, then begin weaving the tape over and under the warp. Continue over and under the right side seat rail, and weave the weft tape into the bottom warp. (The woven pattern on both the top and bottom of the seat should be identical.) Repeat, alternating the weave at the beginning of each new row as needed to continue the pattern.

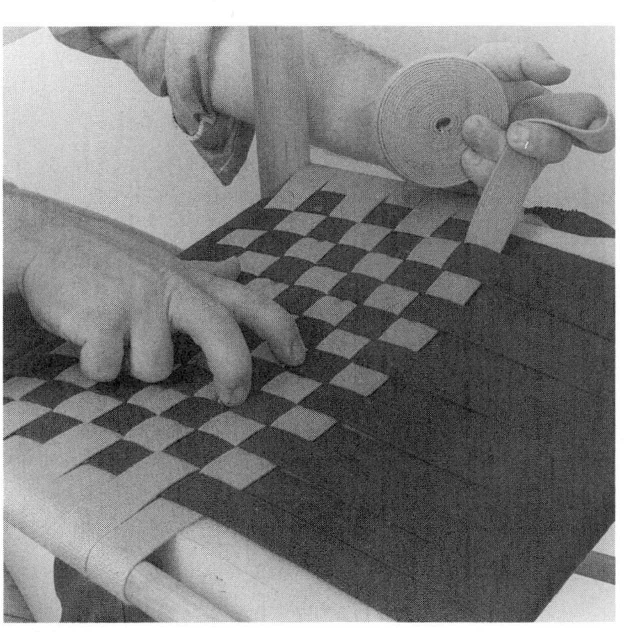

6-34 Every two or three rows, stop weaving and "comb" the weft tapes with your fingers, as shown. Even them out so the rows are straight and the warp and weft are square to one another.

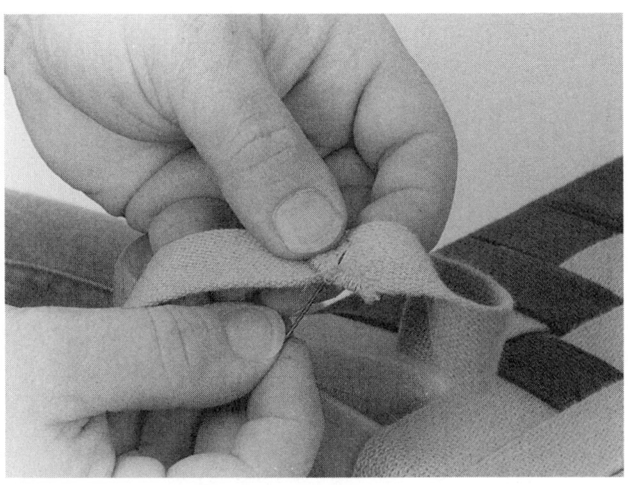

6-35 If the roll of tape runs out in the middle of the warp or weft, splice another roll onto the end of the first. Overlap the ends and sew them together. Make these splices on the *bottom* of the seat, where they won't show.

6-36 As you finish the weft, the weaving will become tighter and more difficult. During the last few rows, you may not be able to weave with your fingers. Instead, use the handle of a spoon to push the weft between the warp tapes. You can also use the spoon to comb the tape.

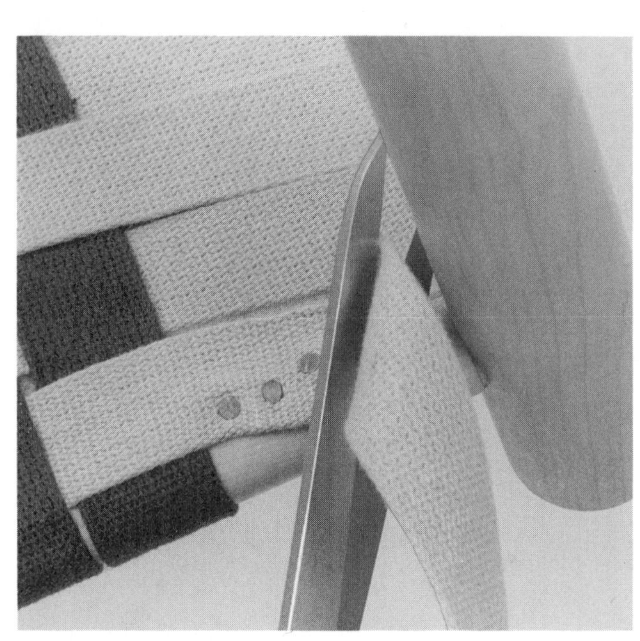

6-37 **When you've covered the** side seat rails with the weft, tack the tape to the underside of the front seat rail near the right front leg and cut it off.

6-38 **Fill in the corners with short** lengths of warp tape, completely covering the front seat rail. Weave these short warp tapes over and under the weft tapes, following the woven pattern.

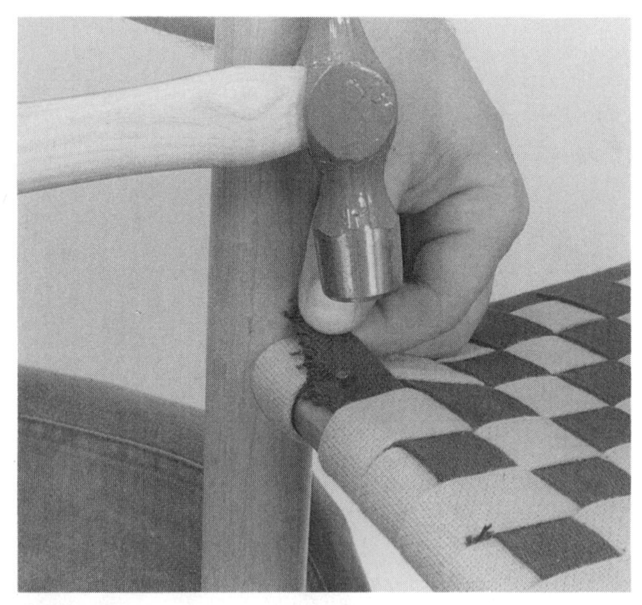

6-39 **When you've completely** covered the front seat rail, spread the weft tapes apart and tack the ends of the short warp tapes to the side seat rails. Pull the weft tapes back in place over the tacks so you won't see where the warp tapes are attached. Comb the weave so it's even, and trim any loose tape ends or threads that may be hanging out.

WHERE TO FIND IT

Purchase cloth tape and other seat-weaving supplies from:

The Connecticut Cane and Reed Co.
P.O. Box 1276
Manchester, CT 06040

or

Shaker Workshops
P.O. Box 1028
Concord, MA 01742

PROJECTS

7

Low-Back Chair

Shaker craftsmen often built tables and chairs to cleverly conserve space, as these low-back chairs testify. The backs are tall enough to provide adequate lumbar support, yet short enough to slip *under* a dining table. When not in use, they can be stored completely out of the way — almost out of sight. An entire dining set takes up no more room than the table itself!

The chair shown was made at the Union Village Shaker community near Lebanon, Ohio, in the early nineteenth century. The back legs are 28 inches high, to fit under the trestle dining tables of that community, which were normally 29 inches high and had ⅞-inch-thick tops. There was just ⅛ inch of space between the top ends of the back legs and the bottom surfaces of the tabletops! If your table is lower than the Union Village trestle tables, shorten the chair backs as needed.

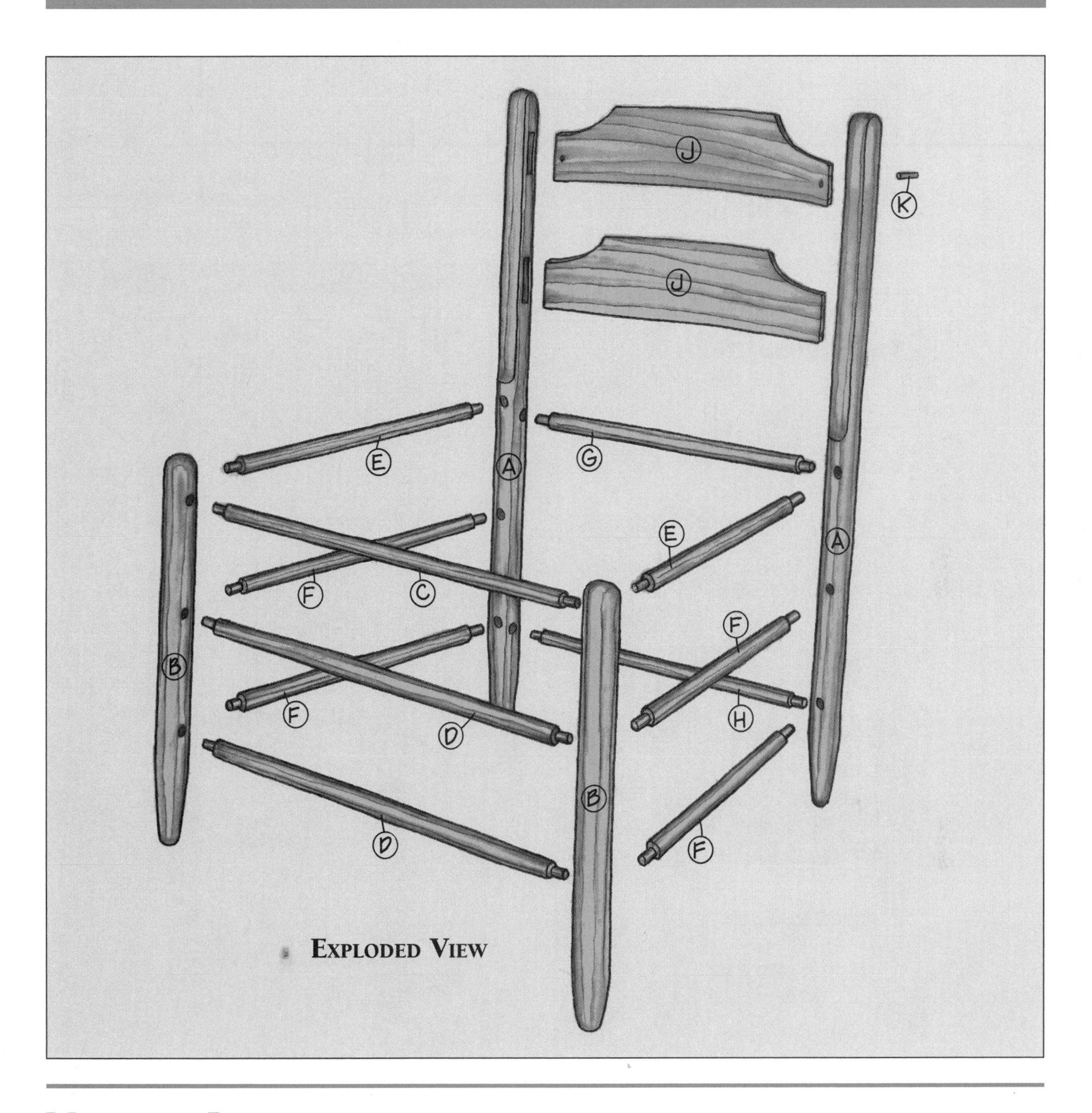

MATERIALS LIST (FINISHED DIMENSIONS)

Parts

	Part	Dimensions
A.	Back posts (2)	1⅝″ dia. x 28″
B.	Front legs (2)	1⅝″ dia. x 18½″
C.	Front seat rail	¾″ dia. x 14¾″
D.	Front rungs (2)	11⁄16″ dia. x 14¾″
E.	Side seat rails (2)	¾″ dia. x 12″
F.	Side rungs (4)	11⁄16″ dia. x 12″
G.	Back seat rail	¾″ dia. x 11¾″
H.	Back rung	11⁄16″ dia. x 11¾″
J.	Back slats (2)	¼″ x 3½″ x 12¼″
K.	Pegs (2)	¼″ dia. x ⅝″

Hardware

1″ Seat tape (25–30 yards)
Upholstery tacks (18–24)

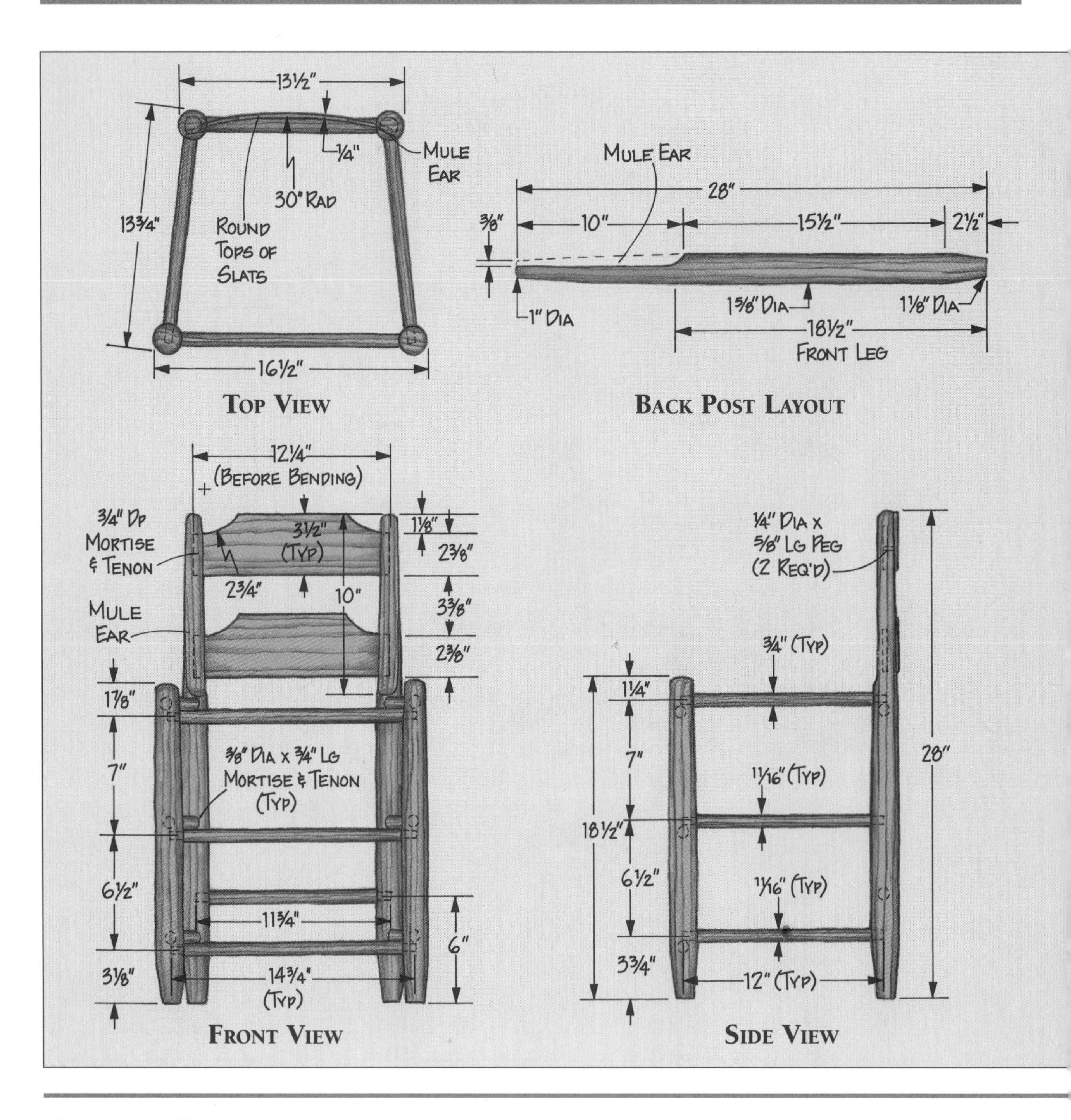

Plan of Procedure

1 Select the stock and cut the parts to size. To make this project, you need about 1 board foot of 4/4 (four-quarters) stock and 3 board feet of 8/4 (eight-quarters) stock, as well as four 36-inch lengths of ¾-inch-diameter dowel rod and a small amount of ¼-inch-diameter dowel rod. Use hardwood for the chair parts — the harder, the better. The Shakers typically used maple, birch, hickory, and oak to make their chair frames. On the chair shown, the back posts, front legs, and slats are made from maple, while the seat rails, rungs, and pegs are oak.

Resaw the 4/4 stock and plane it to ¼ inch thick. Cut the slats to the width and length specified in the Materials List. Cut up the 8/4 stock and the ¾-inch-

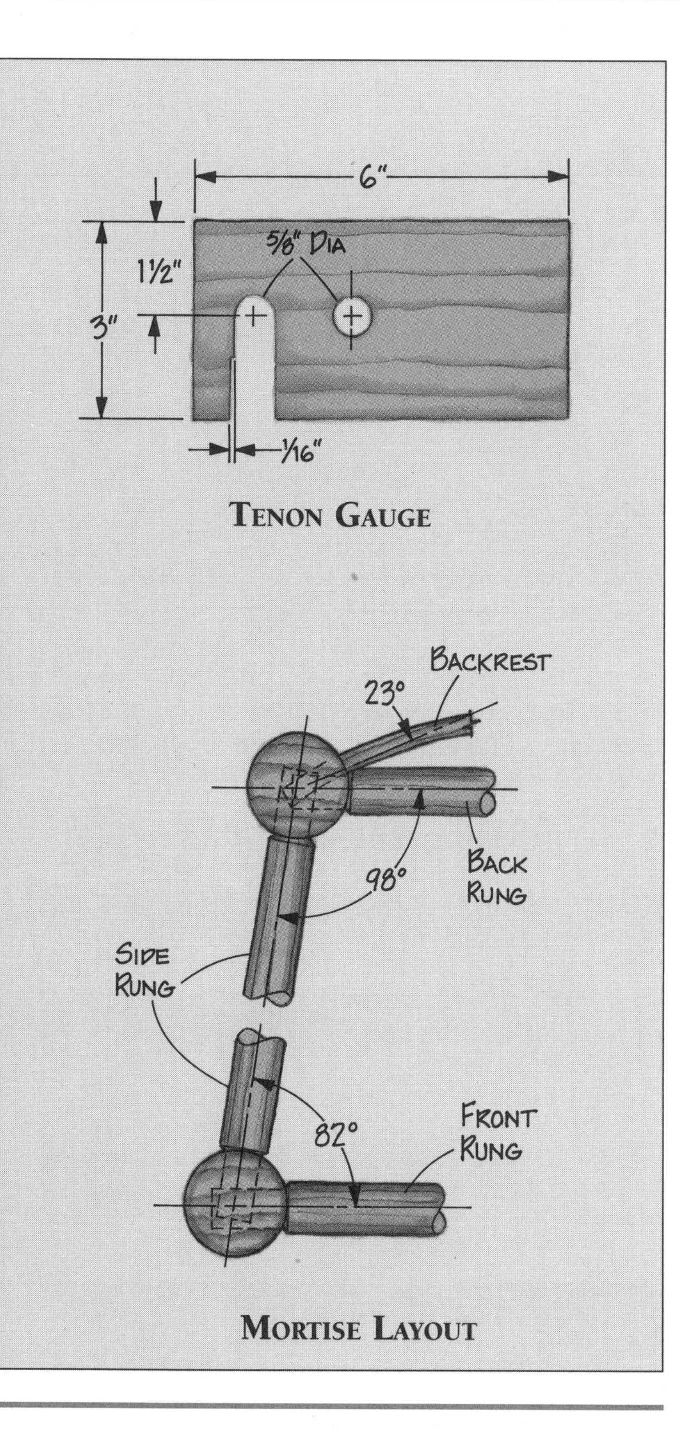

TENON GAUGE

MORTISE LAYOUT

diameter dowel rod to make turning stock for the front and back legs, seat rails, and rungs. Cut each spindle about 1 inch longer than specified — this will give you some extra stock to mount the spindles on the lathe. Also cut the pegs about ¼ inch longer than shown.

2 Turn the front legs, back posts, rungs, and seat rails. Since the turned parts have very little decoration, the turning is straightforward. Simply round the stock and turn the tapers, as shown in the *Front View, Side View,* and *Back Post Layout.* To prevent the slender stock from whipping or bowing on the lathe, support it with a steadyrest. (For more information on this jig, refer to "Lathe Steadyrest" on page 78.)

While the overall diameters of the turned parts are not critical, the diameters of the round tenons on the ends of the rungs are. Turn these carefully, working with calipers to gauge the precise diameter. You can make your own fixed calipers from a scrap of plywood, as shown in the *Tenon Gauge* drawing. Turn each tenon to fit the test mortise in the gauge, as related in "Joining Turned Chair Parts" on page 72.

Finish sand all the spindles on the lathe as you turn them. Remove them from the lathe and cut them to their proper lengths. Round the top ends of the legs with a rasp, then sand them smooth.

3 Make the mortises in the legs. The mortises — the holes and slots in the legs — must line up properly with each other. There are two "lines" of mortises as you sight down the front legs, and three as you sight down the back posts. The first two lines of mortises in each part are for the rungs and seat rails. On the back posts, the third line is for the slats. Each line of mortises must be drilled or cut at the proper radial angle to the other lines, as shown in the *Mortise Layout.*

Make a *Mortising Collar,* as shown in FIGURE 6-7 on page 74, to mark the angles on the ends of the front legs and back posts. (See the *Front Leg Mortising Collar* and the *Back Leg Mortising Collar.*) Use a spindle-marking straightedge to extend these marks down the length of the turnings, as explained in "Joining Turned Chair Parts" on page 72. Then mark the vertical locations of the mortises along these lines, using a story stick.

To make the round mortises, clamp the legs and back posts in a V-jig and drill them on a drill press. To make the slot mortises, drill lines of overlapping holes or rout them with an overhead routing setup.

4 Cut the "mule ears" in the back posts. The upper portions of the back posts are flattened on the front side — this makes the assembled chair back more comfortable. These flats were referred to as "mule ears" by old-time turners and chairmakers.

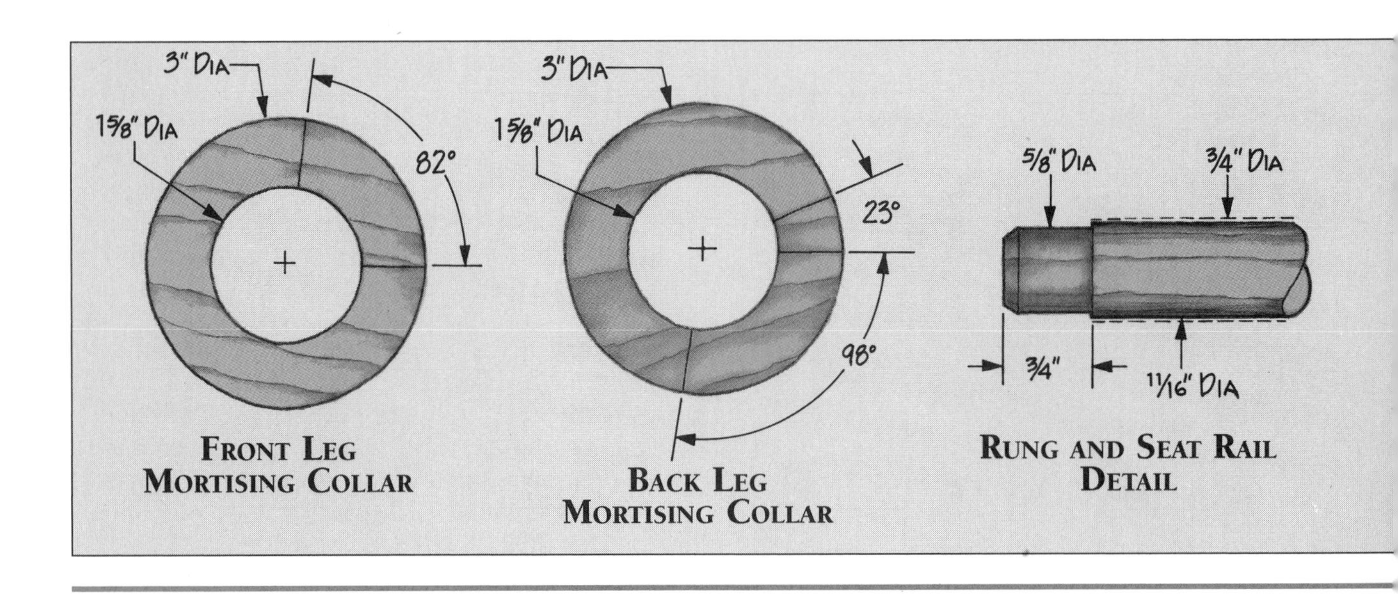

Cut the mule ears on a band saw. Mount each back post in the V-jig, making sure that the metal straps won't interfere with the band saw cut. Also, check that the line of slot mortises are pointing *straight up.* To help determine that they are, temporarily fit a short piece of ¼-inch-thick stock in each mortise.

Mark the end of the mule ear on the stock, as shown in the *Back Post Layout.* Cutting through both the post *and* the V-jig, "eyeball" the shape of the mule ear. *(See Figure 7-1.)* It won't matter if your mule ear is slightly different from the one shown — the shape is not critical. Repeat for the other back post, then sand the sawed surfaces.

5 Cut the shapes of the slats. Lay out the shape of the slats as shown in the *Front View.* Cut the shapes with a band saw or scroll saw, then round the edges so the slats fit in the slot mortises.

To save time, stack the slat stock face to face, sticking the parts together with double-faced carpet tape. Trace the pattern on the top part in the stack, then cut both parts at once.

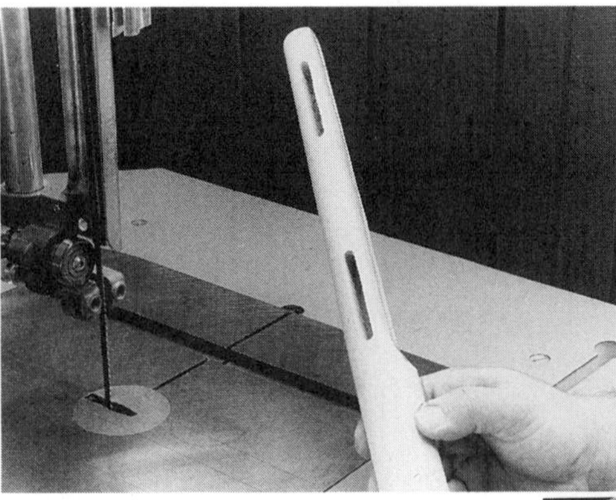

7-1 **To make a mule ear, mount** the back post in a V-jig. Cut the shape on the band saw, cutting through both the post and the jig. Make sure the slot mortises are pointing straight up as you do this.

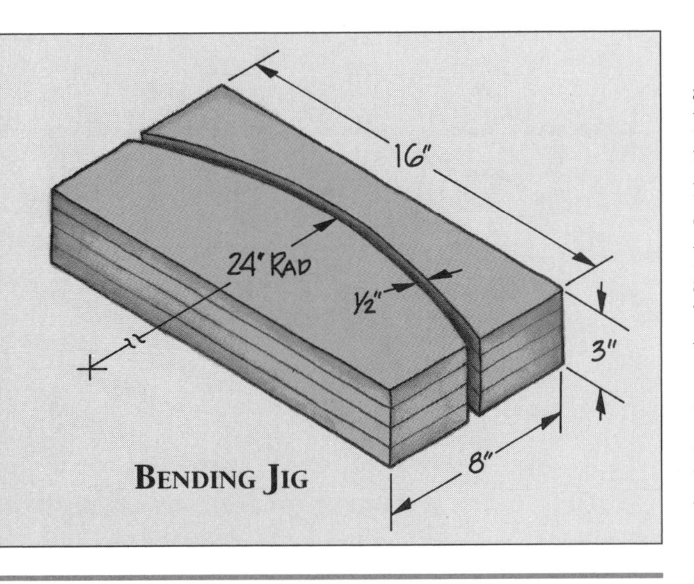

6 Bend the slats. The slats are curved slightly to fit your back. To make these curves, make a bending jig as shown in the *Bending Jig* drawing. Note that the radius of the jig is smaller than the slat radius shown in the *Top View*. Because bent wood typically springs back and loses about 20 percent of its curve after it's removed from a bending jig, the jig curve must be tighter than the final radius of the slats to compensate.

Boil the slats for about 45 minutes in a roasting pan. Remove them from the hot water and *immediately* clamp them in the jig — you can bend both at once. *(SEE FIGURE 7-2.)* Let them dry in the jig for at least a week.

7 Assemble the chair frame. Finish sand the slats and any other wood surfaces that may still need it. Dry assemble the parts of the chair frame to check the fit. If you're satisfied all the parts fit properly, reassemble the frame with glue. However, don't depend on the glue to hold the chair together. The parts of the frame flex every time you sit in the chair, and many of the glue joints will eventually pop. Traditionally, frame chairs are held together by tightly woven seats and a few well-placed pegs.

Drill a ¼-inch-diameter peg hole in each back post, through the back of the post and into the top slat. Stop the hole before it goes through the front of the post. Glue a peg in each hole, then cut it off flush with the surface.

8 Finish the chair frame. Do any necessary touch-up sanding, then apply a finish to the chair. Do this *before* you weave the seat on the frame. The chair shown is finished with a simple hand-rubbed oil finish. Shaker craftsmen also used milk paint or a colored stain made from thinned milk paint.

9 Weave the seat. Although the Shakers used many different materials to cover their chair seats, they are best remembered for their woven cloth tape. For step-by-step instructions on how to weave a tape seat, refer to "Weaving a Chair Seat" on page 87.

7-2 To bend the slats, first boil them to make them pliable. Then clamp them in a bending jig and let them dry for one week or longer.

8

SAWBUCK PICNIC TABLE AND BENCHES

The sawbuck table gets its name from the distinctive X-shaped trestles. Once, every pioneer family had a *sawbuck* standing outside their woodshed, a device that held a log while it was "bucked up" into firewood. This assembly consisted of two or more X-shaped frames tied together with horizontal rails. A wide plank or a door could be thrown across a sawbuck to serve as an outdoor table or workbench. This simple, utilitarian design persists in picnic tables to this day.

The sawbuck design also lends itself to knockdown tables. This particular picnic table is designed to fold flat for storage. You simply remove the lag screws that hold the legs to the rail and pivot the legs under the tabletop. The benches fold up in the same manner.

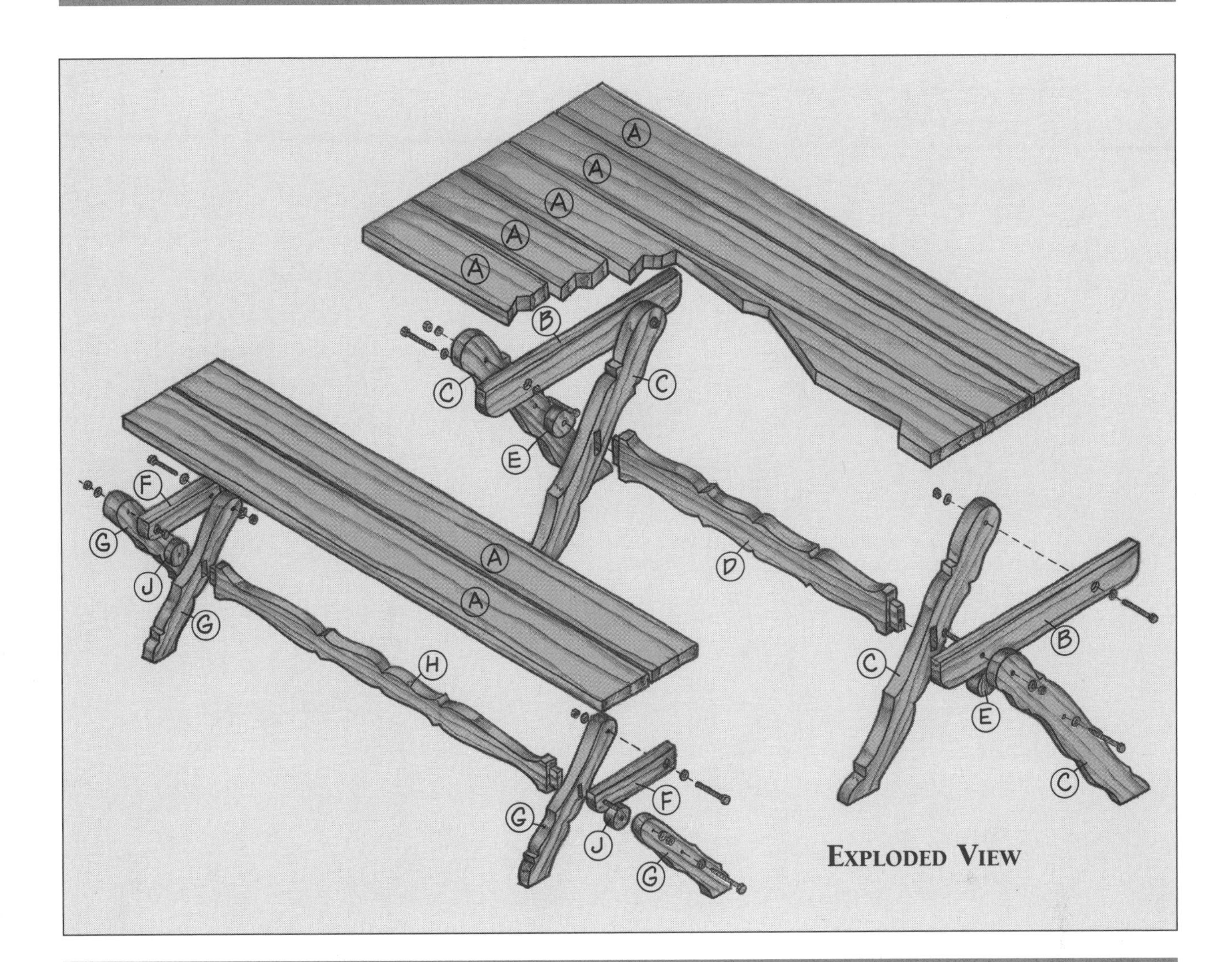

MATERIALS LIST (FINISHED DIMENSIONS)

Parts

Table

A.	Top/seat boards (5)	1½″ x 7″ x 72″
B.	Table battens (2)	1½″ x 4″ x 30″
C.	Table trestle legs (4)	1½″ x 5¼″ x 34¾″
D.	Table rail	1½″ x 5¼″ x 43″
E.	Table spacers (2)	3¼″ dia. x 1½″

Benches (2)

A.	Top/seat boards (4)	1½″ x 7″ x 72″
F.	Bench battens (4)	1½″ x 2¾″ x 11¾″
G.	Bench legs (8)	1½″ x 3½″ x 19⅜″
H.	Bench rails (2)	1½″ x 3¼″ x 53″
J.	Bench spacers (4)	2½″ dia. x 1½″

Hardware

Table

⅜″ x 3″ Hex bolts (4)
⅜″ x 5″ Lag screws (2)
⅜″ Stop nuts (4)
⅜″ Flat washers (10)
#8 x 3″ Galvanized flathead deck screws (20)

Benches (2)

⅜″ x 3″ Hex bolts (8)
⅜″ x 5″ Lag screws (4)
⅜″ Stop nuts (8)
⅜″ Flat washers (20)
#8 x 3″ Galvanized flathead deck screws (16)

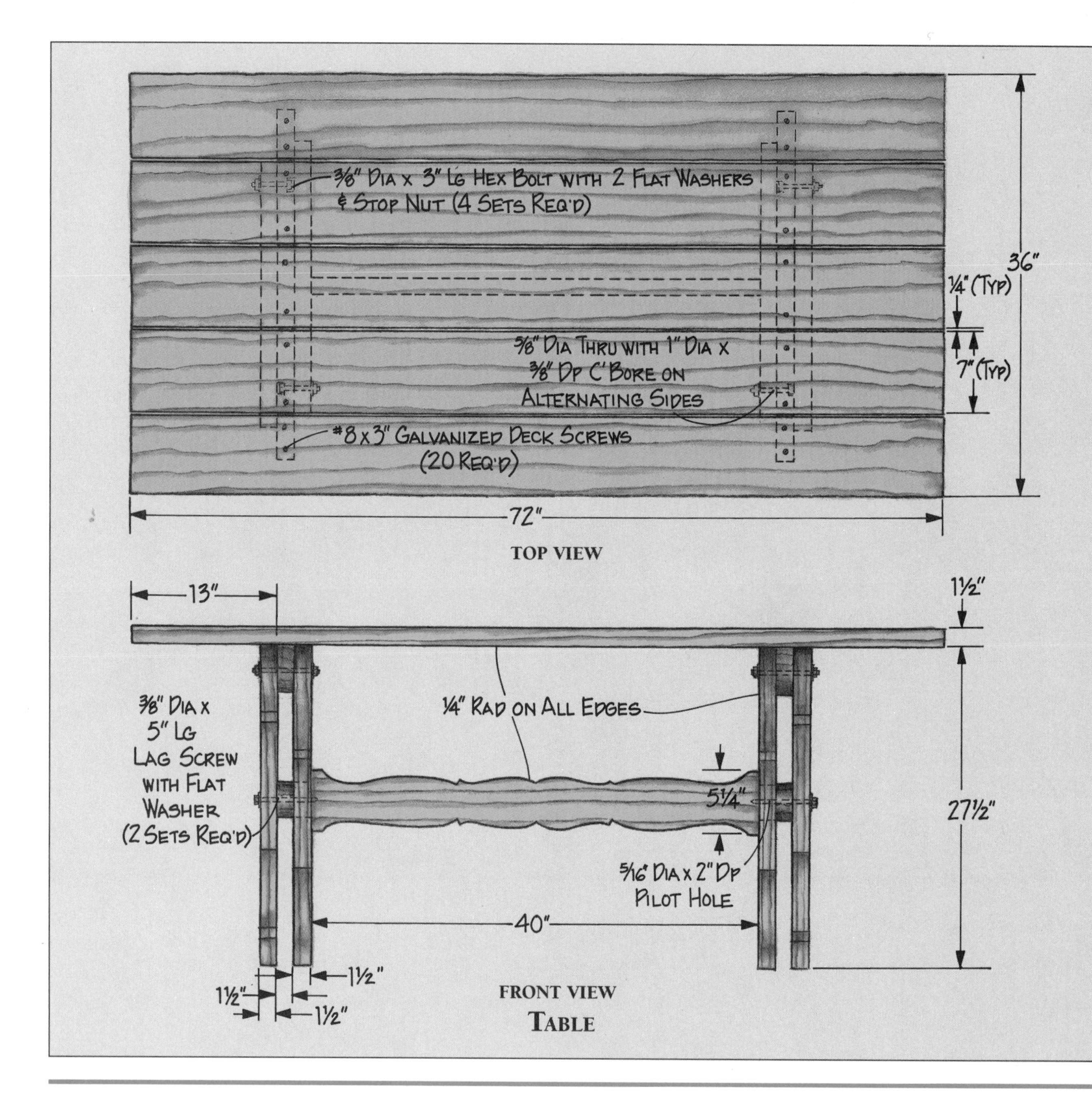

TOP VIEW

FRONT VIEW
TABLE

Plan of Procedure

1 Select the stock and cut the parts to size. You can build the table and benches from construction lumber. Select straight boards with no cracks or checks and as few knots as you can find. You'll need:

- 5 two-by-eights, 12 feet long (top/seat boards)
- 1 two-by-six, 12 feet long (table legs)
- 1 two-by-six, 10 feet long (battens, rail)
- 1 two-by-four, 12 feet long (bench legs)
- 1 two-by-four, 8 feet long (battens, rails, leg)

For Your Information

Construction or "dimensioned" lumber is not dried as thoroughly as cabinet-grade lumber. If you use it just off the rack, the completed table and benches may warp and split. Stack the lumber in a sheltered area with 1 x 1-inch spacers between each board and let it dry for several weeks before cutting the parts.

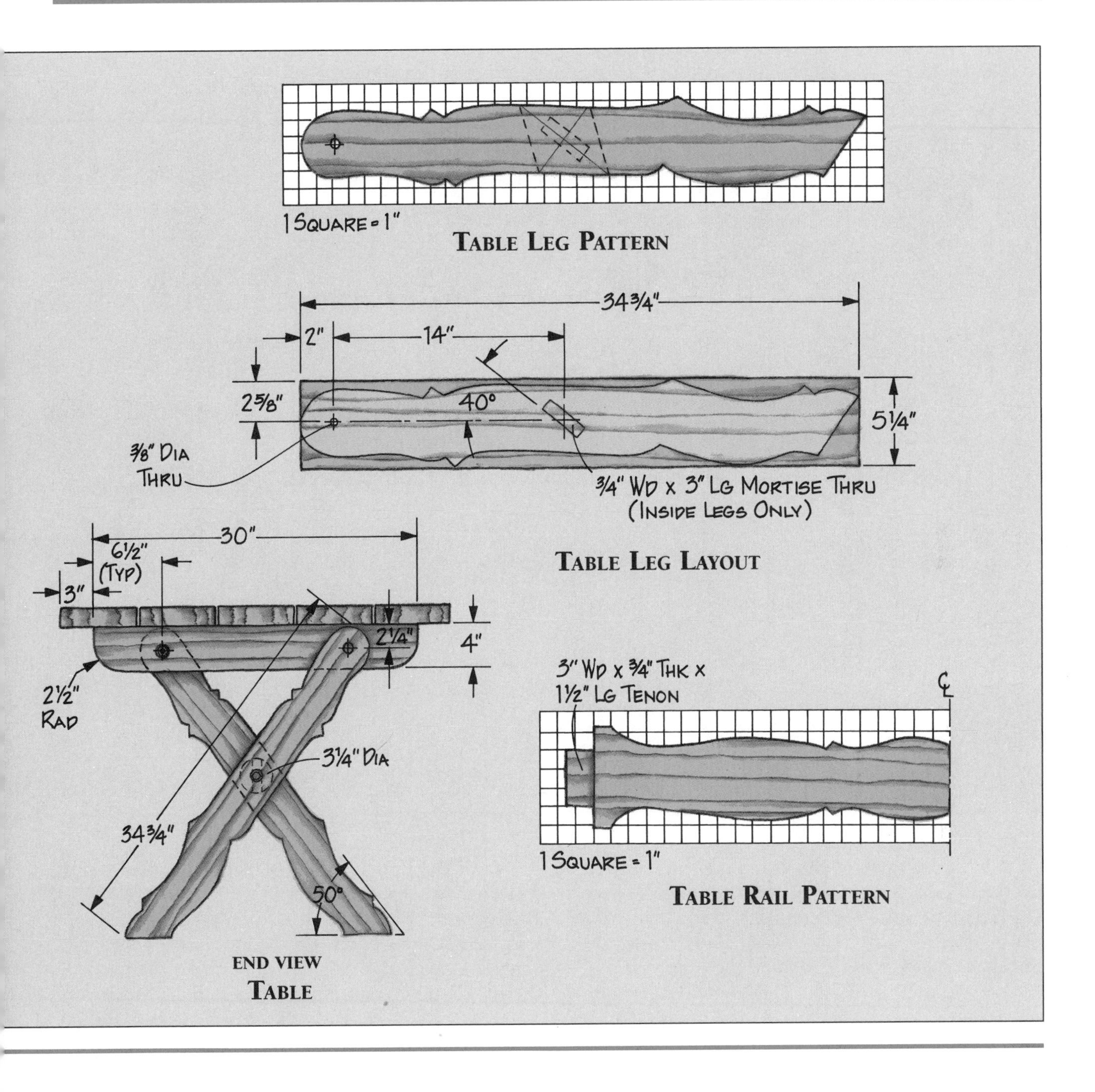

Cut the parts to the sizes specified in the Materials List. Miter the bottom ends of the trestle legs (for both the table and benches) at 50 degrees.

2 Make the mortises and tenons. The inside leg in each X-shaped trestle is mortised to fit a tenon on the end of a rail. Lay out the mortises and the holes on the stock, as shown in the *Table Leg Layout* and the *Bench Leg Layout*. (Note that the long sides of the mortises are not parallel to the sides of the legs — they are angled at 40 degrees.) Also lay out the tenons on the ends of the rails, as shown in the *Table Rail Pattern* and the *Bench Rail Pattern*.

Make the mortises first, then fit the tenons to them. Drill a series of overlapping ¾-inch-diameter holes to rough out the mortises, then clean up the sides and square the corners with a chisel. Cut the cheeks and shoulders of the tenons with a dado cutter.

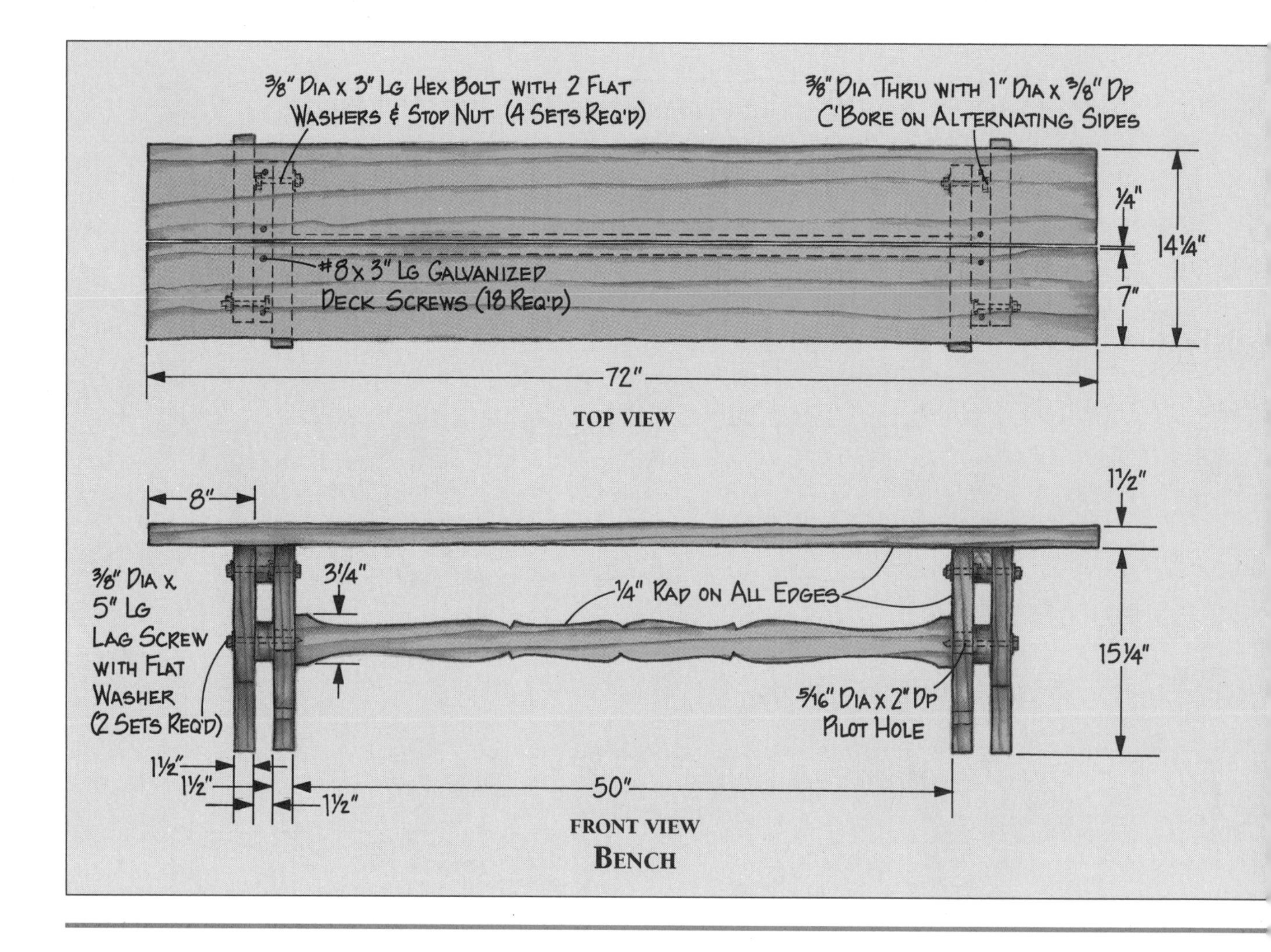

3 Cut the shapes of the legs, rails, spacers, and battens. Enlarge the *Table Leg Pattern* and the *Bench Leg Pattern* to make two templates. Using the templates, trace the shapes of the legs on the stock. Enlarge the *Table Rail Pattern* and the *Bench Rail Pattern* and trace these onto the stock. Also, lay out the rounded corners on the battens and the circular profile of the spacers. Cut the profiles with a band saw or saber saw, then sand the sawed edges.

TRY THIS TRICK

If you have a band saw, save time by pad-sawing and pad-sanding the legs, battens, spacers, and bench rails, making two or more parts at a time. Stack up two or four parts face to face, sticking them together with double-faced carpet tape. Saw through all the parts at once, then sand the edges of the stack. Take the stack apart and discard the tape.

4 Drill the holes in the legs, spacers, and battens. The top ends of the legs are attached to the battens with carriage bolts. Additionally, the spacers and the outside legs are attached to the rails with lag screws. Lay out the ⅜-inch-diameter holes and 1-inch-diameter counterbores for these bolts and screws in the battens as shown in the *Table/End View* and the *Bench/End View*. (SEE FIGURE 8-1.) Also mark the ⅜-inch-diameter holes in the center of the spacers and the 5⁄16-inch-diameter pilot holes centered in the ends of the rail tenons. Drill all the holes.

5 Assemble the table and benches. Finish sand the parts of the table and benches. If you wish, cut a ¼-inch radius on all the edges *except* the top edges of the battens and the edges of the tenons. The rounded edges will make the table and benches more comfortable to use and will protect you from splinters. Glue the rails in the inside leg mortises with waterproof

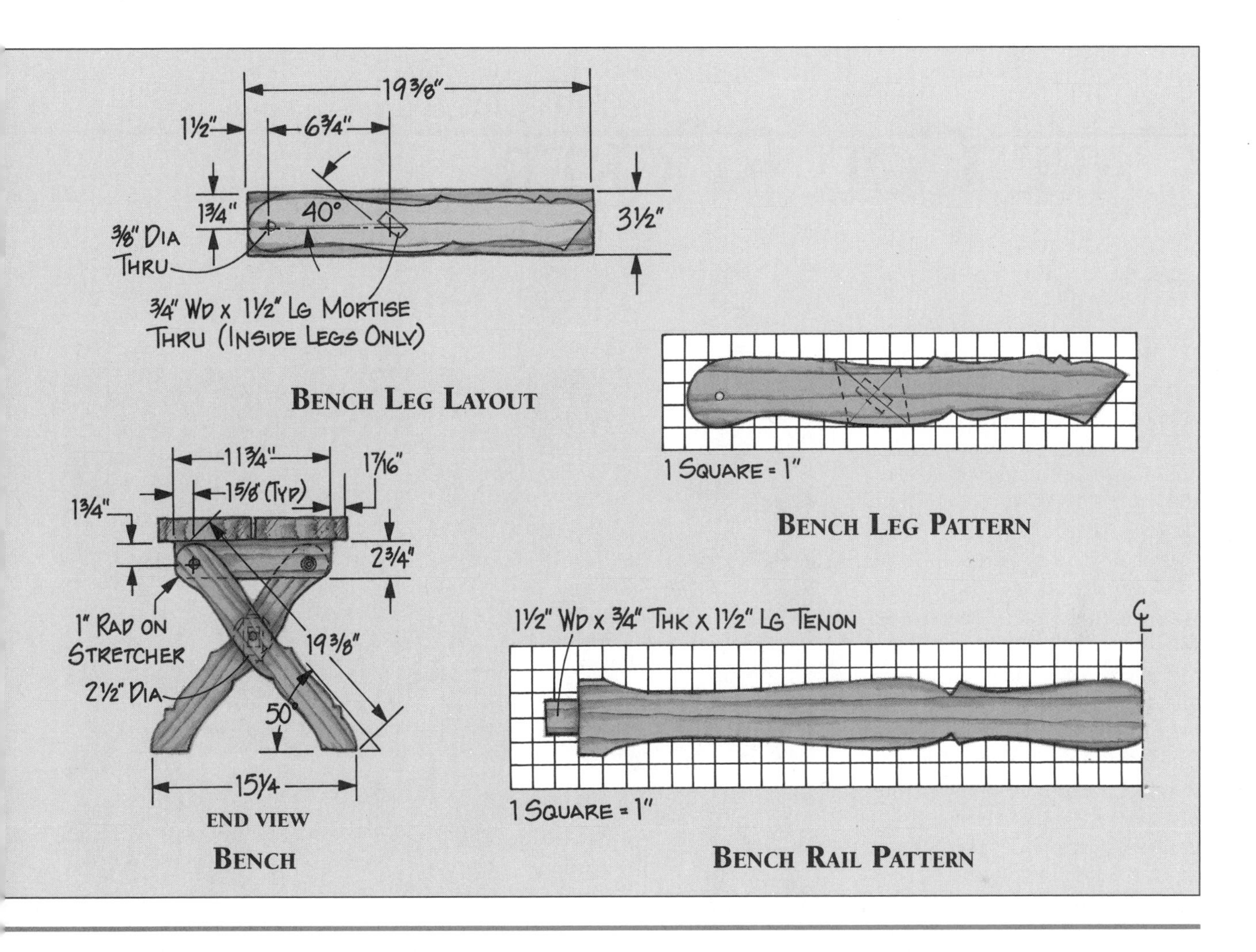

glue. Bolt the inside leg-and-rail assembly to the battens. Bolt the outside legs to the battens, then fasten them to the rail with lag screws and spacers. (The inside and outside legs must cross at the rail.) Turn the assembly right side up and attach the top/seat board with deck screws. Use scraps of ¼-inch plywood to help space the boards.

6 Finish the table and benches. Remove the trestles from the tabletop and seat assemblies, then disassemble the trestles. Set the hardware aside. Do any necessary touch-up sanding, and apply an exterior paint, stain, or water sealant to all wooden surfaces. When the finish dries, reassemble the table and benches.

8-1 **Counterbore the battens so the** heads of the hex bolts rest *below* the surface. This allows you to fold the legs flat against the top/seat boards.

9

Cape Cod Rocker

The rocking chair is an American invention. It first appeared in the colonies in the eighteenth century as an adaptation of the Windsor chair. There is no reliable record of who invented this chair or why, but one woodworking legend says the rocker was originally intended for older folks as a device to soothe aches and pains, increase circulation, and provide a little exercise. Whatever the intention of the inventor, the design quickly became popular among all age groups. Over the last two and a half centuries, craftsmen have built rocking chairs in every style imaginable.

The "Cape Cod" rocker shown was first built in New England in the late nineteenth century. These sturdy chairs can be used either indoors or out, and it's not uncommon to see them on porches and decks along the Atlantic Seaboard.

This design is relatively easy to build. There's no bending needed — the curved rockers, crest rail, and intermediate rail are resawed from thick stock. And the long back post has been divided into two pieces so all the turned parts can be made on an ordinary home workshop lathe.

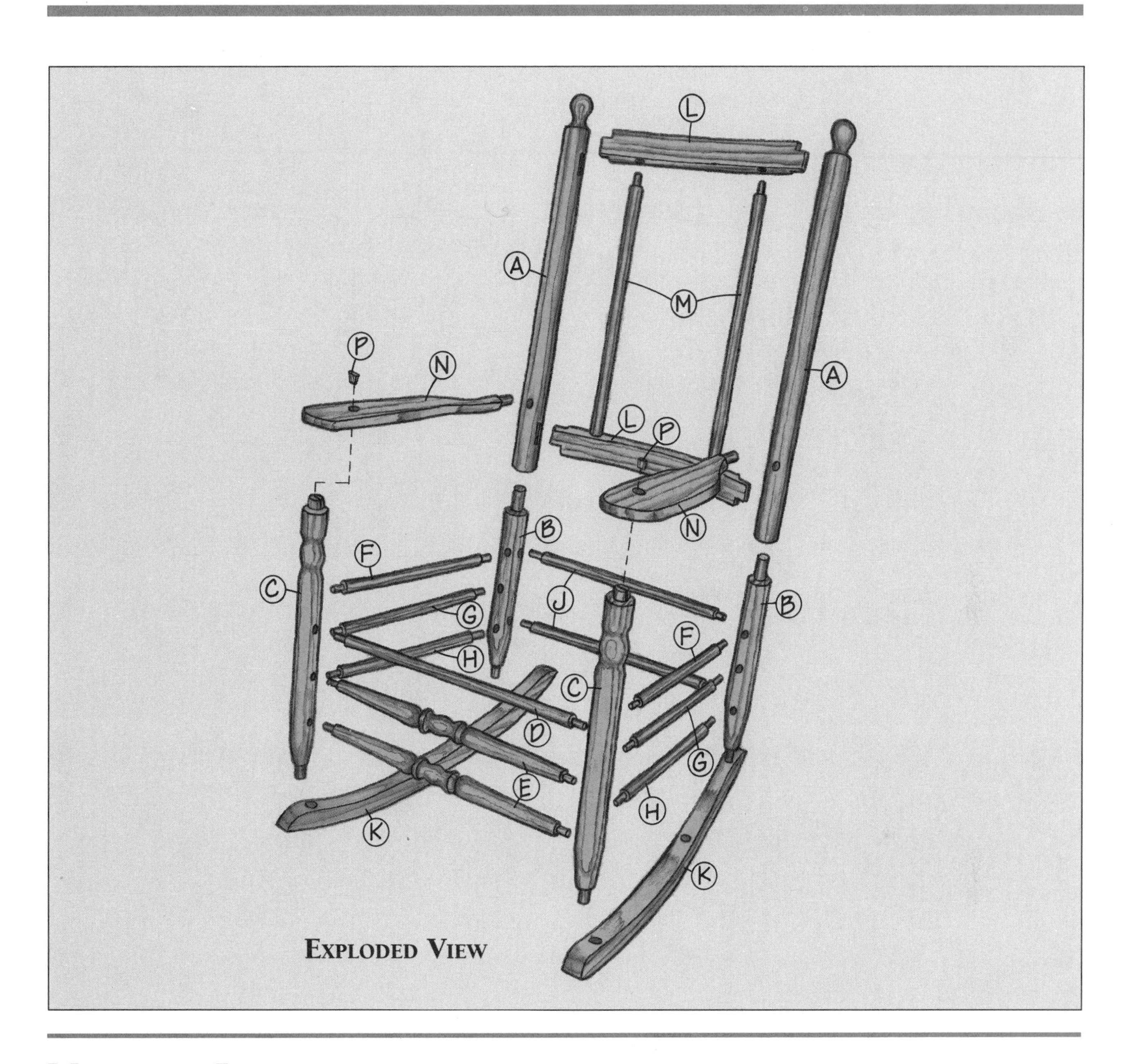

Exploded View

Materials List (FINISHED DIMENSIONS)

Parts

	Part	Dimensions
A.	Top back posts (2)	2" dia. x 30"
B.	Bottom back posts (2)	2" dia. x 16 3/4"
C.	Front legs (2)	2" dia. x 21"
D.	Front seat rail	7/8" dia. x 22"
E.	Front rungs (2)	1 1/2" dia. x 22"
F	Side seat rails (2)	7/8" dia. x 15 3/4"
G.	Middle side rungs (2)	7/8" dia. x 15 5/16"
H.	Bottom side rungs (2)	7/8" dia. x 14 7/8"
J.	Back seat rail/rung (2)	7/8" dia. x 18"
K.	Rockers (2)	1 3/4" x 3 1/2" x 32 1/2"
L.	Crest/intermediate rails (2)	2 3/8" x 2 1/2" x 18"
M.	Back spindles (2)	7/8" dia. x 22"
N.	Armrests (2)	3/4" x 4" x 20 3/4"
P.	Wedges (2)	3/16" x 3/4" x 3/4"

Hardware

For a tape seat:

1" Woven tape (70 yards)
Foam rubber (1" x 24" x 36")
Upholstery tacks (40–48)

For a rush seat:

Fiber cord (7–8 lb.)
Cotton batting (5–6 lb.)
Upholstery tacks (60–72)

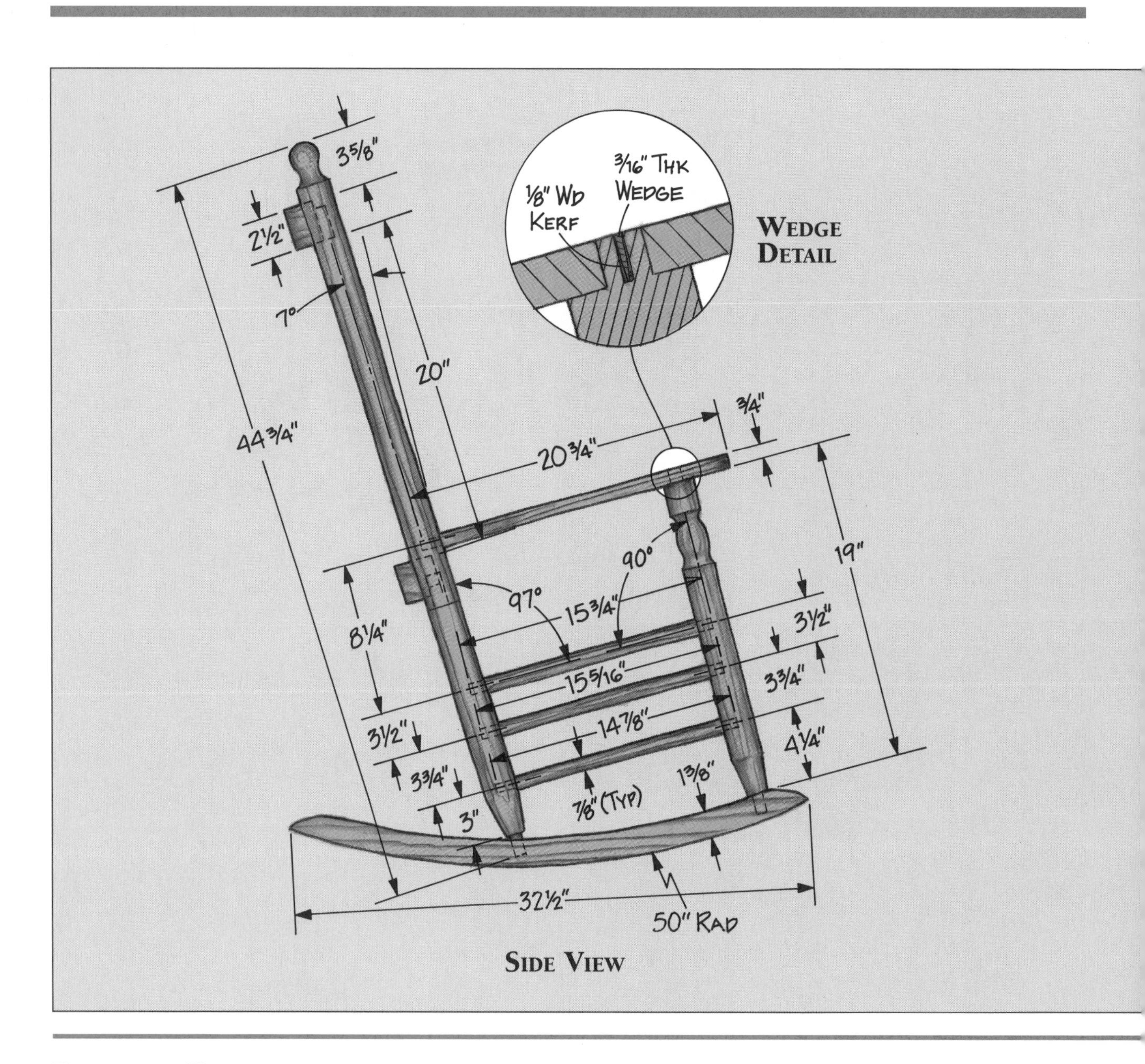

SIDE VIEW

PLAN OF PROCEDURE

1 Select the stock and cut the parts to size. To make this rocker, you need approximately 14 board feet of 10/4 (ten-quarters) and 3 board feet of 4/4 (four-quarters) stock — lumber that has been rough-sawn 2½ inches and 1 inch thick, respectively. Typically, Cape Cod rockers are built from white oak, ash, and hickory. You can also use maple and birch. The rocker shown is made from oak.

Cut the rough lumber into the turning blanks needed to make the turned pieces. Use the 4/4 stock for all ⅞-inch-diameter turnings, and the 10/4 stock for anything larger. Plane the remaining 10/4 stock to 2⅜ inches thick and cut the rockers and crest rail to the dimensions specified in the Materials List. Plane the remaining 4/4 stock to ¾ inch thick and cut the armrests.

2 Turn the posts, legs, rails, rungs, and spindles. Turn the top back posts and bottom back posts as shown in the *Back Post Layout.* Carefully size the tenons on the ends of the bottom back posts, and drill ¾-inch-diameter holes in the bottom ends of the top back posts. Test the fit of the top and bottom parts — they should fit together so the seam is barely visible.

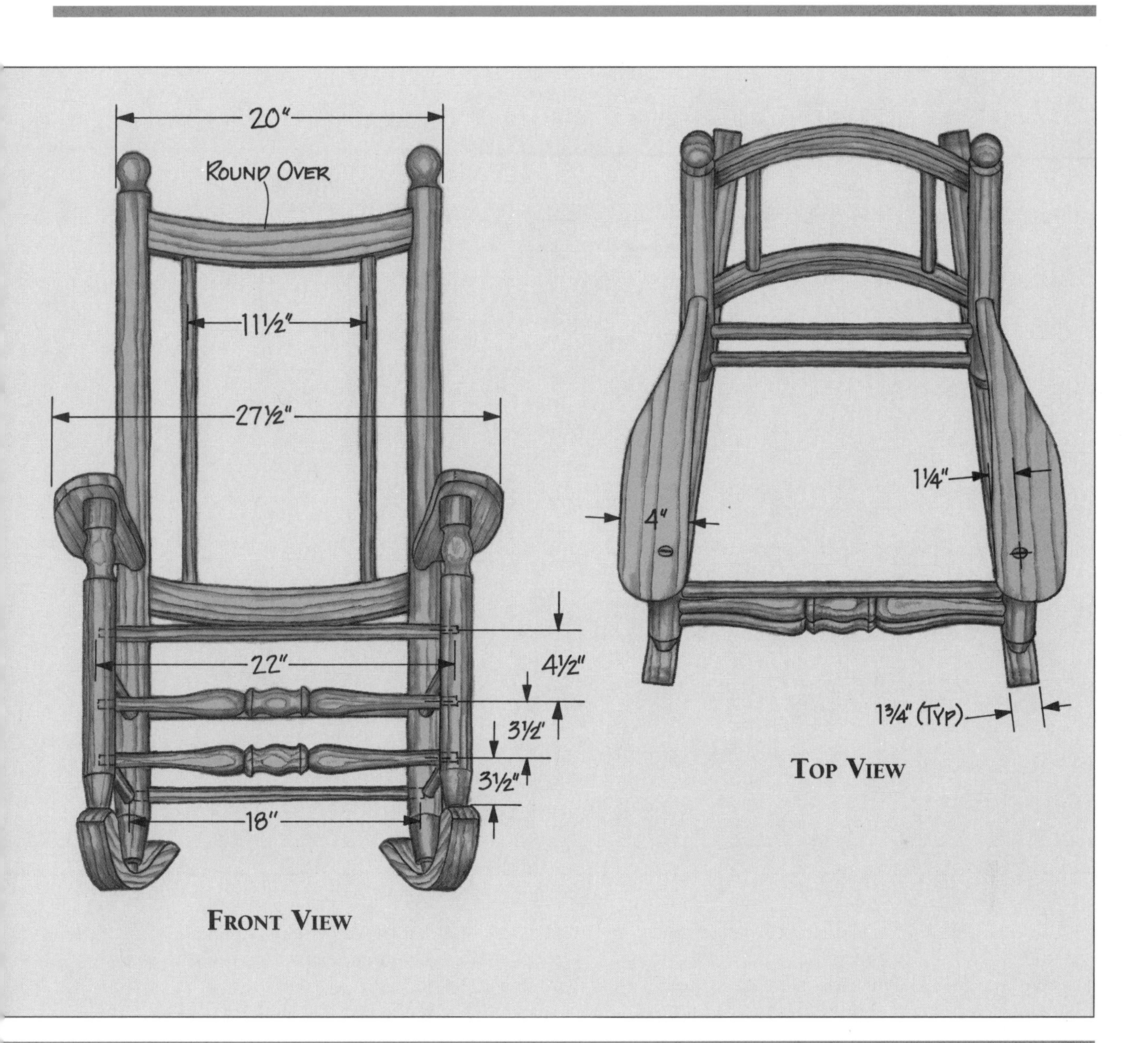

Try This Trick

To match the grain on each top and bottom back post, cut them from the same length of turning stock. To make sure that the top and bottom back posts fit together without a noticeable seam, *undercut* the mating surfaces slightly, as shown, when you turn the parts.

Mating Surfaces Undercut

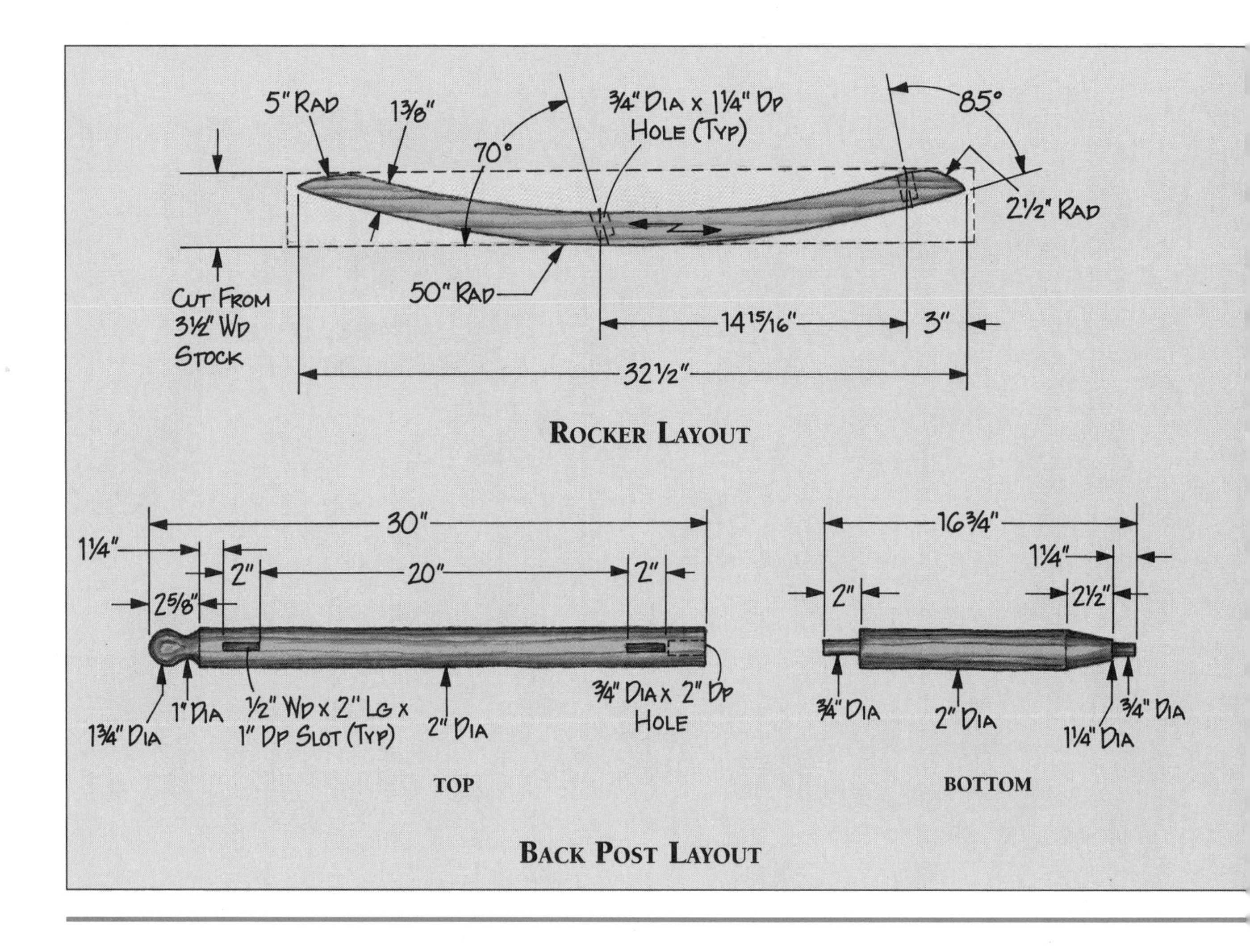

Also turn the front legs, seat rails, rungs, and spindles. Carefully size the tenons on each, and test fit them in either a ½-inch-diameter or a ¾-inch-diameter hole. The fit should be snug but not so tight that you must force the tenons in the holes.

Note: Finish sand all the turned parts on the lathe, but be careful not to sand the tenons after you've sized them.

3 Cut the profiles of the rockers, armrests, crest rail, and intermediate rail. Lay out the shapes of the rockers as shown in the *Rocker Layout,* the armrests as shown in the *Armrest Pattern,* and the crest and intermediate rails as shown in the *Crest/Intermediate Rail.* Cut the profiles with a band saw or a frame saw.

As you cut the crest and intermediate rails, also cut the tenons on the ends. After you have completed the top profile, lay out the side profile as shown in the *Crest/Intermediate Rail Tenon Detail,* and cut it. **Note:** On the crest rail, the *top* edge is notched to form the tenons, while on the intermediate rail, the *bottom* edge is notched.

Round the tenons on the back ends of the armrests, using a rasp and a file. Carefully fit them to a ¾-inch-diameter hole.

4 Drill the round mortises in the back posts, front legs, crest rail, intermediate rail, and rockers. With the exception of the crest rail and intermediate rail, all the rocker parts are assembled with round mortises and tenons. Make a *Back Post Mortising Collar* and a *Front Leg Mortising Collar.* Also make story sticks for the back posts and front legs, using the dimensions shown in the *Front View* and the *Side View*. Mark the radial location of the mortises with the guide collars and a spindle-marking straightedge. Then mark the vertical location with the story sticks or a tape measure. (Refer to "Joining Turned Chair Parts" on page 72 for complete instructions.)

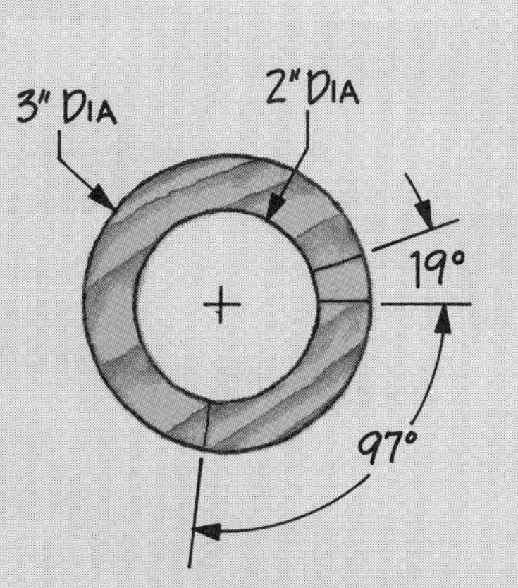

BACK POST MORTISING COLLAR

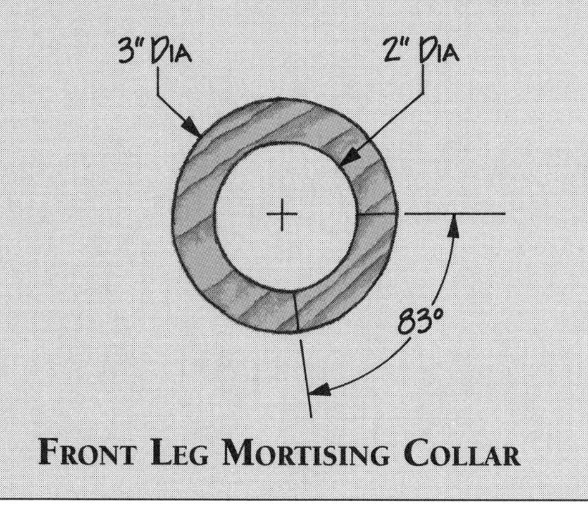

FRONT LEG MORTISING COLLAR

9-1 To drill the mortises in the back posts for the armrests, side seat rails, and side rungs, tilt the drill press table 7 degrees to the right or left. Bore the mortises so they are angled toward the *bottom* ends of the parts.

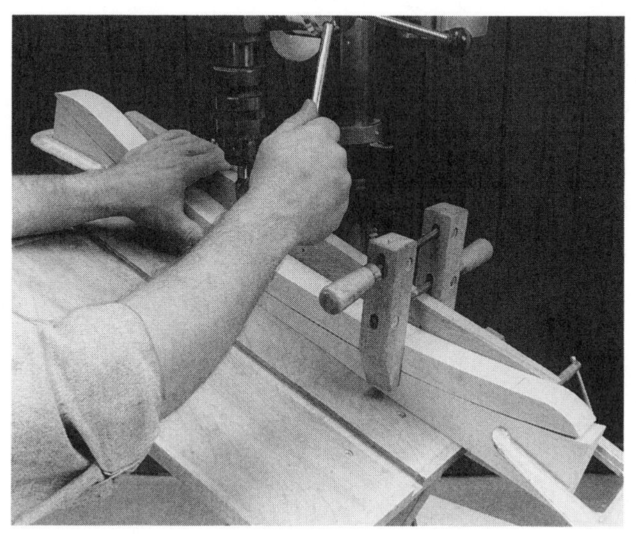

9-2 To drill the angled mortises in the rockers, save the scrap when you cut the profiles. Fasten this scrap to a fence, then clamp the fence to the drill press table, as shown — this will serve as a jig to hold the rockers while you drill them. Tilt the drill press table 5 degrees right (from horizontal) to drill the front mortises and 20 degrees left to drill the back mortises. The front mortises should be angled toward the front of the rockers, while the back mortises are angled toward the back.

Mark the mortises in the crest rail and the intermediate rail as shown in the *Crest/Intermediate Rail,* and the rockers as shown in the *Rocker Layout.*

Drill the mortises on a drill press. Make all the mortises 90 degrees to the surface of the part, with the exception of the mortises for the armrests, side seat rails, and side rungs in the back posts. These must be drilled 7 degrees off perpendicular, as shown in the *Side View*. Tilt the table of your drill press to make these. *(SEE FIGURE 9-1.)*

The mortises in the rockers are also angled. If you draw a line tangent to the curve of the rocker just under the front mortises, they should be angled 85 degrees from that line. If you do the same for the back mortises, they should be 70 degrees from the tangent. These, too, require that you tilt your drill press table. However, you must also build a jig to hold the rockers while you drill them. *(SEE FIGURE 9-2.)*

Note: The armrests also have round mortises, but you don't drill these until *after* assembling the frame.

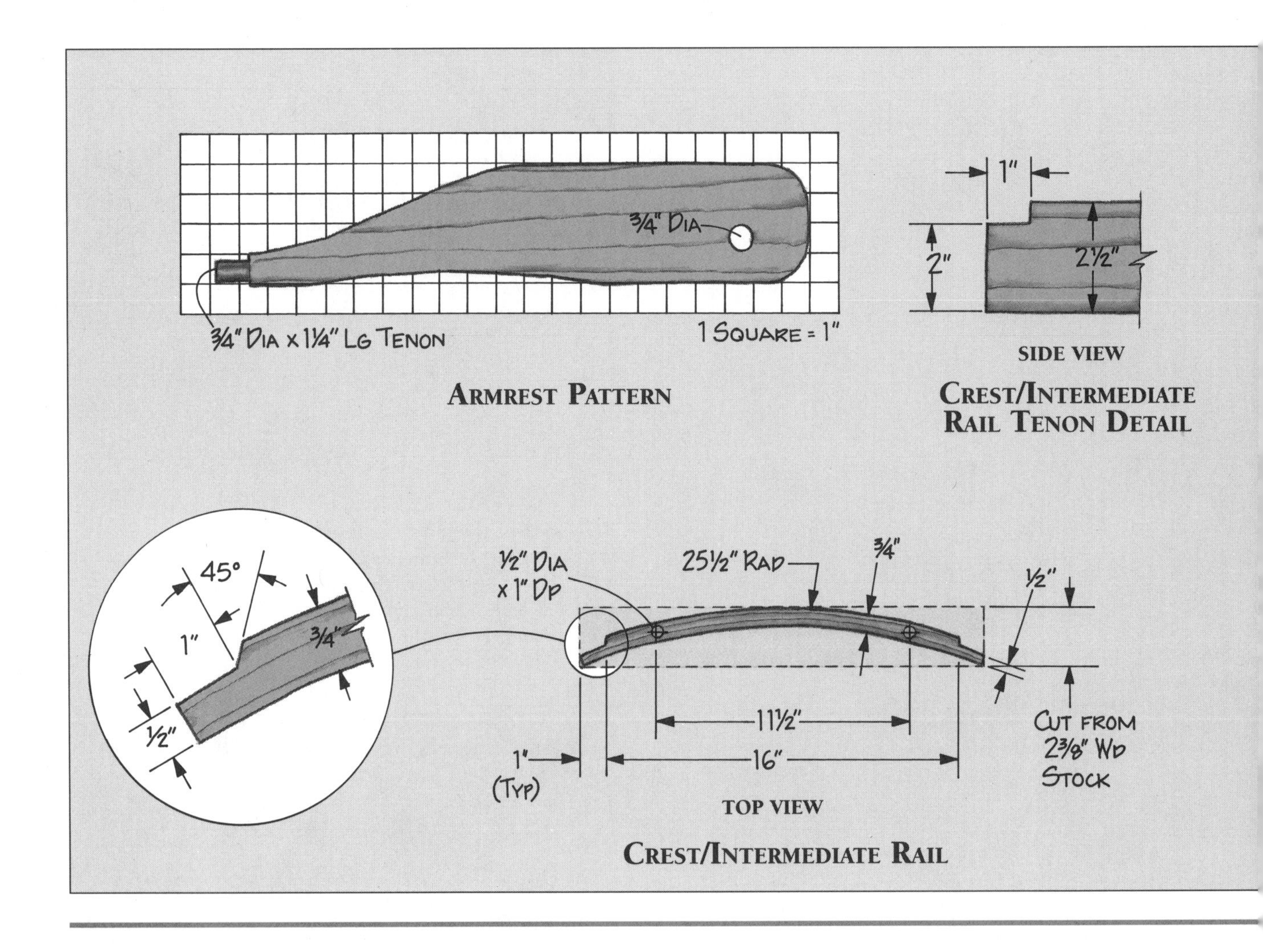

5 Make the slot mortises in the top back posts. The crest rail and the intermediate rail rest in slot mortises in the back posts. Mark these mortises the same way you marked the round mortises, then cut them on a drill press or overhead router. Round the top and bottom surfaces of the crest rail tenons and intermediate rail tenons to fit the mortises.

6 Test assemble the frame. Finish sand the rockers, crest rail, intermediate rail, and armrests. Test assemble the frame members in this order:

- Insert the bottom back posts in the rockers.
- Slide the top back posts onto the bottom back posts.
- Insert the side seat rails and the side rungs in the bottom back posts and the front legs.
- Insert the front legs in the rockers. This may require that you loosen the back posts in the rockers, angle them backward, then wiggle the whole assembly until the legs slide into their respective mortises.
- Insert the spindles in the crest rail and the intermediate rail.
- Join the two side assemblies with the front seat rail, front rungs, back seat rail, back rungs, and back assembly.

7 Drill the mortises in the armrests. At this point, the frame will be complete except for the armrests. Insert the armrest tenons into the top back posts. Position each armrest so the inside surface of the tenon is 7/8 inch from the inside edge of the armrest. (The centers of the tenons will be 1 1/4 inches from the inside edges, as shown in the *Top View.*) Trace around each tenon with a pencil, marking its position on the armrest. Remove the armrests from the assembled frame and drill 3/4-inch-diameter mortises where you've marked them. Replace the armrests, making sure the tenons on the top ends of the front legs fit the armrest mortises.

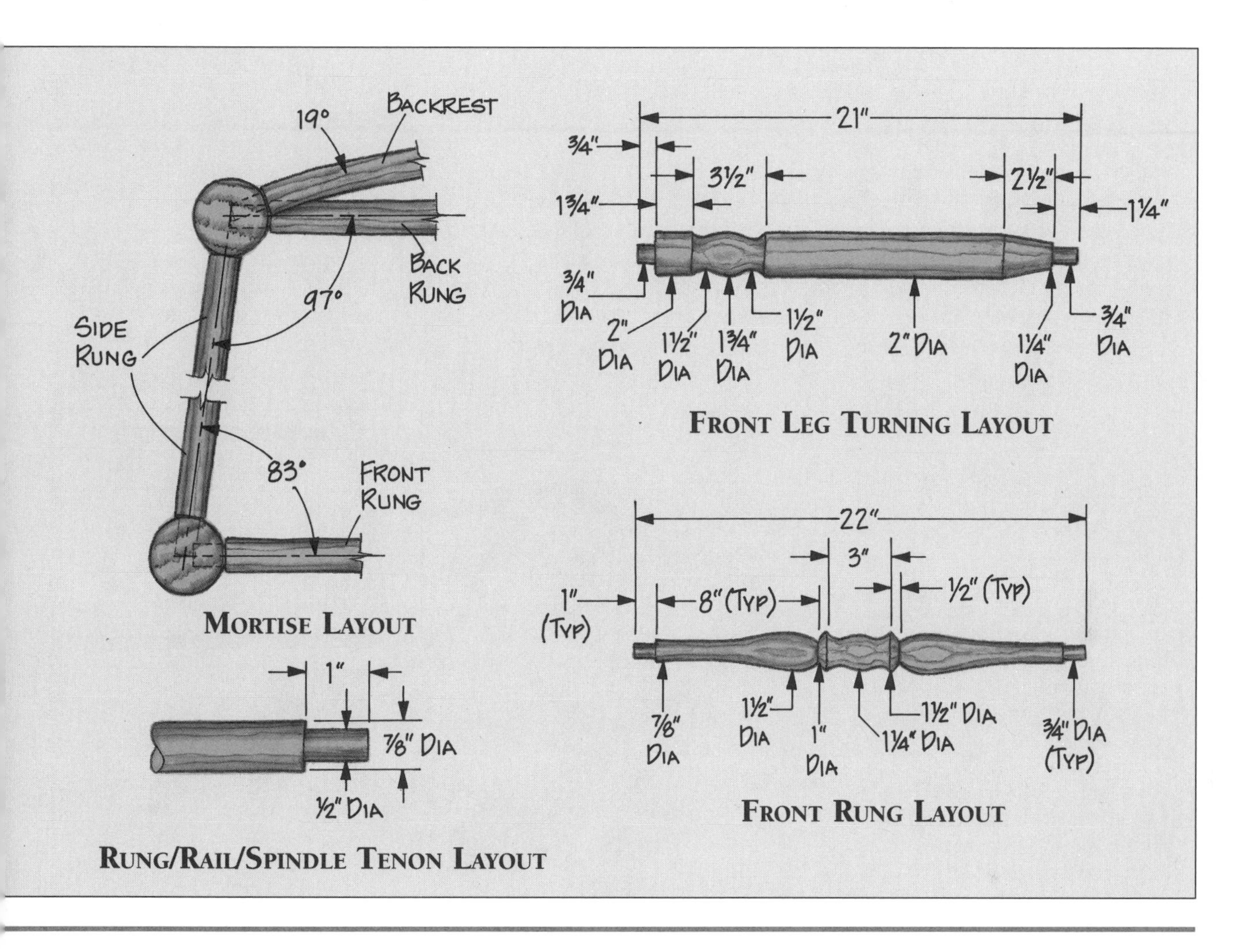

8 Assemble the frame with glue. Disassemble the frame, removing the parts in the reverse order in which you assembled them. Using a band saw or a dovetail saw, cut 1/8-inch-wide, 11/16-inch-long slots in the tenons on the top ends of the front legs. (These slots must run from side to side on the assembled rocker.) From scraps, cut wedges to fit the slots.

Reassemble the frame members with glue. Wipe off any excess glue that squeezes out of the joints as you work, using a wet rag. When you attach the armrests, drive the wedges into the tops of the front leg tenons. Let the glue dry, then cut the wedges flush with the top surface of the armrests.

9 Finish the rocker frame. Do any necessary touch-up sanding, and apply a finish to the rocker frame. You can use almost any durable paint, varnish, or oil finish, but if you intend to leave the rocker out of doors, apply an *exterior* finish with UV protection.

10 Install a seat and a back on the frame. The frame is designed for a *woven* seat and back, made from tape, rush, or a similar material. To weave a cloth tape seat and back, refer to "Weaving a Chair Seat" on page 87. The procedure for weaving the back is exactly the same as for the seat, except that you don't have to "fill in the corners."

To weave a rush seat, refer to "Rush Seats" on page 112. You can also make an upholstered seat. Cut a 1/2-inch-thick piece of plywood to rest on top of the seat rails, notching the corners to fit around the back posts and the front legs. Then cover the plywood with padding, muslin, and upholstery material, as described in "Upholstering a Chair Seat" on page 66.

Rush Seats

Rush once grew in abundance in America; consequently many early American chairs have woven rush seats. Today, rush has been replaced by fiber cord — stiff, twisted strands of paper. Fiber cord looks exactly like rush on a finished chair seat, but it's much easier to work with. You can purchase fiber cord in several different diameters and colors from:

The Connecticut Cane and Reed Co.
P.O.Box 762
Manchester, CT 06040

To weave a single seat, you'll need about 3 pounds of 5/32-inch fiber cord, plus 30 to 40 small upholstery tacks and some cotton batting to pad the chair seat as you weave it.

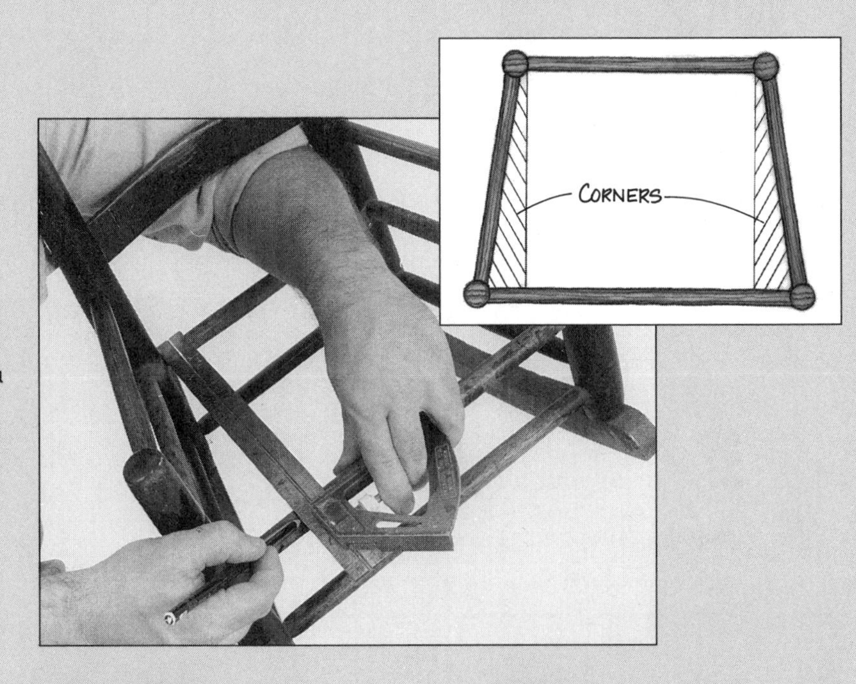

1 Begin a rush seat by "filling in the corners." Turned chair frames are usually trapezoid-shaped, while the weaving forms a rectangle. If you impose a rectangle on the trapezoid, it leaves two triangular "corners" on either side of the frame. These must be filled in with short lengths of cord. Find these corners with a square, as shown. Hold the square against the front seat rail and mark the beginning of each corner with a pencil.

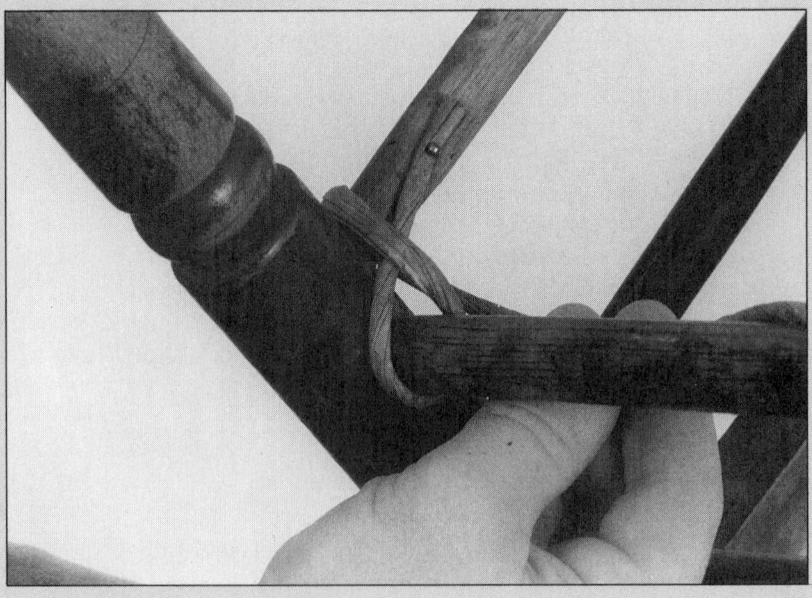

2 Cut a short length of cord from the coil, a little longer than the front rail. Wet it in water a few minutes — wet fiber cord is easier to work with. Tack one end to the left side seat rail, near the front seat rail. Bring the cord forward, *over and around* the front rail, back *over* itself, then *over and around* the side seat rail. This is the basic technique for weaving rush. Every time you come to a corner, go over, over, and over.

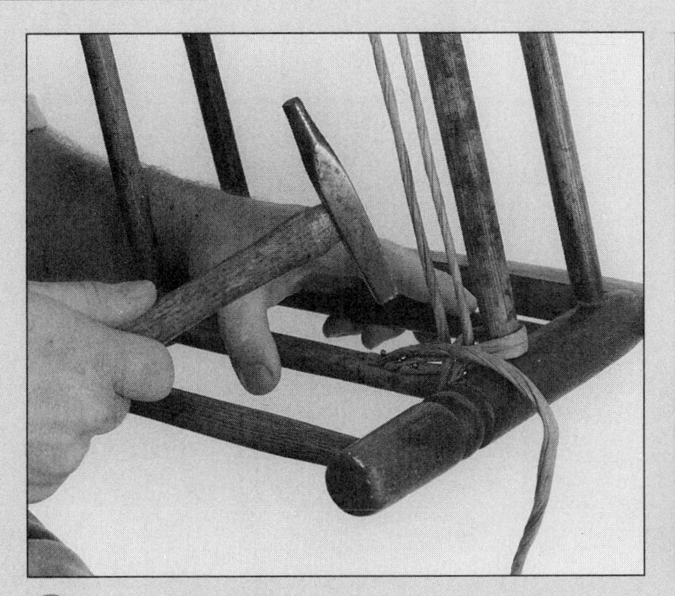

3 **Bring the cord sideways,** over and around the right side seat rail, back over the cord itself, then over and around the front seat rail. Tack the cord to the right side seat rail, near the front rail, and cut off any excess. Repeat this process until you've filled in the corners. Each time you repeat, cut the cord a little longer and tack it to the side seat rails a little farther from the front.

4 **Every third or fourth cord,** check your work with a square. *This is very important!* The warp must be perpendicular to the front rail and the weft must be parallel to it. If they aren't, there will be holes of gaps in your pattern when you finish the seat. **Note:** The secret to keeping the warp and weft square is knowing when to pull the cord taut. Put lots of tension on the cord during the first "over" in each corner, but not as much during the last two "overs."

5 **If the warp and weft are out** of square, there are several ways to bring them back into proper alignment. If the warp takes up too much space on the front rail, place a wooden block against the last cord and tap it toward the corner. If the warp takes up too little space, place the scrap on top of all the warp cords and tap it with a hammer. This will mash the cords, spreading them out along the rail. If the hammer method doesn't work, untwist each cord with needlenose pliers where it loops over the rail — this will spread out the fibers.

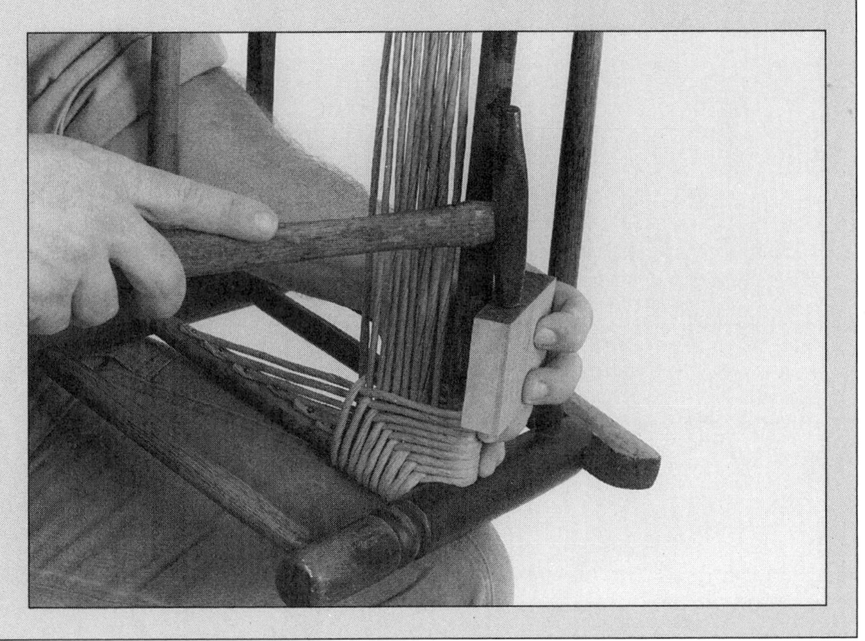

(continued) ▷

Rush Seats — continued

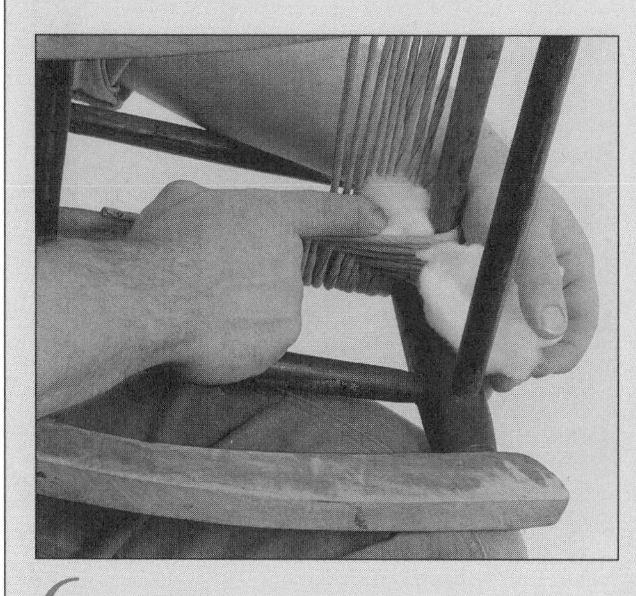

6 **As you work, stuff cotton or** dacron batting between the rush to pad the seat. The weave creates small pockets between the cords at the corners. Weave three or four strands, then fill these pockets with batting. Be careful not to stuff the pockets too full — put in just enough cotton to hold the cords taut.

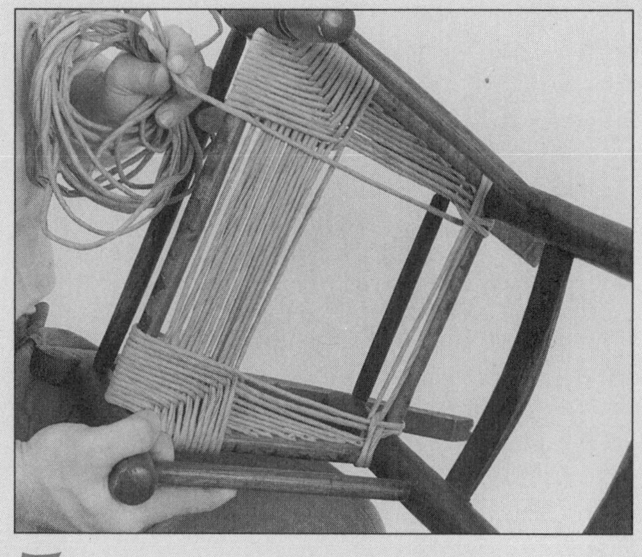

7 **After you fill the corners,** begin a continuous weaving. Cut a length of cord 10 to 20 feet long off the coil — not too long, or it will be difficult to work with. Wet the cord, and tack one to the left side seat rail, as close to the back seat rail as possible. Weave the front left corner, then the front right, back right, and back left, proceeding clockwise around the chair frame.

8 **Continue weaving corner** after corner. Check your work occasionally and keep the cord damp. When you come to the end of a length of cord, splice another length to it. Untwist the tail end of the old length and the leading end of the new one, apply white glue to the paper, then twist the ends together. Wrap the splice with masking tape. Be careful to make these splices where they won't show — *between* the weave that is building out from the corners. This way, they won't show on the completed seat.

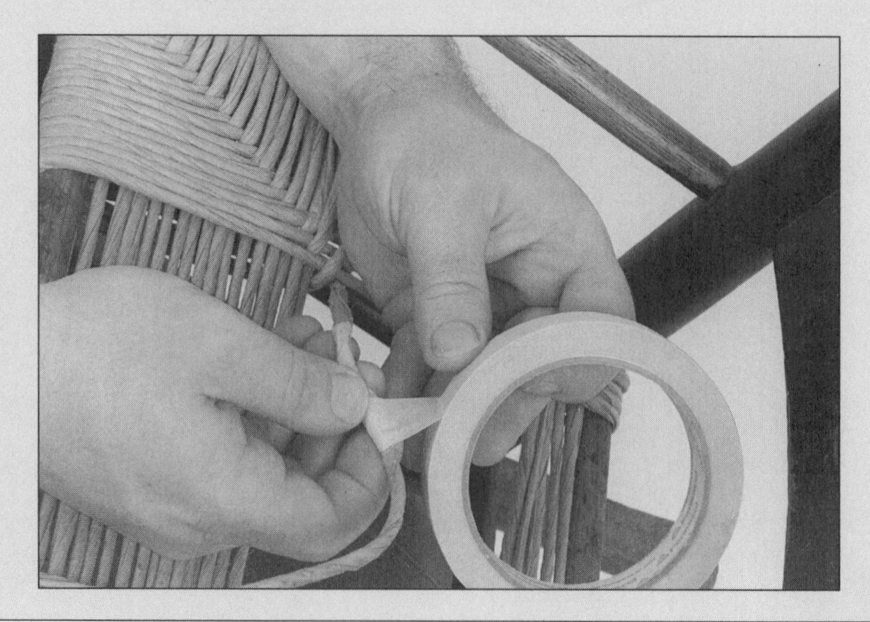

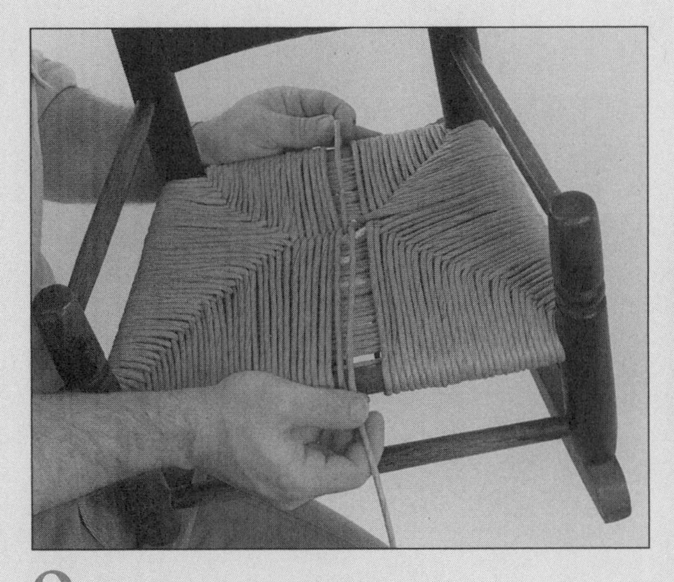

9 On most chairs, the weave will cover the side seat rail before it covers the front and back seat rails. When you get to this point, begin weaving the *warp only,* front to back. Cut an extra-long length of cord before you start this portion of the weave — enough to finish the seat. There will be no place to hide a splice. Weave the cord *over* the front rail, up through the center of the weft, *over* the back rail, and up through the center again.

10 Cover the front and the back seat rails completely, filling in the weave. Then tack the end of the cord to the bottom side of the back rail, where it won't show. Some rush weavers prefer to tie the cord to an adjacent strand and the bottom side of the chair, using string or twine.

11 Wait for the fiber cord to dry completely before using the chair. If you wish, apply a stain or a finish to the cord. Traditionally, rush is finished with either a thin shellac or a mixture of boiled linseed oil and turpentine.

10

Nesting Tables

One of the most ingenious designs for storing small tables is to *nest* them. Nesting tables usually come in sets of three, each one a different size. The smaller tables fit under the larger ones, so the entire set can be stored in the space of a single table. When you need to use the tables, slide them out from under one another.

The set shown was made to serve as side tables, but you can adapt the design to many uses. Lengthen the legs to make a set of portable serving and individual dining tables. Enlarge the tops slightly to make auxiliary sewing or game tables. You can also alter the design of the legs, aprons, and tops to change the style of the tables.

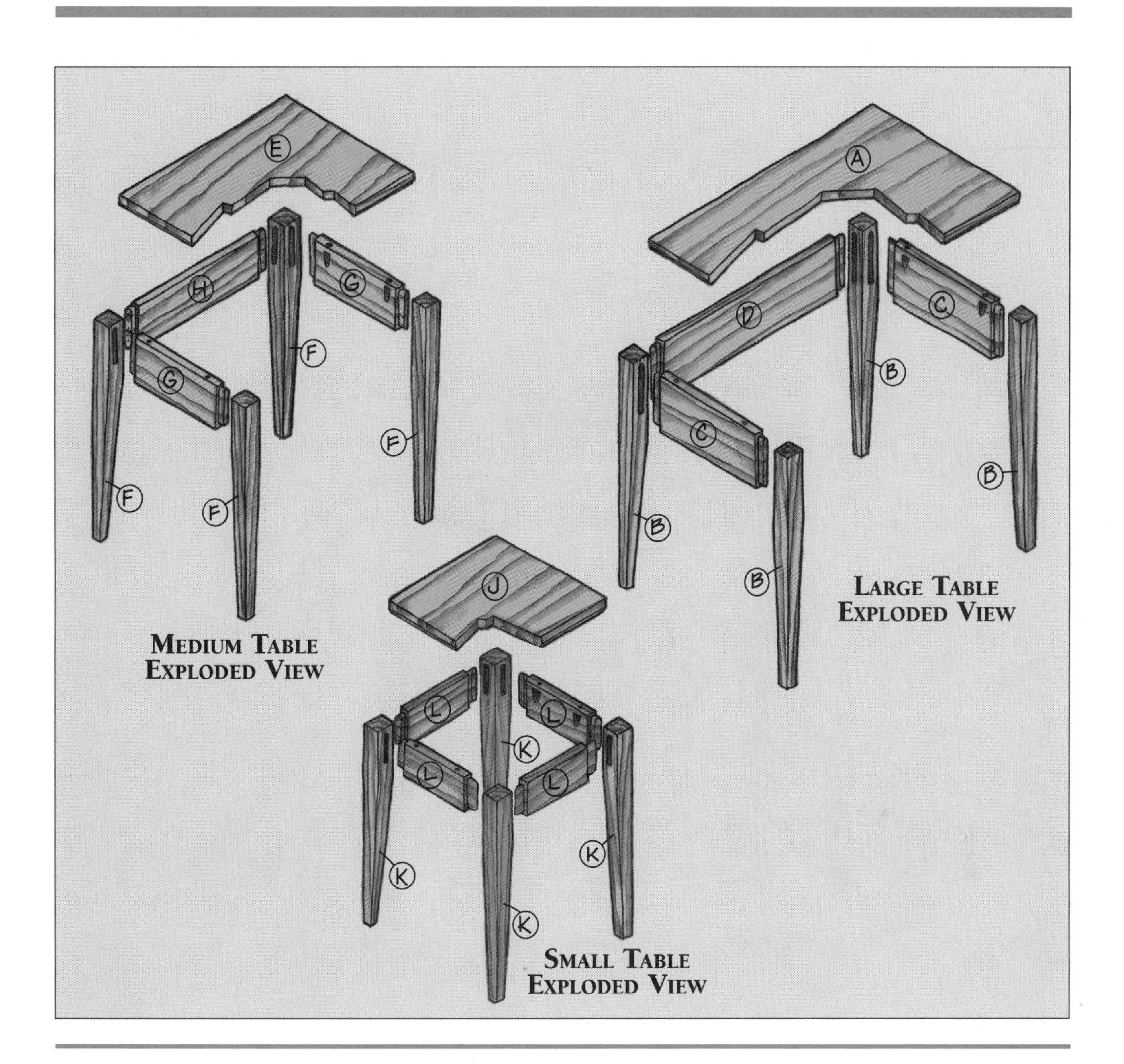

MATERIALS LIST (FINISHED DIMENSIONS)

Parts

Large Table

A.	Top	¾″ x 15″ x 23″
B.	Legs (4)	1⅜″ x 1⅜″ x 19¼″
C.	Side aprons (2)	¾″ x 5″ x 12″
D.	Back apron	¾″ x 5″ x 20″

Medium Table

E.	Top	¾″ x 13″ x 17″
F.	Legs (4)	1⅜″ x 1⅜″ x 18¼″
G.	Side aprons (2)	¾″ x 4″ x 10″
H.	Back apron	¾″ x 4″ x 14″

Small Table

J.	Top	¾″ x 11″ x 11″
K.	Legs (4)	1⅜″ x 1⅜″ x 17¼″
L.	Aprons (4)	¾″ x 3″ x 8″

Hardware

#8 x 1½″ Roundhead wood screws (12)

#8 Flat washers (12)

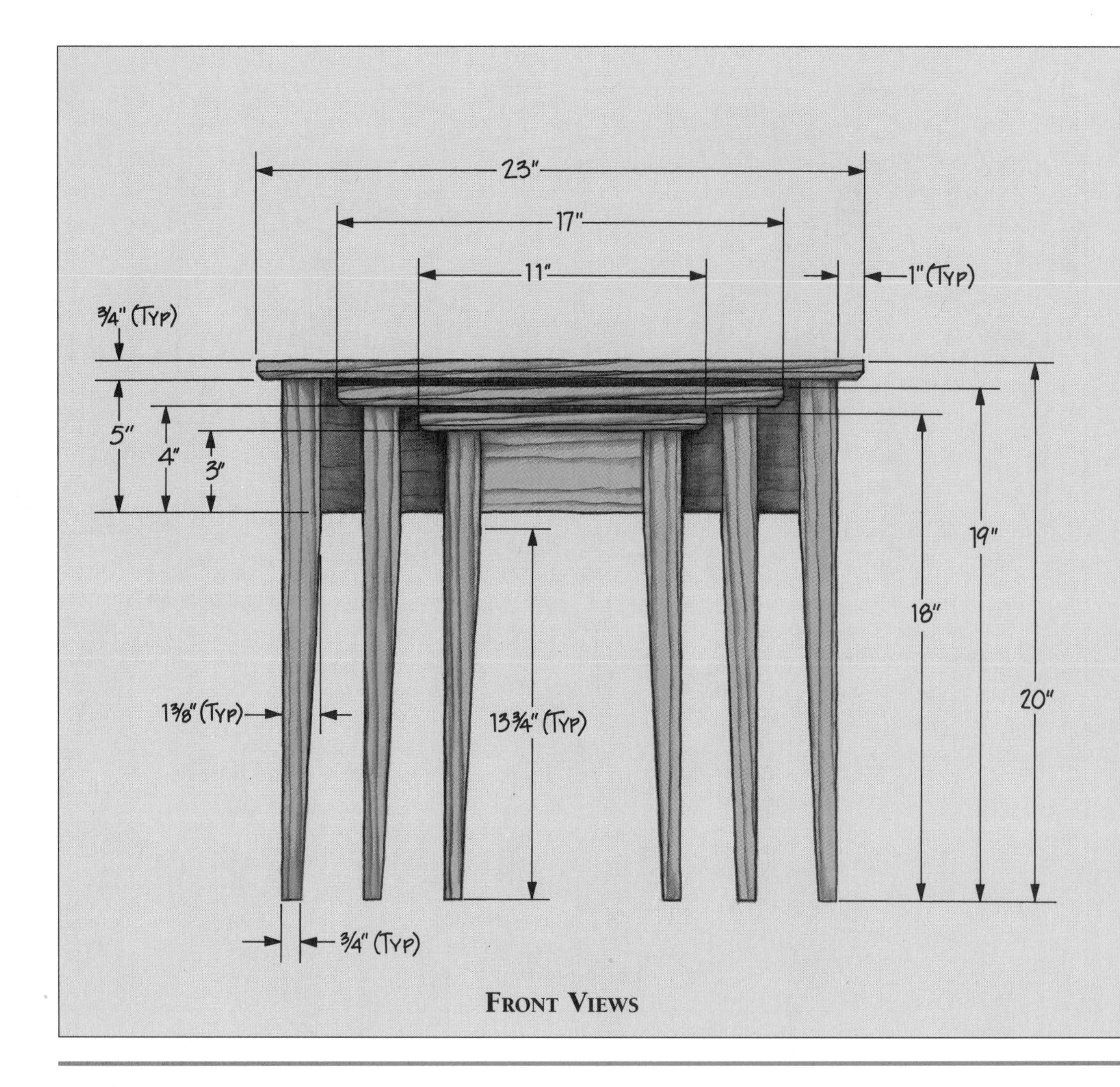

FRONT VIEWS

PLAN OF PROCEDURE

1 Select the stock and cut the parts to size. To make this project, you need approximately 9 board feet of 4/4 (four-quarters) stock, and 6 board feet of 6/4 (six-quarters) stock. You can use any cabinet-grade lumber; the tables shown are made from poplar.

Plane the 4/4 stock to ¾ inch thick. Glue up wide boards to make the tops, then cut the tops and aprons to the sizes specified in the Materials List. Plane the 6/4 stock to 1⅜ inches thick and cut the legs to size.

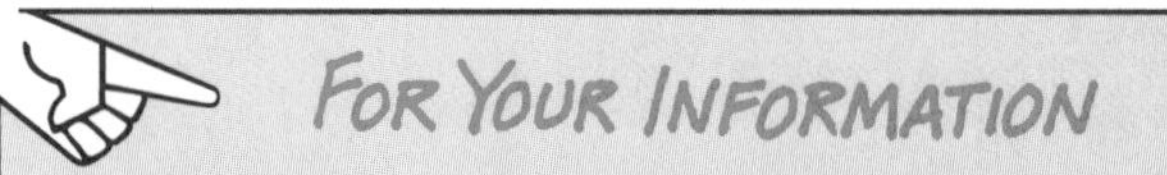

As designed, there is a ¼-inch space between the tabletops when they are nested. This works well if the assembled tables sit on hard, flat floors such as wood or tile. If you plan to rest them on carpet, however, increase the space to ½ inch; cut the legs for the medium and the small tables 18 inches and 16¾ inches long, respectively.

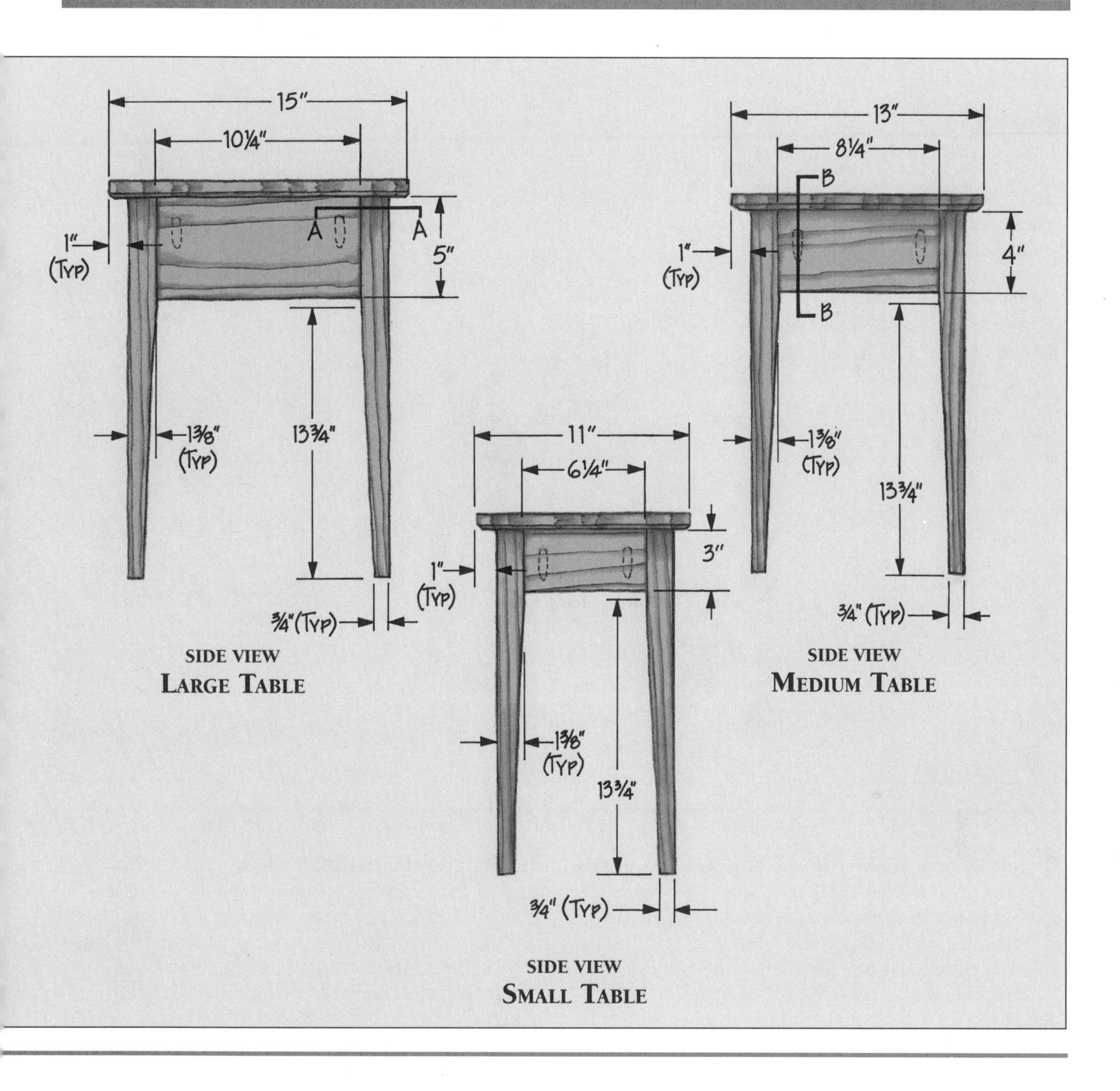

SIDE VIEW
LARGE TABLE

SIDE VIEW
MEDIUM TABLE

SIDE VIEW
SMALL TABLE

2 Cut the mortises and tenons in the legs and aprons. The legs and aprons are joined with mortises and tenons. Make the mortises first, then fit the tenons to them.

Lay out the mortises on the inside surfaces of the legs, as shown in the *Leg-to-Apron Joinery Detail.* The length of the mortises will vary — each mortise should be 1 inch shorter than the width of the adjoining apron. The mortises on the legs for the large table should be 4 inches long, those on the medium table legs should be 3 inches long, and those on the small table legs 2 inches long. Cut the mortises with a table-mounted router, or remove most of the waste by drilling lines of overlapping holes on a drill press and then cleaning up the sides with a chisel.

Lay out the tenons on the ends of the aprons, and cut them with a table-mounted router or a dado cutter. Round the top and bottom surfaces of the tenons to fit the mortises, and miter the ends of the tenons as shown in *Section A.*

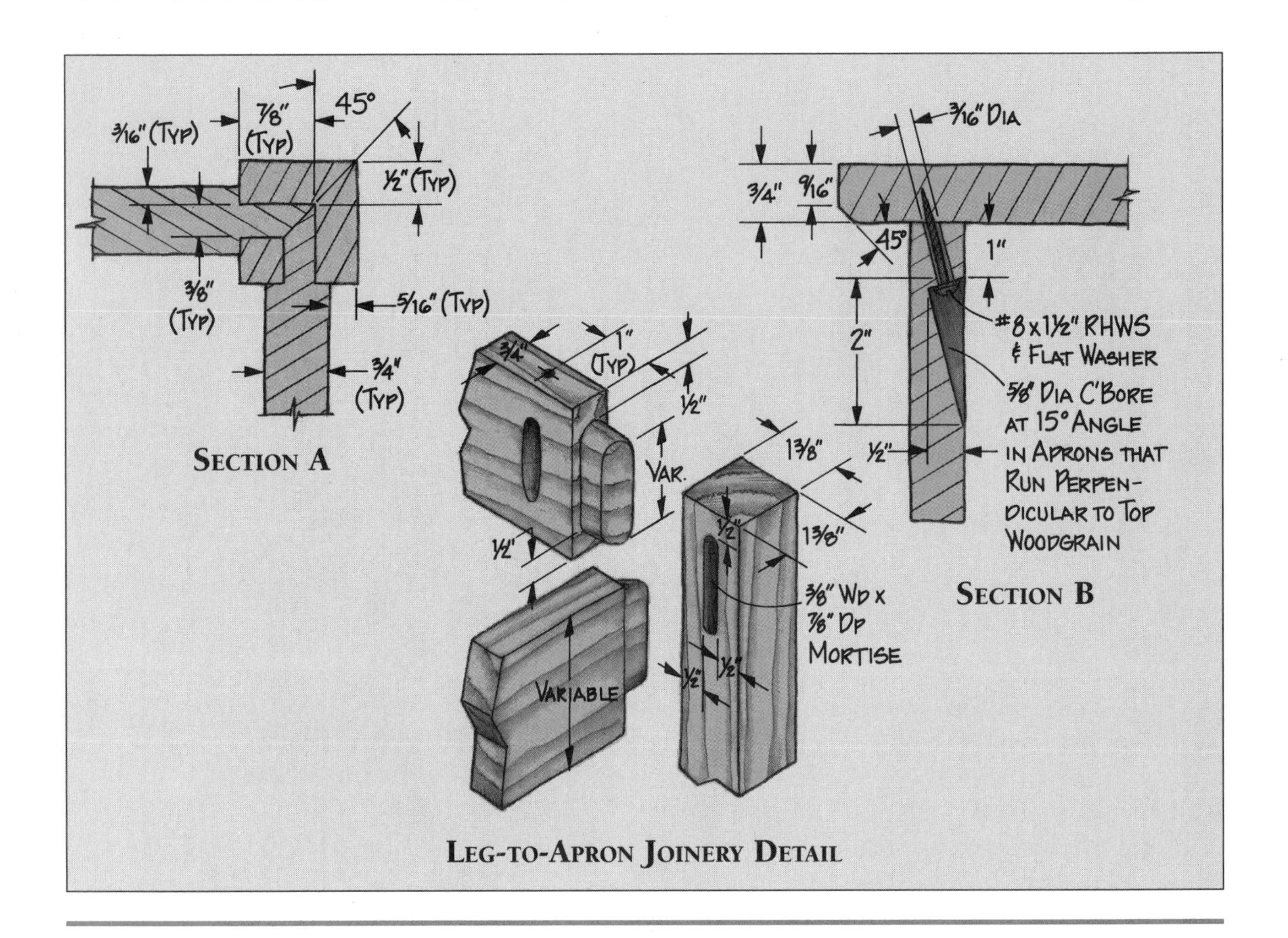

LEG-TO-APRON JOINERY DETAIL

3 Bore screw pockets in the aprons. The aprons are screwed to the tabletops. The screws rest in screw pockets in the inside surfaces of the aprons, as shown in *Section B.*

To make the pockets, tilt your drill press table to 15 degrees and attach a fence to the table on the low side of the bit. Clamp an apron to the fence and drill the pocket with a ⅝-inch Forstner or spade bit. Then drill the shaft hole with a $\frac{3}{16}$-inch twist bit or brad-point bit. Repeat for each screw pocket.

When you assemble the tables, you'll find that the shaft holes are slightly larger than the shafts of #8 screws. This lets the tabletops expand and contract with changes in relative humidity.

4 Taper the legs. Although the legs are three different lengths, they are all tapered exactly the same. The legs all have a single taper on the inside surfaces, tapering from 1⅜ inches to ¾ inch wide over a 13¾-inch run. Cut these tapers on a table saw, using a tapering jig to guide the legs.

5 Chamfer the tabletop edges. The bottom edges of the tabletops are chamfered as shown in *Section B.* Just as the tapers make the legs seem more delicate than they really are, the chamfer makes the tabletops seem thinner. Both the tapers and the chamfers work together to make the tables seem lighter. Cut the chamfers with a router or a table saw.

6 Assemble the tables. Finish sand all the parts. Assemble the legs and aprons with glue; let the glue dry. Then attach the leg-and-apron assemblies to the tabletops with roundhead screws and flat washers. Do *not* glue the tops to the aprons — the tops must be allowed to move with changes in relative humidity.

7 Finish the tables. Temporarily remove the tops from the leg-and-apron assemblies and set the screws aside. Do any necessary touch-up sanding and apply a finish to *all* wooden surfaces, including the underside of the tabletops. Let the finish dry, rub it out, and replace the tops on the aprons.

Index

Note: Page references in *italic* indicate photographs or illustrations. **Boldface** references indicate charts or tables.

V

W

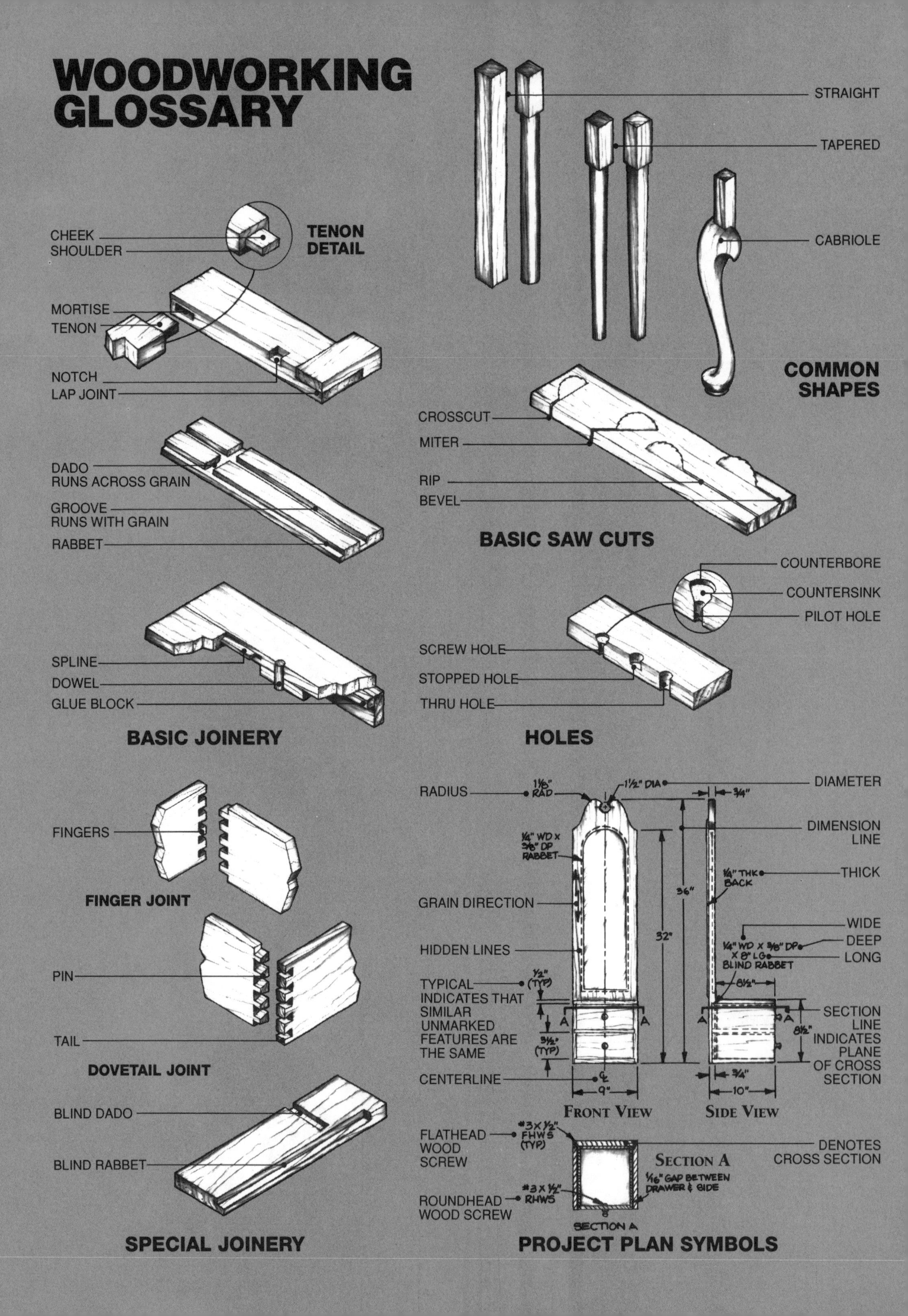
WOODWORKING GLOSSARY
CHEEK
SHOULDER
TENON DETAIL
MORTISE
TENON
NOTCH
LAP JOINT
DADO
RUNS ACROSS GRAIN
GROOVE
RUNS WITH GRAIN
RABBET
SPLINE
DOWEL
GLUE BLOCK
BASIC JOINERY
FINGERS
FINGER JOINT
PIN
TAIL
DOVETAIL JOINT
BLIND DADO
BLIND RABBET
SPECIAL JOINERY
STRAIGHT
TAPERED
CABRIOLE
COMMON SHAPES
CROSSCUT
MITER
RIP
BEVEL
BASIC SAW CUTS
COUNTERBORE
COUNTERSINK
PILOT HOLE
SCREW HOLE
STOPPED HOLE
THRU HOLE
HOLES
RADIUS
1½" RAD
1½" DIA
DIAMETER
¾"
DIMENSION LINE
¼" WD X ⅜" DP RABBET
¼" THK BACK
THICK
36"
GRAIN DIRECTION
32"
WIDE
DEEP
LONG
HIDDEN LINES
¼" WD X ⅜" DP X 8" LG BLIND RABBET
TYPICAL INDICATES THAT SIMILAR UNMARKED FEATURES ARE THE SAME
½" (TYP)
3½" (TYP)
8½"
SECTION LINE INDICATES PLANE OF CROSS SECTION
CENTERLINE
9"
10"
FRONT VIEW
SIDE VIEW
FLATHEAD WOOD SCREW
#3 X ½" FHWS (TYP)
DENOTES CROSS SECTION
SECTION A
1/16" GAP BETWEEN DRAWER & SIDE
ROUNDHEAD WOOD SCREW
#3 X ½" RHWS
SECTION A
PROJECT PLAN SYMBOLS